The Ultimate History of
FAST CARS
Vehicles built for the fast lane

JONATHAN WOOD

p

This is a Parragon Book
This edition published in 2006

Parragon
Queen Street House
4 Queen Street
Bath BA1 1HE, UK

Copyright © Parragon Books Limited 2002

Designed, produced and packaged by
Stonecastle Graphics Limited

Text by Jonathan Wood
Edited by Philip de Ste. Croix
Updated text by Andrew Noaks 2006
Edited by Anthony R John
Designed by Paul Turner and Sue Pressley

ISBN 1-40547-304-5

Printed in China

Photographic credits.

The GP Library: Page 18; page 19 *top*; page 19 *below*.

Andrew Morland: Page 36; page 37 *all three*; page
43 *centre*; pages 164-5 *all four*.

Other pictures © Neill Bruce's Automobile
Photolibrary by:

Ian Dawson: page 168 *below*; page 169 *below*.

Geoffrey Goddard: Page 12 *below*; page 40 *both*;
page 62 *top*; pages 188-9 *all five*; pages 136-7 *all
four*; page 152 *both*; page 160 *centre*.

Christian Gonzenbach: pages 268-9 *all four*; page
280-1 *all three*.

Christian Hatton: Page 141 *centre*.

Stefan Lüscher: Page 94 *below right*; page 95 *top*;
page 170 *below*; page 182 *both*; pages 196-7 *all
four*; page 209 *top right and centre*; pages 210-11
all five; page 258 *below*; page 259 *both*; pages 276-
7 *all three*.

Richard Meinert: Page 134 *both*; page 253 *all
three*; page 253 *centre right and below*; page 254;
page 255 *centre and below*.

F Naef: pages 230-1 *all four*.

All other photographs pages 1-285 © Neill Bruce's
Automobile Photolibrary, with the exception of the
following, which are manufacturer's press pictures
supplied from The Peter Roberts Collection c/o
Neill Bruce: Page 1; page 3; page 6; page 7 *both*;
page 19 *centre*; page 115 *top*; page 155 *centre*;
page 161 *centre right*; page 175 *top*; page 177
below; pages 178-9 *all four*; page 191 *centre*; page
193 *both*; page 195 *top and centre left*; page 205;
page 207 *both*; page 209 *top left*; page 223 *both*;
page 227 *top*; pages 232-3 *all four*; pages 234-5 *all
three*; page 237 *both*; pages 238-9 *all three*; pages
240-1 *all five*; page 242 *centre right*; pages 244-5
all three; pages 246-7 *all three*; pages 248-9 *all
four*; pages 250-1 *all five*; page 253 *top*; page 256
both; page 257 *top*; pages 262-3 *all four*; pages
264-5 *all four*; pages 266-7 *all four*; pages 270-1
all four; pages 274-5; pages 278-9 *all four*; page
282; pages 284-5 *all four*; pages 316-7 *all three*.

Picture research by Neill Bruce, with special thanks
to Bonhams Auctioneers Ltd., Nigel Dawes Ltd.
and Duncan Hamilton Ltd. for making so many
superb cars available.

All photographs pages 286-317 © LAT Photographic
Digital Archive with the exception of the following
manufacturer's press pictures: page 260; page 261
all three; page 273 *all three*; page 286 *top*; page
287 *below right*; page 298; page 299 *all three*.
Picture research by Andrew Noakes.

Please note: Unless
otherwise stated, the
performance figures
of the cars featured
in this book refer to
the speeds recorded
at the time of the
model's introduction.

The Ultimate History of
FAST CARS

Vehicles built for the fast lane

Contents

Introduction

Speed! The very word sends a tingle down the spine, particularly when it refers to a motor car that has been specifically designed for out and out performance *and* driver enjoyment. Such models have evolved over the years, originating with the birth of the sports car in the pre-1914 era and developing through the aerodynamically refined grand tourers of the post-war era to today's supercars which are the latest manifestation of the breed.

All are (or were in their day) fast cars. But how fast is fast? Today there is a handful of models which can attain 200mph (321km/h) while the makers of the projected Bugatti Veyron claim that it will be able to exceed 250mph (402km/h). However, to the pioneers of the automobile in the 1880s even 60mph (96km/h) must have appeared unattainable. Yet such was the growth of the industry and pace of technical development that, by 1902, this speed was perfectly achievable.

In 1901 Daimler had introduced its superlative 35hp Mercedes racer for the road, the model which gave its name to the marque, and its 60hp derivative could reliably and rapidly reach that speed. But it was to be a further 46 years before a production sports car was consistently capable of attaining twice that figure, namely 120mph (193km/h). When Jaguar launched its XK120 sports car in 1948, so-called because it could achieve precisely that speed, the general motoring public could scarcely believe that such performance was possible. Although this stunning open two-seater was powered by an engine with race-proven twin overhead camshafts, this configuration had not hitherto been associated with reliability…

1948 also saw the launch of the first production Ferrari – the company's berlinettas (coupés) initially shared their V12 engines with the firm's Grand Prix cars. Produced in tiny numbers and enhanced with magnificently styled bodywork by

Below: The long-tailed GT version of the McLaren F1. The F1 reigned as the fastest production car in the world from its introduction in 1994, but a decade later it has been surpassed by more modern machines.

some of Italy's finest *carrozzerias* (coachbuilders), these blood-red beauties from Modena were the fastest cars of the 1950s, being capable of 160mph (257km/h) and beyond.

Jaguar E-Type

Jaguar contributed another landmark model in 1961 with the launch of the delectable E-Type. Although slower than some Ferraris, it was mass-produced, even if the 150mph (241km/h) achieved on test by members of the motoring press was not carried over to the production cars!

Then came the supercar, perhaps typified by the Miura of 1966 that was produced by the new Lamborghini marque. It not only looked sensational, it was good for over 170mph (274km/h).

The recession that engulfed the world in the 1970s was swept aside during the 1980s – this was the decade of the Ferrari F40, capable of 201mph (323km/h). By the middle of the 1990s, the ultimate car was the McLaren F1, which was timed at 240mph (386km/h). Today Koenigsegg's CCR has bettered that figure by a whisker – and Bugatti's Veyron looks set to raise the bar still higher…

Above: The long-awaited Bugatti Veyron should finally reach its first customers in 2006. With 987bhp on tap from the mid-mounted 8.0-litre W16 engine, the Veyron is said to be capable of 0-60mph (96km/h) in less than 3 seconds with a top speed of 252mph (405km/h).

Left: Just as Jaguar set the performance pace in the 1960s with the E-Type, it does today with its XK8 sports cars and with this supercharged 4.2-litre R model of the S-Type, which, with 400bhp on tap, makes it the company's most powerful saloon ever. New for 2002, it has a claimed governed top speed of 155mph (249km/h).

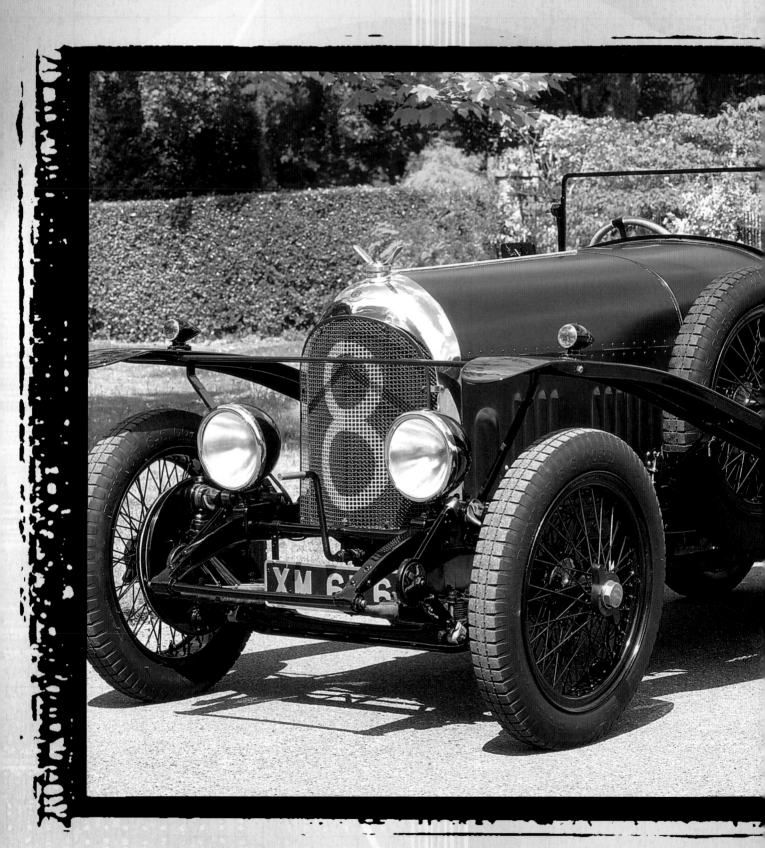

1886–1940
Birth of the Sports Car

Performance motoring has now been with us for over 100 years. The arrival in 1901 of the assured, innovative Mercedes, a car that was specifically designed with speed in mind, marks the birth of the sports car.

Initially such vehicles were expensive and thus exclusive, as the Bentley, Bugatti and Alfa Romeo marques of the inter-war years proved. But the appearance in the 1930s of the lower cost, visually attractive MG brought the sports car within the reach of a far wider public and created a buoyant market that continues to this day.

Birth of the Sports Car

 In the years prior to the outbreak of the Second World War fast cars were predominantly the preserve of an exclusive club of wealthy, young enthusiasts. They owned sports cars to capture the sheer delight and exhilaration of speed and to enjoy the sensation of rapid acceleration, the rip-roaring rasp of straight-cut gears or the scream from a supercharger that came in its wake.

And it was essentially an European passion. For the world's fastest road cars emanated principally from Germany, Italy, France and, to a lesser extent, Great Britain.

When Karl Benz and Gottlieb Daimler, each working independently of the other, first created motor cars in Germany in 1886, the 'horseless

carriages' they produced were capable of only around 10mph (16km/h). Both were powered by rear-mounted single-cylinder engines. It was only when, in 1891, French engineer Emile Levassor transferred the power unit to the front of the car, from where it drove the rear wheels via a clutch and in-line gearbox, that a configuration was born that was capable of almost infinite development.

Just 15 years after the German duo's pioneering efforts, the vehicle that should be accorded pole position on the historic starting grid of fast cars first saw the light of day. The 35hp Mercedes of 1901 was the work of Daimler's company, but it was designed after its founder's death by his able assistant, Wilhelm Maybach. Named after Mercedes Jellinek, the 10-year-old daughter of a

Below: A sports car in everything but name, this 60hp Mercedes dates from 1903 and in that year it won two major races. The absence of windscreen and doors was clearly no deterrent to the indefatigable motorists of the day.

valued Daimler customer, the designation was adopted to allay anti-Germanic feeling then prevalent in the all-important French market.

Featuring a low-slung pressed steel chassis and a fan-cooled honeycomb radiator, the Mercedes' engine used a throttle in the modern sense and employed soon to be universal mechanical inlet valves, rather than the atmospheric type then commonly in use. This potent car, capable of 60mph (96km/h) in its best known 60hp guise, was thus a design of great technical competence and it laid the foundations of a corporate high-performance image that endures to this day. (The merger with Benz to create the Mercedes-Benz marque did not occur until 1926.)

Mercedes was also in the forefront of motor racing although the grand prix, as such, did not exist until the first running of the French event in 1906. From then on racing cars would be in the vanguard of technological innovation that would then be passed down to the benefit of their roadgoing first cousins.

The French Peugeot company was responsible for the introduction in 1912 of the high efficiency twin-overhead-camshaft engine; this racing initiative was soon extended to sports cars which still use 'twin-cam' power units to this day. Prior to Peugeot's initiative most sporting models were powered by relatively simple side-valve engines. This certainly applied to Marc Birkigt's exquisite race-bred Alfonso Hispano-Suiza of 1911 which used a 3.6-litre 'four' that featured a dated T-head design. It was capable of a sparkling, safe and reliable 70 to 75mph (113-121km/h).

Later in the same year came Laurence Pomeroy's magnificent Prince Henry Vauxhall powered by a high revving 3-litre side-valve engine. It is often acclaimed as the world's first true sports car. This in turn gave birth to the equally impressive 4.5-litre 30/98 Vauxhall of 1913 which set the standard for British sports models of the 1920s. Able to attain over 80mph (129km/h) on the road, examples prepared for the racetrack could hit the magic 100mph (161km/h).

Above: Laurence Pomeroy's landmark Prince Henry Vauxhall, so named because two examples entered the 1910 Prince Henry Trials enjoying a trouble-free run and proving themselves capable of 72mph (116km/h), a respectable speed from a 3-litre engine. The road cars were sold with a guaranteed speed of 65mph (105km/h). The company described them as 'light carriages suitable for travelling or speed work'.

Above: A 3-litre Bentley of this type won the second Le Mans race of 1924 at 53.78mph (86.55km/h).

Below: A continental sports coupé: the 1938 Touring-bodied Alfa Romeo 8C2900B which ran at Le Mans in 1938.

The new 3.0-litre Bentley was the Vauxhall's great rival of the 1920s. W.O. Bentley steadily developed his cars throughout the decade, and the big green cars from Cricklewood dominated the Le Mans 24 hour race in its early years. John Duff and Frank Clement chalked up Bentley's first success there in the second 24-hour race, in 1924, and Bentleys won every race from 1927 to 1930.

Though Britain was a force to be reckoned with in sports car racing, the same could not be said in Grand Prix events, which were dominated in the interwar years by the car makers of continental Europe. Fiat and Alfa Romeo from Italy, Bugatti from France and, later, the mighty Mercedes-Benz and Auto Union teams from Germany pushed forward the frontiers of competition technology. The science of aerodynamics began to be applied to racing car bodywork, to reduce wind resistance and improve a vehicle's performance. By the 1930s this principle was being extended to road cars.

Design and innovation

While Britain remained faithful to the traditional open two-seater, Europeans recognized that closed bodywork was more aerodynamically efficient and provided greater comfort for the occupants. This concept was to give birth to the 'grand tourer' or GT. The trend was being given extra impetus by the arrival of straight, purpose-built motorways on which cars could be driven at high speed: the Italian autostradas date from 1924, and Germany's first autobahn was opened in 1933.

The most significant mechanical innovation was the supercharger – an engine-driven pump which forces air into the cylinders to improve power. Introduced in 1923 on the Fiat 805, the 'blower' continued to be standard wear for Grand Prix cars until the 1950s. Most of the manufacuturers in Grand Prix racing also produced supercharged road cars. Vittorio Jano's visually stunning Alfa Romeo 8C of 1931, for instance, which could attain 115mph (185km/h).

But a revolution was coming. The BMW 328 sports car of 1936 made practically all of its competitors look dated overnight. Its chassis was a sophisticated and lightweight tubular frame, and it was clothed in an aerodynamically efficient open body with a swept-back grille and integral headlights. The steering was by rack and pinion, the brakes were hydraulically operated, the front suspension independent in an era when beam front axles were the norm. The BMW beat most of its rivals for power-to-weight ratio, and trounced the rest with its grip and predictable handling.

While the BMW catered for well-heeled enthusiasts, MG produced sports cars for the less wealthy. Cecil Kimber's delightful boat-tailed M-type Midget of 1928, based on the Minor saloon from MG's parent company Morris, might only have achieved 65mph (105km/h) from its tiny 847cc engine, but it cost just £175. More than 3000 were built in four years, making it by far the world's most popular sports car. MG sports cars would delight British, and later American, enthusiasts for decades to come.

MG's formula – taking off-the-shelf engines and chassis, modifying them and clothing them in fashionable sporting bodywork – would be widely copied by manufacturers at home and abroad in the austerity years after the Second World War. Though the motor industry at large had a tough time in the 1940s, it would be an era which would give birth to some of the most extraordinary fast cars of all time.

Below: Bugatti, like Alfa Romeo, produced costly and exclusive supercharged sports cars that were closely related to their grand prix cars. This 1932 Type 55 is powered by a 2.3-litre twin-overhead-camshaft straight eight engine that was based on the Type 51 racer. Its price new was £1200.

1945–1950
Enter Ferrari and Porsche

With the ending of the war in 1945, most fast car makers dusted off their 1939 models which were quickly snapped up by a car-hungry public. While Britain remained faithful to its open two-seaters, which attracted American buyers in the wake of a UK government-directed exported drive, Continental Europe saw the birth of two new marques that would spawn some of the greatest performance cars of the post-war years – usually built in coupé form.

In 1948 Enzo Ferrari in Italy began the production of his 166 model and in the same year Porsche built the 356, the first of a legendary line. In this new world order times were certainly a-changing.

MG TC

**Top speed
75mph**
121km/h

*Right: The dashboard of a
sensitively restored 1947
TC. The steering wheel was
telescopically adjustable
and the seat back could
also be altered.*

*Below: Essentially carried
over from the pre-war TB,
the TC's distinctive lines
still delight enthusiasts
today. The exposed horn
and the spotlight were
standard fitments.*

 Like the HRG, the TC's design dated from the 1930s. However, here the similarities end because the MG became the world's most popular sports cars of the early post-war years. With the British government encouraging its car makers to export their products to gain valuable foreign currency, the stylish, practical two-seater, that was good for a top speed of 75mph (121km/h), brought MG a global audience, first in Australia and then, even more significantly, in America.

MG stands for Morris Garages and the company was the creation of its general manager, Cecil Kimber, who possessed a formidable flair for style and form. The TC's visual origins are to be found in the J2 Midget of 1932. This open two-seater with its wire spoked wheels, double humped scuttle, cutaways doors and bolster petrol tank, with all enveloping wings following in 1933, fathered an impressive stylistic line that was destined to survive until 1955.

The J2 was succeeded by the P-type Midget of 1934, but the TC's mechanical forebear was the larger Wolseley-engined 1.3-litre TA of 1936. This was replaced by the outwardly similar but Morris-powered 1.2-litre TB of 1939. The war interrupted production and when the MG factory at Abingdon, Berkshire restarted motor manufacture in 1945, the TB was dusted off, mildly updated and renamed the TC. Initially it was only available in black.

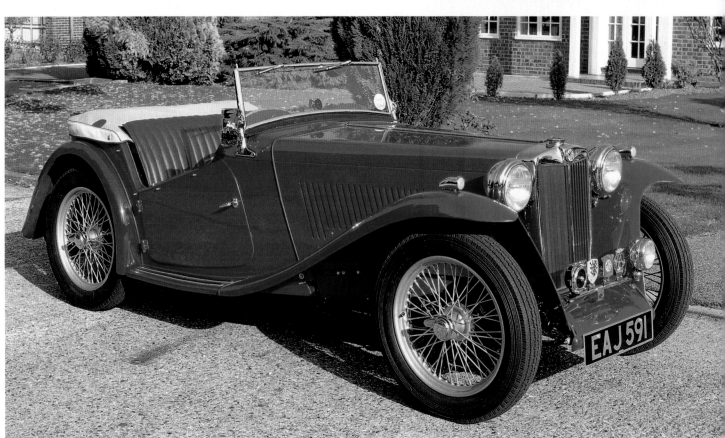

Although by then an archaic design which lacked independent front suspension and sporting a body that did not possess a whiff of aerodynamic refinement, the public nevertheless responded to its undoubted charm. A car-hungry marketplace that was singularly bereft of open two-seaters, and a selling price of a little over £500 did the rest.

Wind through the hair

When the TC's hinged windscreen was in the fold-flat position with the wind blowing through the driver's hair, it felt as though this harshly sprung little car was doing 90mph (145km/h), rather than the 75mph (121km/h) of which it was capable.

By the time production ceased in 1950, an unprecedented 10,000 of these MGs had been sold, of which 65 per cent were dispatched overseas. It was, to coin the company's corporate advertising slogan, 'the sports car America loved first', and the TC paved the way for the outwardly similar TD. This was enhanced with independent front suspension. A total of 30,000 were produced, of which some 80 per cent found American customers. This was in its turn replaced by the TF of 1953, the last of the line, which survived until 1955.

But MG's transatlantic successes had not been wasted on its competitors at home and abroad. The race for the American sports car market was on!

Specification	MG TC
Engine location	Front, in-line
Configuration	Four-cylinder
Bore and stroke	66 x 90mm
Capacity	1250cc
Valve operation	Pushrod
Horsepower	54bhp @ 5200rpm
Transmission	Manual four-speed
Drive	Rear
Chassis	Channel section
Suspension – front	Half-elliptic spring
Suspension – rear	Half-elliptic spring
Brakes	Hydraulic drum
Top speed	75mph (121km/h)
Acceleration	0-60mph (0-96km/h): 22.8 seconds

Left: The TC was powered by a twin-carburettor version of the durable EXPAG engine. In a more basic form the same unit powered Morris and Wolseley cars.

Below: The 1947 TC showing its cutaway doors and elegantly shaped rear wings which combined to convey a sense of speed.

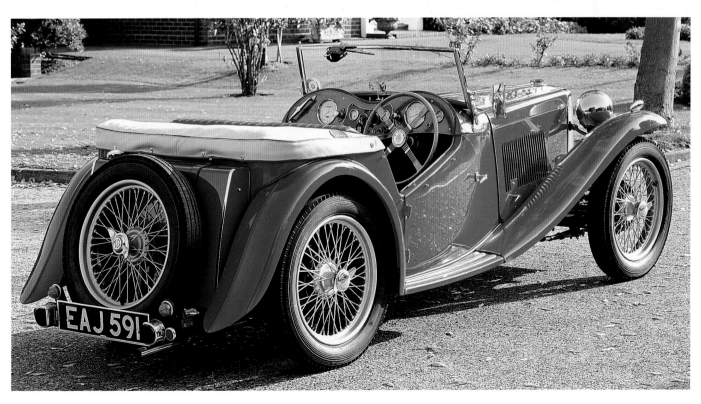

Cisitalia 202 Gran Sport

**Top speed
99mph**
159km/h

*Below: Although the
Cisitalia was principally
produced in coupé form,
there was also an open
version of which about 20
examples were built in
1947/48. With bodies by
Garella and Stabilimenti
Farina and originally
called the Spyder Sport
Special, it was soon re-
named the Spyder Nuvolari
as the great Tazio Nuvolari
drove one to second place
in the 1947 Mille Miglia.*

Although the little Cisitalia coupé of 1947 was only powered by an 1100cc engine, which was significantly smaller than the HRG and MG power units, it was capable of close on 100mph (161km/h).

No model more expresses the potential of Italy's post-war motor industry than the newly-minted Cisitalia make, created by Turin industrialist Piero Dusio. It had an impressive pedigree, having been designed by Dante Giacosa, the distinguished Fiat engineer who was responsible for the Fiat 500 *Topolino* of 1936, one of the most significant European small cars of the interwar years.

Giacosa undertook his Cisitalia work on a freelance basis. In the first instance he designed, in 1946, a single-seater racer with tubular space-frame chassis and transverse leaf independent front suspension, powered by an 1100cc Fiat engine. It was intended as a curtain-raiser at grand prix events but Dusio also wanted a roadgoing version for which Giacosa was also to be responsible.

However, Fiat was soon demanding all his time and attention and his place was taken by a colleague, Giovanni Savonuzzi, who joined Dusio's company. He, like Giacosa, designed a coupé, rather than a convertible body in the British tradition, because a closed car is aerodynamically more efficient, and thus potentially faster, than an open one.

His first wind tunnel-refined design, which featured two large stabilizing fins, was capable of 122mph (196km/h) but it did not lend itself to production. At Dusio's behest Savonuzzi tried again and created an exquisitely proportioned coupé that was shorn of any unnecessary decoration. Its construction was entrusted to Pinin Farina.

Excellent aerodynamics

Powered by a 55bhp engine, the Cisitalia 202 Gran Sport was launched at the 1947 Paris Motor Show. Production began in the following year but its size proved to be deceptive; it was found to be faster

than many larger-engined vehicles because of its excellent aerodynamics and low weight of 1713lb (777kg). When enhanced with an optional 60bhp engine, top speed was pushed to beyond the 105mph (169km/h) mark.

Then the car's styling attained international recognition when in 1951 it was lauded, along with seven others, by the New York Museum of Modern Art. The display enhanced Pinin Farina's coachbuilding reputation, although the Cisitalia's body was by then being built by Stablimenti Farina and Vignale.

Unfortunately Piero Dusio became distracted by a costly and complicated four-wheel-drive grand prix car and lost interest in his road model which ceased production in 1952. By then only 170 or so lucky customers had been able to sample the results of his inspired creation.

Above: A Cisitalia of a type which Taruffi ran in the 1948 Mille Miglia in 1200cc form before succumbing to piston failure.

Left: The definitive Cisitalia coupé of 1948 with a body by Pinin Farina that secured the stylist's international reputation.

Below left: Extraordinarily modern for 1947, like many other prestigious Italian marques of the day, it is right-hand drive.

Specification	Cisitalia 202 Gran Sport
Engine location	Front, in-line
Configuration	Four-cylinder
Bore and stroke	68 x 75 mm
Capacity	1089cc
Valve operation	Pushrod
Horsepower	55bhp @ 5500rpm
Transmission	Manual four-speed
Drive	Rear
Chassis	Unitary
Suspension – front	Transverse leaf spring and wishbones
Suspension – rear	Half-elliptic spring
Brakes	Drum
Top speed	99mph (159km/h)
Acceleration	0-60mph (0-96km/h): N/A

Jaguar XK120

**Top speed
120mph**
193km/h

*Below: This 1949 XK120 is
a rare aluminium-bodied
example. Most of these are
identifiable by the curved
windscreen pillars and
accompanying large rubber
grommets; the rest of the
outward features are shared
with the steel-bodied cars.
Although this is a right-
hand-drive version, the vast
majority of 120s were left
hookers destined for the
American market.*

 The first of Jaguar's fabled XK sports car
line, the 120 was so named because it
could attain 120mph (193km/h), an
unprecedented speed for a production model of its
day. Announced at the 1948 London Motor Show,
the line was destined to survive until 1961 when
the XK150 made way for the sensational E-Type.

The 120's powerful performance came courtesy
of a 3.4-litre, twin-overhead-camshaft, six-cylinder
engine, the legendary XK unit, that had been
conceived during the war to power the company's
new 100mph (161km/h) Mark VII saloon. This,
paradoxically, appeared in 1950, *after* the open
two-seater sports car.

Manufactured for export

William Lyons, Jaguar's accomplished chairman
who also styled his company's products, ensured
that his new model had the looks to match its
performance. It was conceived at a time when the
British government was directing the country's
motor manufacturers to export their products
overseas and the overwhelming majority of the
Coventry-built XK120s were produced in left-
hand-drive form for the American market.

Based on the chassis of the simultaneously
announced Mark V saloon, the public was
astounded by the new Jaguar's much publicized top
speed. Lyons confounded his critics by carefully
preparing a mildly streamlined test car which, in
1949, attained 132mph (212km/h) on the Jabbeke
motorway in Belgium.

Demand for the 120 was intense. After the first
240 cars, which used aluminium bodywork, had
been completed, steel panels replaced the
aluminium – a change that modestly increased the
model's weight.

The new XK engine undeniably proved its
worth. While the twin-cam concept had a pre-war
reputation for unreliability, the new Jaguar unit was
durable and dependable, to the extent that it
remained in production until 1992.

Left: How it achieved 120mph (193km/h): the 120's legendary twin-overhead-camshaft XK engine. The absence of studs on the front of the cam covers indicates an early car.

Left below: Most 120s had a black steering wheel, but white was occasionally offered during the XK150 production run. The hood was stored behind the seats when not in use.

Below: This fine XK120 fixed-head coupé in rallying guise has optional wire wheels in place of the usual discs and bonnet straps. Unlike the roadster, this possessed a walnut dash and door cappings, courtesy of Jaguar's saloon line.

Enter the drophead coupé

In 1951 the XK120 roadster was joined by a drophead coupé version. This was not only stylistically successful but it also had an enhanced interior with walnut veneer replacing the open car's leathercloth-covered instrument panel.

A Special Equipment package was offered for both versions from 1952 and this included high lift camshafts, a lightened flywheel, twin exhaust pipes and handsome centre-lock wire wheels which replaced the original discs. These ministrations added 20bhp to the 160bhp the XK unit developed in 1948.

The final variation on the XK120 theme was a drophead coupé which appeared in 1953. This combined the comfort of the fixed head coupé with the fresh air of an open car. Mechanically there was little to choose between all three models although the later versions used a quieter Salisbury rear axle.

XK 120 production ceased in the autumn of 1954. By then, Jaguar had established itself as one of the world's leading sports car manufacturers.

Specification	Jaguar XK120
Engine location	Front, in-line
Configuration	Six-cylinder
Bore and stroke	83 x 106mm
Capacity	3442cc
Valve operation	Twin overhead camshafts
Horsepower	160bhp @ 5000rpm
Transmission	Manual four-speed
Drive	Rear
Chassis	Box section
Suspension – front	Wishbone and torsion bar
Suspension – rear	Half-elliptic spring
Brakes	Drum
Top speed	120mph (193km/h)
Acceleration	0-60mph (96km/h): 12 seconds

Ferrari 166 Inter

**Top speed
100mph**
161km/h

The 166 has the distinction of being Enzo Ferrari's first road car, but it was not his first model, that accolade being accorded to the competition-honed Type 125 of 1947. Unusually for the day Ferrari opted for a V12 engine and the 2-litre, 60 degree unit which had a single overhead camshaft per bank was designed for him by Gioacchino Colombo, creator of Alfa Romeo's famous Alfetta racing car of 1938.

The 166's engine was mounted in an oval tubular chassis enhanced by transverse leaf front suspension although the live axle was sprung with conventional half-elliptic rear springs. A five-speed gearbox with synchromesh on third and top gears was employed.

Enzo Ferrari

Enzo Ferrari had managed Alfa Romeo's racing team in the 1930s, and so (not surprisingly) he adopted a similar approach to competition when he established a marque under his own name. During 1947 and 1948 all the cars produced at the Maranello works were either campaigned by the factory or by their prosperous owners.

Introduced in competition-proven 166 Sport form in 1947, the 166 Inter was a touring Ferrari, if that is not a contradiction in terms. Announced at the 1948 Turin Motor Show, the first two examples were fitted with coupé bodies by the respected Carrozzeria Touring concern and built to its superleggera (super light) principles featuring a sub-structure of small diameter tubes.

The closed car conjured up echoes of the body that Touring had already produced for Alfa Romeo; the finely proportioned, austere open version with its distinctive sculptured front was named the barchetta (little boat) and it was widely imitated.

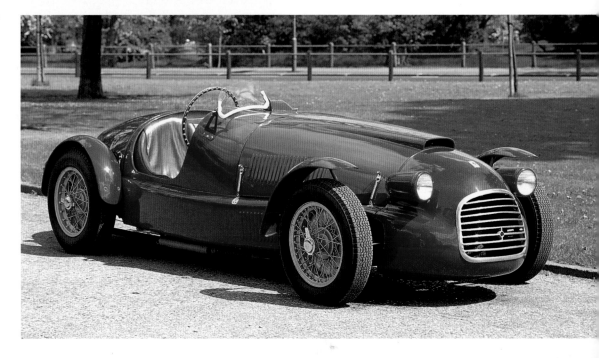

Above: One of a handful of pillarless coupés that Touring built on the 166 chassis, each differing slightly from one another. Even though produced in Italy, these early Ferraris are right-hand-drive cars.

Right: A Spyder Corsa competition version of the 166 with an open two-seater body for sports racing events, but with the minimum of weather equipment. Note the length of the bonnet which concealed a V12 engine, a feature of the marque that still endures.

Specification	Ferrari 166 Inter
Engine location	Front, in-line
Configuration	V12
Bore and stroke	60 x 58mm
Capacity	1995cc
Valve operation	Single overhead camshaft per bank
Horsepower	110/115bhp @ 6000rpm
Transmission	Manual five-speed
Drive	Rear
Chassis	Oval tubular
Suspension – front	Wishbones and transverse leaf spring
Suspension – rear	Half-elliptic spring
Brakes	Drum
Top speed	100mph (161km/h)
Acceleration	N/A

Above left: Although Ferrari maintained that he chose a V12 engine because of its use by Packard in 1915, it was a configuration employed in Mercedes-Benz and Alfa Romeo racing cars in the immediate pre-war years.

Left: The no-frills barchetta two-seater created for the 166MM chassis by Touring. The company's famous Superleggera badge can be seen on the front right-hand side of the bonnet with the nearby cold air intake serving the engine's carburettors.

At that time Ferrari only sold his cars in chassis form – they were then bodied in response to a specific customer or dealer order. This is why no two 166s are exactly alike! In all Touring created the bodies for some five cars, but other examples were the work of a variety of talented Italian coachbuilders, namely Stablimenti Farina, Vignale, Bertone, Allemano and Ghia.

Three prestigious road race wins

Capable of a reliable and sustainable 100mph (161km/h), in 1949 Ferrari 166s won the world's three most prestigious road races, namely the Mille Miglia, the Targa Florio and Le Mans. The 24 hour race in 1949 was the first to be held since the end of the Second World War, and Chinetti and Selsdon averaged 82.27mph (132.4km/h). Ferrari would go on to take the chequered flag at the Sarthe circuit on no less than nine occasions.

Below left: The barchetta's cockpit with the distinctive leather beading around its edge readily apparent, as is Ferrari's prancing horse motif on the steering wheel boss. Unusually for the day, the 166 was fitted with a five-speed gearbox.

In two years about 39 examples of the 166 were produced, three Sports and 36 Inters. Although the 166 was listed into 1953, it had been replaced the previous year by the 2.5-litre 212. Ferrari was on his way!

Frazer Nash Le Mans Replica

**Top speed
130mph**
209km/h

Below: This 1950 Le Mans Replica has a colourful history. It was displayed in chassis form at the 1950 Turin Motor Show, being acquired by Italian racing driver/collector Count 'Johnny' Lurani, who had a coupé body built by Motto. It later returned to Britain where the Italian coachwork was removed and restorer Dick Crossthwaite produced this copy of a Le Mans Replica body

Capable of speeds approaching 130mph (209km/h), Frazer Nash's Le Mans Replica was a well-engineered, expensive sports racer in the continental manner, being a derivative of BMW's fabled 328 sports car of 1936. Its origins are, however, somewhat convoluted! From 1935 until the outbreak of war in 1939, Frazer Nash had marketed the German make in Britain under the Frazer Nash-BMW name.

With the coming of peace in 1945, 'Nash's H.J. Aldington formed an association with the Bristol Aeroplane Company, which wanted to join the ranks of motor manufacturers. It was decided that as well as making the Filton-built Bristol, the firms would jointly create a new generation of Frazer Nashes that would continue to be assembled at Isleworth, Middlesex.

BMW designs and personnel were accordingly 'liberated' from Germany and the Bristol 400 coupé, a selective cocktail of proven BMW concepts, entered production in 1947. In that year

the association between the two businesses was unscrambled and Frazer Nash car production, similarly BMW-based, began in 1948. There were two models, a Fast Tourer with full-width two-seater coachwork, and the more powerful, stark and purposeful High Speed.

The work of former BMW engineer Fritz Fiedler, both shared the same 328-derived twin tubular chassis, while the 2-litre, six-cylinder, high efficiency pushrod engine sprang from the same source and was already being used in the Bristol.

Streamlined two-seater

Developing 120bhp when fitted in the High Speed 'Nash, 40hp more than the Fast Tourer, it was clad in a functional, streamlined, open two-seater body, complete with cycle wings, for which Fiedler was also responsible. But at £3073 it was expensive and would have bought no less than six MG TCs!

It was clearly geared for the competition owner-driver. One such was Norman Culpan who entered

his car for the first post-war Le Mans race held in 1949. With Aldington as co-driver, the duo averaged 78.53mph (126.38km/h) for the 24 hours and attained a creditable third placing. As a result the High Speed name was discontinued, and the Le Mans Replica was born for the 1950 season. It remained in production until 1953 – a revised simpler chassis having arrived in 1952. A total of 34 were completed.

The touring car had passed through Fast Tourer, Roadster and Millie Miglia guises, and in 1952 it was again updated and became the Targa Florio. The Fixed Head Coupé was created for the 1953 Le Mans event where it won the 2-litre class but the racing Sebring roadster of 1954 was the last of the line and only three were built. The final cars were assembled in 1956 and that, effectively, was the end, after 32 years, of the Frazer Nash.

Left: Instrumentation was impressive and dominated by a 5in (127mm) diameter 120mph (or 200km/h) speedometer and 6000rpm revolution counter. Other dials included water and oil temperature gauges. The driver could also activate a foot-operated pump for a 'one-shot' chassis lubrication system.

Below left: The view other drivers experienced as a Le Mans Replica overtook them. The hinged tail was a feature of the later cars, it was originally made in one piece. An aluminium 20-gallon (91lit) petrol tank was fitted. The external exhaust system is an original feature and the small silencer at its end is another authentic touch.

Bottom left: The Frazer Nash's Bristol engine of BMW ancestry. The triple Solex carburettors are mounted on the top of the alloy cylinder head, rather than on its side, a layout necessitated by the ingenious cross pushrod design.

Specification	Frazer Nash Le Mans Replica
Engine location	Front, in-line
Configuration	Six-cylinder
Bore and stroke	66 x 96mm
Capacity	1971cc
Valve operation	Pushrod
Horsepower	120bhp @ 5200rpm
Transmission	Manual four-speed
Drive	Rear
Chassis	Twin tube
Suspension – front	Transverse leaf spring and wishbones
Suspension – rear	Torsion bar
Brakes	Drum
Top speed	130mph (209km/h)
Acceleration	0-60mph (0-96km/h): 7.5 seconds

Allard J2

**Top speed
130mph**
209km/h

*Below: Stripped for action:
a J2X destined for the
American market and fitted
with aero screens rather
than the usual full-width
windscreen. The longer
nose concealed the coil
springs that had been
exposed on the J2.*

Sydney Allard had campaigned Ford V8-based specials in pre-war days and in 1938 he began limited production of such cars at his garage in the south London suburb of Clapham. Work stopped during the Second World War but manufacture resumed in 1946. Allard offered the chunky no-frills K1 open two-seater with its distinctive waterfall-style cowled radiator.

The accent was on simplicity and a good power-to-weight ratio. Allard used a straightforward chassis and a simple but effective divided independent front suspension axle although he retained Ford's crude Model T-inspired transverse leaf springing. The three-speed gearboxes came from the same source.

Monte Carlo Rally

The robust 3.6-litre side-valve V8 engine provided both reliability and acceleration and the K1 was joined by L and M1 four-seaters, while Sydney Allard himself won the 1952 Monte Carlo Rally in the P1 saloon version.

But the sports-racing J2 of 1949 saw a return to first principles. The open two-seater body did away with doors and was removable; it was even starker than its predecessors and came complete with cycle wings. It was ideal transport for the enthusiast who wanted to drive to the racetrack and then compete there. The J2's mechanicals differed from the earlier models with the use of a de Dion rear axle and all-round coil springs.

Even when Ford V8-powered, with a 4.4-litre Mercury ohv conversion, the J2 was capable of over 100mph (161km/h), but when one of the new generation of American V8s was installed, then the Allard really went motoring. These engines, it should be said, were usually fitted in those cars sold on the US market, because import restrictions prevented the Allard company from spending precious dollars on the purchase of new units.

However, the firm was able to acquire a few engines for experimental purpose and the prototype 331cid (5.4-litre) Cadillac-engined J2 with 160bhp on tap was capable of a spirited 130mph (209km/h), no less than 100mph (161km/h) in second gear and 80mph (129km/h) in first cog!

Specification	Allard J2 (Cadillac engine)
Engine location	Front, in-line
Configuration	V8
Bore and stroke	3.81 x 3.63in (97 x 92mm)
Capacity	331cid (5.4 litres)
Valve operation	Pushrod
Horsepower	160bhp @ 4000rpm
Transmission	Manual three-speed
Drive	Rear
Chassis	Box section
Suspension – front	Divided beam and coil spring
Suspension – rear	De Dion axle and coil spring
Brakes	Drum
Top speed	130mph (209km/h)
Acceleration	0-60mph (96km/h): 7 seconds

With such acceleration it could pull away from a Jaguar XK120. American enthusiasts also delighted in fitting alternative Oldsmobile or Chrysler V8s. This latter unit, also of 331cid, was a feature of the revised J2X for the 1952 season. This outwardly resembled its predecessor although it had a longer nose section because the engine was mounted 7in (178mm) further forward to allow more room for the occupants.

Built until 1952, the X was succeeded by the Cadillac-engined JR of 1953, the last of the line. Its aerodynamic body was in stark contrast to the functional appeal of its predecessor. In all 187 J Series cars were built, 99 J2s, 83 J2Xs and just five JRs. By 1960 the Allard was no more.

Above: A J2 showing its original windscreen and distinctive triangulated side pieces in place. The spare wheel could be fitted on either side of the body.

Left: A J2 fitted with a 3.6-litre British-built Ford V8. Although a side-valve unit, aluminium cylinder heads were added to extract 90bhp rather than the usual 85.

Healey Silverstone

**Top speed
105mph**
169km/h

*Opposite top: The
Silverstone's cockpit. This
1950 car is an example of
the E-type model with a
bench-type front seat in
place of the original two
buckets. It is also slightly
wider than the original
version and a telescopic
steering column adds a
further refinement.*

*Opposite below: The E-type
Silverstone is instantly
identifiable by the air scoop
on the bonnet top. The
wings were easily
detachable for racing and
the headlamps, concealed
for aerodynamic
considerations behind the
radiator grille, are a
notable feature. Note the
alloy trailing arm
independent front
suspension, a costly
refinement!*

*Right: The Silverstone's tail
contained a 17-gallon
(77lit) petrol tank while the
protruding segment of the
spare wheel did double duty
as a rear bumper, one not
being fitted for cost
considerations. It was held
in place by a fixing, access
to which was obtained
through a small panel
located directly above the
number plate.*

Rally driver Donald Healey began manufacturing cars under his own name in 1946. In the next eight years he produced no less than eight mostly Riley-engined models from a small factory at Warwick. Of these the best known is the 105mph (169km/h) Silverstone of 1949/50.

The first Healeys, the Westland Roadster and Elliott saloon, were some of the fastest cars of their day – an example of the latter model was timed at 104.7mph (168.5km/h) on an Italian *autostrada*. This was because Healey had adopted Riley's potent and efficient 104bhp 2.5-litre engine. These were expensive cars, the saloon cost £1598, and, as a small, newly established manufacturer, Donald Healey recognized his vulnerability when in 1948 the British government doubled the rate of purchase tax, from 33⅓ to 66⅔ per cent, on all cars that sold for over £1000.

The result was the cost-conscious two-seater Silverstone of 1949, named after Britain's newly opened motor-racing circuit. Aimed at the club racing fraternity in Britain and America, it sold for £975 and was thus liable for the lower 33⅓ per cent rate of duty. Based on the standard Healey 100 chassis, the engine and gearbox were moved 8in (203mm) back in the frame and its rear was modified to accommodate an enlarged 16 gallon (73lit) petrol tank.

Streamlined headlamps

As the emphasis was placed on simplicity and low cost, the bodywork was of straightforward construction. Designed by Len Hedges of the Birmingham-based Panelcraft concern, in the interests of aerodynamics the headlamps were contained within the cowled radiator grille in the manner of pre-war streamlined Peugeots.

The windscreen was a novel feature as it could be lowered into the bodywork for racing. To keep costs down there was no rear bumper; instead the horizontally mounted spare wheel, which resided in a sort of letterbox-like slot, performed that function too. Weighing some 448lb (203kg) less than the earlier Healeys, the Silverstone could easily exceed 100mph (161km/h) and was able to hit 80mph (128km/h) in third gear.

In 1949 an example won the manufacturers team prize in the British Racing Drivers' Club Production Car Race, appropriately held at Silverstone. No less than eight participated in the following year's event and Duncan Hamilton won his class at 79mph (127km/h).

By the time that production ceased in September 1950 a total of 105 Silverstones had been completed. But Healey was beginning to recognize that his cars were too big, heavy and expensive. The result was the Healey 100 which appeared in 1952.

Specification	**Healey** Silverstone
Engine location	Front, in-line
Configuration	Four-cylinder
Bore and stroke	80 x 120mm
Capacity	2443cc
Valve operation	Pushrod
Horsepower	104bhp at 4500rpm
Transmission	Manual four-speed
Drive	Rear
Chassis	Box section
Suspension – front	Trailing link and coil spring
Suspension – rear	Torque tube and coil spring
Brakes	Drum
Top speed	105mph (169km/h)
Acceleration	0-60mph (0-96km/h): 11 seconds

Porsche 356

**Top speed
101mph**
163km/h

*Below: Early days: the
Porsche marque had only
been in existence for three
years when this 356 coupé
was completed in 1951.
This example was owned
for many years by arch-
enthusiast Betty Haig. The
smooth body contours
reflect a shape that was the
product of scrupulous
aerodynamic refinement.
The divided windscreen was
replaced by a single curved
screen for 1952.*

Porsche is one of the great German
sporting marques of the post-war years.
However, the 356, the first of the line,
actually began life in Austria. In the autumn of
1944 Dr Ferdinand Porsche's engineering
consultancy business, which was principally
located in Stuttgart, had also established a base at a
former sawmill which the family owned at Gmund,
high in the Austrian mountains. It was thus out of
reach of Allied bombing raids.

In 1948 Porsche's son Ferry, inspired by the
Fiat-powered Italian Cisitalia, decided to produce a
sports car using Volkswagen mechanicals, Dr
Porsche having been responsible for the design of
the famous Beetle in 1933-38. The first
experimental 356 coupé was completed in June
1948 and, although VW-based, it had its own
distinctive aerodynamically refined body. However,
beneath the louvred engine cover sat the Beetle's
rear-mounted, air-cooled, 1131cc flat-four engine
with twin carburettors, which produced 40 rather
than 25bhp. By contrast, most production Porsches
used a 1086cc version to bring the model within the
1100cc sports racing class.

Capable of 85mph (137km/h), this
unconventional sports car was also produced in
open (cabriolet) forms, and it continued to be built
in Austria until 1951. But in the previous year
assembly had been transferred to Stuttgart and that
was when 356 development began in earnest.

In 1951 a supplementary 1286cc engine was
introduced, and this was followed for 1952 by a
1.5-litre version available in 54bhp and Super
69bhp states of tune. The latter designation was to
remain a 356 feature from then on.

For the revised 356A of 1956 the existing 1.3-
litre and 1.5-litre engines were supplemented by a
1582cc unit. This '1600' model, which would continue
until the end of 356 production, was capable of
over 100mph (161km/h) in Super specification. But
already an even faster 356 was available.

It was called the Carrera, after the Carrera
Panamericana road races in which Porsche had
been successful in 1952 and 1954. Those successes
had come with the 550 Spyder sports racer, which
donated its engine to the new Carrera, a 100bhp
1.5-litre unit with twin overhead camshafts on each
bank of cylinders and a built-up roller bearing

crankshaft. Raucous and rapid, the Carrera soon won the hearts of enthusiasts all over the world.

The mainstream 356B arrived for 1960. The basic 1600 now developed 60bhp and the Super was a 90bhp car capable of 110mph (177km/h). In 1962 the Carrera 2 arrived, with a 2.0-litre 130bhp engine which significantly improved acceleration.

The last of the line, the 356C, was introduced for the 1963 model year. Horsepower was up again, with 75bhp now available from the basic version and 95 from the Super. The 356C survived until 1965, when it was replaced by the 911 – and a new chapter in Porsche's history began.

Above: This 1955 Speedster was also owned by Betty Haig. This no-frills model was supplied with a hood which looked unsightly when raised and also leaked in the rain!

Left: It could be no other car. The rear-located engine of this 356A is revealed by the presence of an air intake grille.

Below left: The 1582cc engine of the 356A, still displaying its flat-four Volkswagen Beetle ancestry and its twin carburettors readily apparent.

Specification	Porsche 356A
Engine location	Rear, in-line
Configuration	Horizontally opposed four-cylinder
Bore and stroke	82 x 74mm
Capacity	1582cc
Valve operation	Pushrod
Horsepower	70bhp @ 4500rpm
Transmission	Manual four-speed
Drive	Rear
Chassis	Platform
Suspension – front	Trailing arm and torsion bar
Suspension – rear	Swing axle and torsion bar
Brakes	Drum
Top speed	101mph (163km/h)
Acceleration	0-60mph (0-96km/h): 15.4 seconds

Aston Martin DB2

**Top speed
118mph**
190km/h

*Right: Unusually, the entire
front end of the DB2 hinged
forward to permit access to
the Bentley-designed twin-
overhead-camshaft engine
and independent front
suspension.*

*Below: The DB2 in its
original form with body
lines inspired by the Italian
berlinettas of the day. At this
stage only two occupants
could be accommodated.*

 The famous Aston Martin marque was
effectively reborn with the appearance, in
April 1950, of the DB2. Named after
David Brown, the company's owner since 1947, the
model was destined to survive until 1959.

It represented the union of Aston Martin with
the Lagonda make that Brown had acquired in
1947. The chassis, of square section tubes, came
courtesy of a 1939 Aston Martin prototype saloon
named the Atom, while the 2.6-litre, 100bhp, twin-
overhead-camshaft, six-cylinder engine was the
work of W.O. Bentley, no less. It had been designed
to power the post-war Lagonda saloon car line
which Brown also perpetuated.

However, his first Aston Martin was the 2-litre
Super Sports of 1948, retrospectively dubbed the
DB1. This, like the pre-war cars, was an open
model and used the Atom's chassis and ohv engine.
But it was an expensive concept and only 15 were
sold. Production ceased in 1950.

It was replaced in that year by the DB2 which
boasted closed coachwork in the manner of the
latest sporting *gran turismos* from Italy. The work
of talented Lagonda stylist, Frank Feeley, it was
every inch a thoroughbred and performed as well as
it looked. Top speed was in the region of 110mph
(177km/h), but later in 1950 a more powerful
116bhp Vantage version appeared and a drophead
coupé body was also introduced.

Arrival of the new DB2/4

The 1954 season saw the arrival of the DB2/4 which turned the mainstream coupé into an occasional four-seater which had a rear-opening door, an innovation at that time. A curved windscreen replaced the original divided one. The extra weight meant that the Vantage engine was fitted as standard but it was soon replaced, from April 1954, by an enlarged, race-proven, 3-litre unit. Top speed rose to 118mph (190km/h).

A Mark II version followed for 1956 which was outwardly similar but identifiable by its more angular rear wings. Although the drophead option continued, there was also a notchback version which lacked the rear door.

The final version, the DB Mark III, was launched at the 1957 Geneva Motor Show. This differed visually by having a new front end with a curved radiator grille and lower bonnet line. It concealed a revised 162bhp engine and the company's competition experience was reflected in the optional fitment of front Girling disc brakes that had been developed on the company's DB3S sports racer. Originally only available for export, American influence was reflected when an automatic gearbox became available for 1959. Production ceased that year as the III made way for the DB4, a total of 1724 examples of the line having been built since 1950.

Above: A DB2/4 with a one-piece windscreen rather than the divided one of its predecessor and two small seats introduced in the rear.

Left: The DB2's interior. The rubber heel pad on the driver's side is an original fitting, as is the grab handle on the passenger's.

Specification	Aston Martin DB Mark III
Engine location	Front, in-line
Configuration	Six-cylinder
Bore and stroke	83 x 90mm
Capacity	2992cc
Valve operation	Twin overhead camshafts
Horsepower	162bhp @ 5500rpm
Transmission	Manual four-speed
Drive	Rear
Chassis	Tubular square section
Suspension – front	Trailing arms and coil spring
Suspension – rear	Radius arm and coil spring
Brakes	Front disc, rear drum
Top speed	118mph (190km/h)
Acceleration	0-60mph (0-96km/h): 9.4 seconds

DDD 5

1951–1960
The Sports Car Boom

With the American economy booming in the 1950s, Britain became the world's largest provider of fast cars with Jaguar and MG roadsters joined by the newly minted Austin-Healey and a revived Triumph marque.

In Europe the grand touring theme was given expression in the delectable gullwing-doored Mercedes-Benz 300SL coupé, a reminder that Germany was, once again, a force to be reckoned with.

France produced the Facel-Vega that used a powerful but low-cost American engine, while the ubiquitous V8 was also to be found under the bonnet of the United States' own Chevrolet Corvette. After years of mass producing family saloons, the Americans were now building a fast car of their own.

Triumph TR2

**Top speed
103mph**
169km/h

*Below: Although created
with the American market
in mind, a fair proportion,
some 30 per cent, of TR2
production was sold in the
home market. This was a
much higher figure than
Triumph's Jaguar and MG
rivals, so right-hand-drive
Triumph roadsters are
nothing like as rare. Its
functional lines reflect a
very cost-conscious product.
This example is fitted with
optional wire wheels.*

Triumph's famous family of TR sports cars first took the stage in 1953 with the appearance of the TR2. It was destined to endure until the TR7, the last of the line, ceased production in 1981.

In 1944 the moribund Triumph company had been acquired by Standard's Sir John Black with the intention of challenging the growing stature of Jaguar. Its superlative XK120 had been created at governmental behest for the American public, a market which had been first exploited by MG's TC Midget. The TR line (standing for Triumph Roadster) was intended to occupy the territory between these two models.

Triumph's tentative design appeared at the 1952 London Motor Show. Retrospectively designated the TR1, this used a pre-war Standard Flying 9 chassis enhanced by a chunky, open two-seater body essayed by Standard's Walter Belgrove and powered by a 1991cc version of the engine used in the new Vanguard saloon.

In truth, these unrelated components required 'sorting out' and the task was successfully accomplished by Standard's Harry Webster and ex-BRM driver Ken Richardson. The most significant modification was the introduction of a stronger purpose-designed chassis. Their ministrations resulted in the definitive TR2 which entered production in August 1953.

Rally success

With engine output boosted from 75 to 90bhp and capable of exceeding the magic 100mph (161km/h), Triumph's new sports car got off to a flying start when it won the 1954 RAC Rally. This was to prove to be the first of many successes in such events. But in sales terms the TR2's achievement was more modest and by the time that production ceased in the autumn of 1955, a total of 8628 had been completed. Of these about 70 per cent had found American owners.

Its TR3 replacement for 1956 was outwardly

similar, although it was identifiable by its egg-crate radiator grille in the Ferrari idiom. Front disc brakes arrived for the 1957 season and were a notable first for a British car. This model lasted until mid-1957 when the TR3A was announced. Sharing the same body style, it was fitted with a full-width radiator grille while under the bonnet the engine was boosted to 100bhp. The A was initially sold exclusively on the American market.

The four-cylinder TR line came of age with this model and between the autumn of 1957 and October 1962 some 61,000 examples were produced – of these an overwhelming 98 per cent were exported, mostly to the United States.

Throughout, TR performance had remained at about the same level with the accent on continual refinement. These first models of the line were noted for their mechanical simplicity and, in consequence, for reliability. These were sound foundations on which the company built when it planned its next generation of TR sports cars for the 1960s.

Above: The TR2 line would not acquire a forward-mounted radiator grille until the TR3's arrival.

Left: This is a 1954 car, for 1955 the doors were decreased in depth and sills were added.

Below left: The TR2's engine was shared with the in-house Standard Vanguard and Ferguson tractor.

Specification	Triumph TR2
Engine location	Front, in-line
Configuration	Four-cylinder
Bore and stroke	83 x 92mm
Capacity	1991cc
Valve operation	Pushrod
Horsepower	90bhp @ 4800rpm
Transmission	Manual four-speed
Drive	Rear
Chassis	Box section
Suspension – front	Wishbones and coil spring
Suspension – rear	Half-elliptic spring
Brakes	Drum
Top speed	103mph (169km/h)
Acceleration	0-60mph (0-96km/h): 11.9 seconds

Bentley Continental

**Top speed
115mph**
185km/h

*Right: The Continental's
driving compartment with
the polished walnut
dashboard almost wholly
occupied by instruments.
The right-hand gear change
is clearly visible.*

*Below: This is the prototype
Continental of 1951,
affectionately known as
'Olga' on account of its
distinctive number plate,
which happily escaped from
the factory. Its roof is 1in
(25mm) higher than the
production versions.*

 With a top speed of 115mph (185km/h), and clothed in a handsome and distinctive fastback body by H.J. Mulliner, the Bentley Continental of 1952 was, in its day, the fastest production four-seater car in the world.

Destined for a seven-year manufacturing life, the Continental was a spiritual successor of the Bentley Corniche, an experimental aerodynamic saloon of 1939 that did not enter production because of the outbreak of war. As such, it was a model that carried on the traditions of the well-appointed intercontinental grand tourers that were popular in the 1930s.

In 1946 Rolls-Royce introduced its Silver Wraith and related Bentley Mark VI lines. While the former was only available with bespoke coachwork, over 80 per cent of the Bentleys were fitted with a standardized four-door saloon body by Pressed Steel.

Corniche II

Based on the R-Type chassis that was to replace the Mark VI frame in 1952, Rolls-Royce had begun work on what had been internally coded 'Corniche

II' in 1950. The emphasis was placed firmly on aerodynamic refinement and weight-saving and the memorable body was styled by RR's Ivan Evernden. However, the saloon's 4.6-litre, overhead inlet/side exhaust engine had its compression ratio raised from 6.4 to 7.3:1 and a new exhaust system was fitted.

The prototype, completed in August 1951, was taken to the Montlhéry racing circuit near Paris where it proceeded to average 118.75mph (191.1km/h) over five laps.

Announced in February 1952, the Continental was priced at £6929, which made it one of the most expensive cars on the market. Initially it was only available for export but a right-hand-drive version appeared for the 1953 season.

In the event the overwhelming majority of the 208 R-Type Continentals built were sold in Britain, which accounted for 108 of them. France was in second place with 33, followed by America's 28, and Switzerland's 24. Belgium, Canada and Portugal each took two cars apiece.

Engine capacity increased

After two years in production, in July 1954 the capacity of the Continental's engine was increased to 4.9 litres and four-speed automatic transmission became an option.

In 1955 came the S-Series saloon, the Bentley version of the Rolls-Royce Silver Cloud, both of which used Pressed Steel bodywork. However, the bespoke Continental option was perpetuated although the resulting car was slightly longer than its predecessor because of a new lengthened chassis. The model remained in production until 1959. Its demise spelt the end, for the time being at least, of a Bentley with a purpose-designed body. However, the concept was later revived with the Continental R of 1991.

Specification	Bentley Continental (R-Type)
Engine location	Front, in-line
Configuration	Six-cylinder
Bore and stroke	92 x 114mm
Capacity	4566cc
Valve operation	Overhead inlet/side exhaust
Horsepower	Not disclosed
Transmission	Manual four-speed
Drive	Rear
Chassis	Channel section
Suspension – front	Wishbones and coil spring
Suspension – rear	Half-elliptic spring
Brakes	Drum with mechanical servo
Top speed	115mph (185km/h)
Acceleration	0-60mph (0-96km/h): 13.5 seconds

Above: The view that most other drivers experienced when a Bentley Continental overtook them! To help keep weight down, the bumpers were made of heavy-gauge light alloy. The boot was commodious and the tools and jack were carried in a separate compartment.

Left: Originally the rear wheels were covered with spats in the interests of aerodynamic efficiency. The stop lights mounted on each wing doubled as flashing indicators at a time when semaphore units were the norm. There were also twin reversing lights positioned alongside the number plate.

Pegaso Z102

**Top speed
125mph**
201km/h

*Right: The Pegaso seats
are unusual with a one-
piece shaped aluminium
backrest to which leather
upholstery was clipped.*

*Below: One of the 19
coupés Touring built for
Pegaso in 1954. Produced
in Milan on the Z102B
chassis to its superleggera
principles, this featured a
sub-structure of strong
load-bearing tubes.*

 Cars built regardless of cost were not uncommon in the interwar years but they did not feature much in the harsher realities of the early post-war era. However, the Spanish Pegaso was precisely that. Capable of 125mph (201km/h), it was looked upon by its makers as a publicity vehicle to draw attention to its truck, bus and coach lines.

The business in question was the nationalized ENASA, the acronym for *Empresa Nacional de Autocamiones SA*, which was established in Barcelona in 1946. Its products were named Pegaso, after Pegasus, the winged horse of Greek mythology, and this name was extended to the car that was unveiled at the 1951 Paris Motor Show.

It was the work of Spanish engineer Wilfredo Ricart, who in the 1920s had been responsible for the Ricart Espania car and who subsequently became technical director of Alfa Romeo. Hand-built in the Barcelona factory which had previously produced the costly and prestigious Hispano-Suiza,

the Z102 Pegaso was a car in very much the same idiom. All its mechanical components, with the exception of the Bosch electrics, were produced in the Calle de Segrera works while the bodies were respectively by two of the world's finest coachbuilders, Touring in Milan and the Paris-based Saoutchik concern.

Left: This Z102B chassis was unconventionally bodied by the Parisian coachbuilder Saoutchik and was named El Dominicano on its completion in 1954.

Below: Rear view of this uncompromising two-seater. Note that the lines of the boot lid echo those of the nose. And no conventional bumpers were fitted to detract from the body lines. The flush-fitting door handles reflect aerodynamic considerations.

Chain drive replacement

The engine was a fearsome, light, alloy 2.5-litre V8 with twin overhead camshafts per cylinder bank. Although initially chain driven, they were soon replaced by more efficient but costly and noisy gears. A single twin-choke Weber carburettor was specified although a more potent version was listed with no less than four. The five-speed gearbox was mounted in unit with the De Dion rear axle.

The steering gear was a study in its own right and passed through the fascia rather than the floor. Its subsequent contortions made it probably the most complex such system ever fitted to a production car. And, unusually for any car, the interior controls were set out on the dash rather like a row of piano keys!

But such ambitious specifications were expensive and the Z102 cost £3000. Customers were initially offered an alternative 2.8-litre engine, then a supercharged 2.5. Handling, brakes and steering were, not surprisingly perhaps, in the Alfa Romeo league and the Pegaso could attain 100mph (161km/h) in fourth gear.

Later, in 1954, came yet another engine variation in the shape of a 3.2-litre V8 with twin Roots superchargers and magneto ignition. A perhaps optimistic 185mph (298km/h) was quoted as its top speed. Finally in 1956 came the Z103 with a new pushrod V8 and, again, varying capacities of 4 or 4.7 litres. Just four were completed, making a total of 84 Pegasos built by 1958 which was when ENASA ceased car-making to concentrate on its more popular commercial vehicle lines, an activity that continues to this day.

Specification	Pegaso Z102 (2.5 litres)
Engine location	Front, in-line
Configuration	V8
Bore and stroke	75 x 70mm
Capacity	2474cc
Valve operation	Twin overhead camshafts
Horsepower	165bhp @ 6500rpm
Transmission	Manual five-speed
Drive	Rear
Chassis	Unitary
Suspension – front	Wishbones and torsion bar
Suspension – rear	De Dion axle and torsion bar
Brakes	Drum
Top speed	125mph (201km/h)
Acceleration	0-60mph (0-96km/h): 10.3 seconds

Fiat 8V

**Top speed
120mph**
193km/h

*Below: Although the
majority of 8Vs were bodied
by the factory, some chassis
were enhanced by specialist
Italian carrozzerias, namely
Ghia, Bertone, Zagato and
Vignale. This 1953 example,
arguably more attractive
than the standard car, is the
work of Bertone. This
coachbuilder's associations
with Fiat stretched back to
a time soon after Giovanni
Bertone established his
business in Turin in 1912.*

Fiat is best known for providing small,
distinctive cars for the ordinary 'Italian in
the street'. But in 1952 it introduced what
can be regarded as a 'poor man's Ferrari' in the
shape of the 8V, a hand-built coupé for the
discriminating few that was capable of 120mph
(193km/h) and proved its worth in GT class races.

This was Fiat's first sports cars since the Ballila
of 1934. The 8V, *Otto Vu* in its native land and so
called because Ford owned the rights to the V8
name, was launched at the 1952 Geneva Motor
Show. Work on the project had begun in 1950
under the direction of chief engineer Dante
Giacosa. The compact 2-litre alloy V8 engine was
initially designed for use in a prestigious Pinin
Farina-styled version of Fiat's impending 1900
saloon, but this never actually got into production.

It was used in the 8V in no less than three states
of tune: the standard model was powered by a
105bhp unit, but there were alternative versions,
with higher compression ratios and different
camshafts, which variously produced 115 and
127bhp. So there was plenty of choice!

The bodies, the styling was by Rapi, were
produced by Fiat in its experimental workshops.
However, the cars were assembled by SIATA, the
Turin-based tuning business that specialized in
Fiats, and this company developed a five-speed
gearbox for the 8V. The model also had the
distinction of being the first Fiat to employ all-
independent suspension.

The body panels were built around a tubular
framework and were invariably finished in metallic
cellulose. Later versions featured twin vertical
headlamps, a styling feature that was rediscovered
by the Americans in the early 1960s. The bumpers
and body mouldings were made of stainless steel, a
nice touch.

Competition successes

Strictly a two-seater with the spare wheel
occupying the space behind, the 8V was able to
attain a noisy 89mph (143km/h) in third gear and
120mph (193km/h) in top. It enjoyed some
competition successes, notably taking the Italian 2-
litre GT Championship in 1954. However, a works

Above left: This body on an 8V chassis is by Alfredo Vignale, who established his own carrozzeria in Turin in 1948, having been foreman at Stabilimenti Farina.

Above: An 8V by Zagato of Milan. Its owner, Elio Zagato, son of the founder, ran such an 8V himself in which he achieved many sporting successes.

Left: Not a production 8V but an experimental gas-turbine-powered version completed in 1954, hence the excess of dashboard instrumentation!

sortie to Le Mans in the previous year had been less successful when an example fitted with an experimental SIATA five-speed gearbox proved to be quicker in fourth gear than in top!

In addition to the usual factory coachwork, there were versions by Ghia and Zagato. The factory also exhibited an emerald green glass-fibre-bodied example at the 1954 Geneva show but the idea was not taken any further. An experimental gas turbine version produced in the same year suffered a similar fate.

A lack of demand resulted in production ceasing at the end of 1954 after a mere 114 examples of this all too exclusive Fiat had been completed but its memory lingers on.

Specification	Fiat 8V
Engine location	Front, in-line
Configuration	V8
Bore and stroke	72 x 61mm
Capacity	1996cc
Valve operation	Pushrod
Horsepower	105bhp @ 6000rpm
Transmission	Manual four-speed
Drive	Rear
Chassis	Unitary
Suspension – front	Wishbone and coil spring
Suspension – rear	Wishbone and coil spring
Brakes	Drum
Top speed	120mph (193km/h)
Acceleration	0-60mph (0-96km/h): 12.3 seconds

Chevrolet Corvette

**Top speed
105mph**
169km/h

*Right: A 1955 Corvette's
dashboard with centrally
positioned rev counter. This
is one of a few cars built in
that model year to be fitted
with a manual gearbox.*

The first of a legendary line, the Corvette
was created by America's General Motors
Corporation in response to the British
open two-seaters that were increasingly appearing,
albeit in modest numbers, on American roads
during the early 1950s.

The result was distinctly transatlantic in flavour
with, to European eyes, a garish open two-seater
body created by GM's styling supremo, Harley
Earl. Because of the low production volumes
envisaged, it was made of glass fibre. This was
mounted on a bespoke chassis and under the bonnet
was a 235cid (3.8-litre) six-cylinder engine; two-
speed automatic transmission, with a floor gear
change, was fitted.

In truth this first Corvette of 1953 was a bit of a
horror but then America's last true sports car had
been the Mercer Raceabout of 1911! Only available
in that first year in polo white with a red interior,
GM's first performance model was marred by
indifferent handling, a worrying characteristic when
the top speed was an alarming 105mph (169km/h).

Against a background of poor sales, the
Corporation contemplated scrapping the 'Vette but
wisely, in 1955, replaced the six with a 265cid (4.3-
litre) V8. A three-speed manual gearbox arrived for
the 1956 season. Performance perked up and the
car was now capable of speeds nudging the
120mph (193km/h) mark.

All-new design

The body was rethought for 1956 with the
unveiling of an all-new design – the hitherto rather
bland profile was enhanced by the introduction of
sculptured side panels which were sometimes
finished in a contrasting colour. A detachable
hardtop was an option and quadruple headlights
followed in 1958.

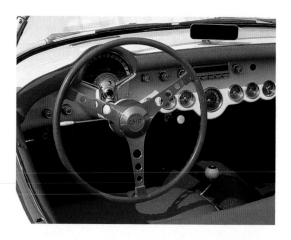

*Right: Exterior of the same
1955 car with smoother
body panels than previously
– teething production bugs
of the two previous years
had been ironed out.*

*Opposite below: This is one
of only a handful or so '55
Corvettes to be six-cylinder-
powered. Most used the V8
engine, a configuration
which would apply to every
'Vette from then on.*

Millionaire racer

The engine's capacity had been upped to 283cid (4.6 litres) for the 1957 season and, interestingly, fuel injection was available as an option although initially it proved to be unreliable. More significantly, in 1960 American millionaire Briggs Cunningham entered a team of three Corvettes in that year's Le Mans race. Although he crashed in the third hour, one car was placed a creditable eighth and the other also finished.

More changes were in store: in 1961 further body refinements included a neatly sculptured tail, which was the work of William Mitchell who had replaced Earl in 1958. Performance was now top of the agenda and in 1962 the engine was again enlarged, this time to 327cid (5.3 litres).

With the Corvette now capable of 150mph (241km/h), Mitchell opted for a complete facelift. The result for the 1963 season was the Sting Ray, arguably the most memorable Corvette of all.

Below: A 1955 Corvette, the first year in which the model was powered by a V8. A 265cid unit was fitted, the CheVrolet script on the side of the front wing being so embellished.

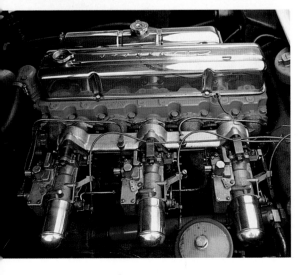

Specification	**Chevrolet** Corvette (1953)
Engine location	Front, in-line
Configuration	Six-cylinder
Bore and stroke	3.56 x 3.93in (90 x 100mm)
Capacity	235cid (3.8 litres)
Valve operation	Pushrod
Horsepower	150bhp @ 4200rpm
Transmission	Automatic two-speed
Drive	Rear
Chassis	Box section
Suspension – front	Wishbones and coil spring
Suspension – rear	Half-elliptic spring
Brakes	Drum
Top speed	105mph (169km/h)
Acceleration	0-60 mph (96km/h): 11.2 seconds

AC Ace

**Top speed
118mph**
190km/h

*Right: The 2-litre Bristol
engine, as fitted to the Ace
from 1956. At £1340 it cost
a significant £240 more
than the AC-powered
version.*

*Below: A 1955 AC-engined
Ace. It was owned for some
years by photographer Neill
Bruce, whose work appears
in this and many other
motoring books.*

The handsome, sure-footed, open two-seater Ace, a car capable of over 115mph (185km/h) in its most potent form, enjoyed a respectable ten-year production life. More significantly it is best remembered for having formed the basis of the legendary Cobra.

Paradoxically, the Ace did not begin life at AC's Thames Ditton, Surrey factory but at the Hertfordshire premises of engineer John Tojiero who designed, for the club racing fraternity, a tubular chassis fitted with all-independent transverse leaf suspension. Cliff Davis was one such competitor and in 1952 he acquired a Tojiero frame in which he fitted a Bristol engine. The mechanicals were then enclosed by an open two-seater body inspired by the Ferrari 166 Barchetta that had won the 1949 Mille Milgia race.

Following a successful 1953 racing season, by chance AC's Charles Hurlock heard of this car and decided to acquire it. There followed a rapid

transformation which turned it into the Ace which the company then displayed at the 1953 London Motor Show. The only principal difference was the removal of the Bristol engine and its replacement by AC's long-running, 2-litre, overhead-camshaft, six-cylinder alloy unit. However, while this was extraordinarily advanced when it was unveiled in 1919, 34 years on it was nearing the end of its life.

Choice of engines

Nevertheless, it was destined to remain available in triple carburettored 85bhp form throughout the Ace's production span; so powered, this lively open two-seater was able comfortably to exceed 100mph (161km/h). Early in 1956 the Ace was also offered with a choice of 105 and 120bhp Bristol engines which transformed its performance. So equipped, the Ace could now exceed 115mph (185km/h).

By this time the model had spawned a derivative in the shape of the Aceca coupé of 1955 that was also available in Bristol-powered form. Yet a further variant was the longer-wheelbase Greyhound coupé of 1960 with coil spring and wishbone independent front suspension.

Unfortunately in its latter years the Ace was threatened with a loss of engines. AC's six was nearing the end of its development, while Bristol was making the switch to a Chrysler V8 and so its potent and versatile six was destined for extinction. As a result in mid-1961 the Ace was offered with a 2.6-litre Ford Zephyr engine in varying states of tune. Perhaps surprisingly, the Ford-powered open two-seater could exceed 110mph (177km/h).

The model ceased production in 1963. But this was far from being the end of the story because American racing driver Carroll Shelby proposed that it should form the basis of the Cobra (see page 82). So the Ace survived, in essence, for a further six years.

Specification	AC Ace (Bristol 100D engine)
Engine location	Front, in-line
Configuration	Six-cylinder
Bore and stroke	66 x 96mm
Capacity	1971cc
Valve operation	Pushrod
Horsepower	120bhp @ 6000rpm
Transmission	Manual four-speed
Drive	Rear
Chassis	Twin tubular
Suspension – front	Transverse leaf and wishbone
Suspension – rear	Transverse leaf and wishbone
Brakes	Drum
Top speed	118mph (190km/h)
Acceleration	0-60mph (0-96km/h): 9.2 seconds

Left: Cockpit of the 1955 Ace, the 50th built. Owners occasionally specified that the handbrake should be moved from the transmission tunnel to the right of the driver's seat.

Below: The earlier cars had circular rear lights while later versions had a shorter boot lid to improve aerodynamics when the hood was raised.

Mercedes-Benz 300SL

**Top speed
140mph**
225km/h

*Right: The steering wheel
hinged along its centre to
allow the driver to get in.
Only left-hand-drive cars
were built.*

*Below: The gullwing 300SL
in all its glory. The
distinctive grille in the front
wing was intended to permit
hot air to escape from the
engine compartment.*

One of the truly delectable dream cars, the
300SL coupé is forever remembered for
its upward-opening gullwing doors to the
extent that its 140mph (225km/h) top speed, fast
now but truly sensational in 1954, is often
overlooked. It was an instant thoroughbred.

The 300SL, signifying 3-litre super light, was
competition bred, its sports-racing predecessor
having appeared in 1952. It was powered by a six-
cylinder overhead camshaft engine, courtesy of the
300S road car, but this and other production
components imposed a weight penalty. The
Stuttgart engineers strove to save precious
kilograms by the use of a light, strong, but complex
tubular space-frame chassis. This demanded that
the tubes should be continued as high as possible
along the sides of the driving compartment which,
in turn, ruled out the use of conventional doors.
The answer was the imaginative and ingenious
gullwing units that opened vertically and were
hinged along the coupé's roof line.

These cars had dominated the 1952 racing
season but they were not campaigned in the
following year because corporate resources were
dedicated to the successful launch and running of
the W196 Formula 1 car.

However, in New York, Max Hoffman, a car
dealer *par excellence* who specialized in the import
of European sports models, convinced Mercedes-

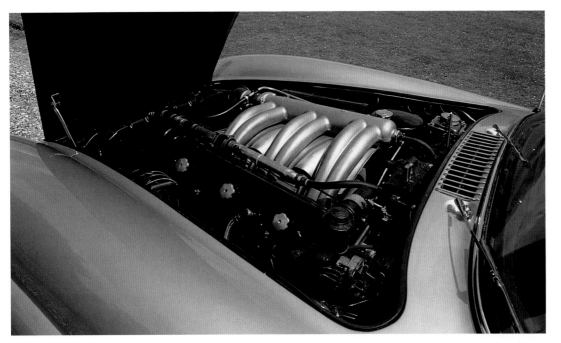

Left: The 300SL's 3-litre, six-cylinder, single-overhead-camshaft engine inclined 50 degrees from the vertical to permit a low bonnet line. Fitted with Bosch fuel injection, it was the first production car to be so equipped. A dry sump unit, it was a modified version of that used in the company's 300 model which appeared in 1951.

Benz of the viability of a roadgoing version of the gorgeous gullwing coupé and promptly ordered 1000. The resulting model was the star of the 1954 New York sports car show.

Racing pedigree

Under the bonnet the 3-litre, six-cylinder, Bosch fuel-injected engine, the first to be fitted in a production car, was inclined to the left to permit a low body line, although this ruled out a right-hand-drive version. The use of dry sump lubrication was a further reminder of the model's racing pedigree while an all-synchromesh gearbox with a floor change, rather than Mercedes' usual column system, was employed.

With room for only two occupants, the steering wheel hinged forward at its lower edge to permit the driver to get in. There was some space behind the seats for luggage but, although the boot outwardly appeared reasonably large, most of the space was occupied by the spare wheel and the large petrol tank.

The coupé's acceleration was phenomenal: it could reach 70mph (113km/h) in second gear and 98mph (158km/h) in third. But handling was tricky and maintenance costs formidable. Nonetheless exactly 1400 examples had been completed when production ceased in 1957. Of these, 29 were lightened cars. These desirable models had all-alloy bodywork and enhanced engines, and were capable of 155mph (249km/h).

Left: One of the famous gullwing doors in the open position. They do take a little time to open and Mercedes-Benz experimented with a variety of handles before finalizing the design. Luggage was stored behind the front seats, the manufacturer offering bespoke suitcases that were held in place with straps to fit into the space.

Specification	Mercedes-Benz 300SL
Engine location	Front, in-line
Configuration	Six-cylinder
Bore and stroke	85 x 88mm
Capacity	2996cc
Valve operation	Single overhead camshaft
Horsepower	190bhp @ 6100rpm
Transmission	Manual four-speed
Drive	Rear
Chassis	Tubular steel space-frame
Suspension – front	Wishbones and coil spring
Suspension – rear	Swing axle and coil spring
Brakes	Drum
Top speed	140mph (225km/h)
Acceleration	0-60mph (0-96km/h): 8.9 seconds

Facel Vega HK500

**Top speed
147mph**
237km/h

*Below: Unmistakable and
rapid, the Franco/American
Facel Vega HK500 of 1959,
by which time right-hand-
drive was available. The
sills were protected by
stainless steel pressings
which also made a visual
contribution to the design.
The deep screen and low
bonnet resulted in excellent
visibility for the driver.*

Take a powerful American V8 engine and
install it in a distinctive coupé body,
complete with aircraft-style controls, and
you have the essentials of the Facel Vega, a French
make that only survived a mere ten years.

Launched at the 1954 Paris Salon, the model
was the brainchild of Jean Daninos, whose
business, *Forges et Ateliers de Construction d'Eure
et Loire* (hence Facel), produced specialist car
bodies for the likes of Panhard, Simca and Ford
France. However, as the mass-produced saloon
moved centre stage, this aspect of Daninos'
business began to decline, so he decided to produce
his own cars. The two-door Facel Vega FVS was
the result. The car's appearance was chunky, the
twin vertically mounted headlamps distinctive and
the well appointed interior was awash with
aeronautical themes.

Luxury seating

The instruments extended into a console located
between the front seats, establishing a trend in car
design that continues to this day. Occupants
luxuriously reclined in 'roly-poly' seats.
Refinements included such transatlantic influences
as electric windows and the twin radio aerials that
sprouted from the rear fins. In fact only one of
them was operative!

The engine compartment was pure Detroit.
Initially Daninos chose a 4.5-litre 'hemi' Chrysler
V8 which had been used in its De Soto make.
There was, inevitably, Powerflite two-speed
automatic transmission although a manual gearbox
was available at extra cost. Even in this form the
FVS was capable of some 130mph (209km/h) in
the manner of the pre-war *grand routiers* which
mopped up the kilometres with such ease.

Specification	Facel Vega HK500
Engine location	Front, in-line
Configuration	V8
Bore and stroke	104 x 85mm
Capacity	5910cc
Valve operation	Pushrod
Horsepower	360bhp @ 5200rpm
Transmission	Manual four-speed
Drive	Rear
Chassis	Unitary
Suspension – front	Wishbones and coil spring
Suspension – rear	Half-elliptic spring
Brakes	Disc
Top speed	147mph (237km/h)
Acceleration	0-60mph (0-96km/h: 8.5 seconds

Nevertheless, it was not long before Daninos began to opt for larger engines, their capacity first being increased to 4.8, then 5.4 and, ultimately, 5.8 litres. The less popular and unwieldy four-door Excellence followed in 1958.

The HK500, the definitive Facel, appeared in 1959. It was essentially an uprated FVS although it was by then packing a 5.9-litre V8 and 360bhp under its bonnet. Power steering was then well established and the 500 was a 147mph (237km/h) car, even if disc brakes did not arrive until 1960.

The end of the line

The 6.3-litre Facel II, the last of the line, appeared in 1962. It was outwardly more attractive, being lower and more angular, although this was to the detriment of the driving position. There was even more power with a 390bhp option but the model only survived for two years.

Sadly, Daninos' business foundered in 1964, partly because of his decision to introduce the smaller and cheaper Facellia with its own purpose-designed engine.

Above left: The Facel Vega's unusual deeply dished steering wheel. Note the quantity of instrumentation and that the minor controls are located within the innovative central console. The leather-trimmed seats were particularly comfortable, and the cockpit was roomy when judged by the standards of the day.

Left: The twin vertically mounted headlamps dated from the marque's origins in 1954 and were later adopted by the American motor industry in the early 1960s. The steering was moderately low-geared. By this time all-round Dunlop disc brakes had been fitted. In truth, the expensive, well-equipped HK500 had no direct rivals.

Alfa Romeo Giulietta SS

**Top speed
124mph**
199km/h

 An inspired union of Alfa Romeo's sophisticated mechanicals and Bertone's extravagant styling resulted in the Giulietta SS coupé, a car that was able to exceed 120mph (193km/h) when it appeared in 1957. It is considered by many enthusiasts to be one of the most beautiful Alfa Romeos of the post-war years.

Its origins are to be found in the Giulietta Sprint of 1955, a Bertone-styled coupé capable of attaining 110mph (177km/h). This, perversely, appeared before the four-door saloon on which it was based! In both instances power came from a 1.3-litre, twin-overhead-camshaft engine which developed 55bhp in its most basic form. The Sprint, by contrast, had an 80bhp unit which was also available in 90bhp Sprint Veloce guise.

Styling by Bertone

Then, at the 1957 Geneva Motor Show, the SS was unveiled. The initials stood for Sprint Speciale. This creation had a daring and extravagantly styled Bertone body that revealed the influence of a series of experimental aerodynamically related BAT (*Berlina Aerodinamica Tecnica*) cars produced between 1953 and 1955.

Unlike the Sprint which was built by Alfa Romeo, Bertone had responsibility for the SS's production. The aim was to produce a lighter, more aerodynamically efficient coupé, and although aluminium was originally used for its construction, from 1959 this was changed to steel. The model was based on shortened version of the Sprint's sub-structure with a 7ft 5in (2260mm) wheelbase; this was 4in (101mm) less than its predecessor. There was only room for two people, and understandably not much space for their luggage. However, the SS was cheaper than the more spacious Sprint.

Ministrations to the SS's 100bhp engine included the fitment of twin Weber carburettors and a higher 9.7:1 compression ratio. A five-speed gearbox was employed. There was also a version

Above: The Bertone-bodied Giulietta Sprint Veloce, this version boasting 90bhp rather than the customary 80. In consequence it could attain 110mph (177km/h), rather than the usual 100mph (161km/h) plus. Handling was excellent.

Right: A 1961 Guilietta SZ. Zagato arrived at this shape without the aid of a wind tunnel but rather by trial and error on the autostrada. Unveiled at the 1960 Turin Motor Show, it featured a light steel frame clad with alloy panels.

Specification	**Alfa Romeo** Giulietta SS
Engine location	Front, in-line
Configuration	Four-cylinder
Bore and stroke	74 x 75mm
Capacity	1290cc
Valve operation	Twin overhead camshaft
Horsepower	100bhp @ 6500rpm
Transmission	Manual five-speed
Drive	Rear
Chassis	Unitary
Suspension – front	Wishbones and coil spring
Suspension – rear	Live axle, coil spring
Brakes	Drum
Top speed	124mph (199km/h)
Acceleration	0-60mph (96km/h): 11.3 seconds

with a chunky Zagato body called the SZ; 200 of these were built. This was lighter than the Bertone-built car as Zagato dispensed with much of the original underframe. Designed for racing, its top speed remained about the same although it accelerated harder than its stablemate.

Of the two, the SS was the more practical and thus the more popular car, and 1366 examples were completed by the time that the Giulietta, on which it was based, ceased production in 1962. Its replacement that year was the Giulia saloon. The SS remained in production and was accorded the new name. A further 1400 were duly completed with the last of the line being built in 1965, the final 30 examples being fitted with all-round disc brakes, a somewhat belated refinement.

Above: A 1963 Giulietta Sprint Speciale, the most beautiful of the post-war Alfa Romeos.

Above left: The Sprint Speciale's dials were readily visible to the driver.

MGA Twin Cam

**Top speed
113mph**
182km/h

*Below: The standard
pushrod-engined MGA
roadster of 1959, then the
most popular sports car in
the world. This 1.6-litre
version was enhanced by
front disc brakes and wire
wheels were available at
extra cost. Most were
exported to the USA.
However, side screens were
still fitted; winding windows
would have to wait until
the MGB.*

The long awaited replacement for the T-Series family, the MGA of 1955 was destined to become the world's most popular sports car. Over 100,000 had been completed by the time that production ceased in 1962 with about 80 per cent of this output having been sold in America.

If MG had been left to its own devices, the A could have entered production in 1952. That was when the Abingdon factory produced a prototype, designated EX 175, which closely resembled the finished product, but in the same year Morris Motors, of which MG was a part, had merged with Austin to form the British Motor Corporation. And the chairman, Leonard Lord, chose the Healey 100 (see page 72) as BMC's corporate sports car.

The MGA eventually reached public view three years later, but because the model had not yet been officially announced, a trio of cars were run at the 1955 Le Mans race under the EX 182 name. Two were placed 12th and 17th while the third one crashed in the fifth hour.

Open two-seater

Designed by MG's chief engineer, Syd Enever, the MGA was officially launched at the 1955 London Motor Show as a well proportioned, full-width, open two-seater. As befitted the merged businesses, the 1.5-litre pushrod engine was of Austin origin, and was known as the B- Series in corporate parlance. It endowed the A with a top speed of over 95mph (153km/h).

The 1957 season saw the roadster joined by a coupé version. The engine was enlarged to 1588cc in 1959 although top speed remained about the same. A Mark II version of the design followed in 1961 with the engine's capacity again being increased, this time to 1622cc; the revised cars were outwardly identifiable by a recessed radiator grille. The A was replaced in 1962 by the even more successful MGB.

In the meantime a more potent version of the MGA had entered production in 1958. This was the Twin Cam that was somewhat faster than the original, being able to exceed 110mph (177km/h).

Available in both roadster and coupé forms, it outwardly resembled the originals, with the exception of handsome centre-lock Dunlop disc wheels. All-round disc brakes were a further departure from the original specification. Under the bonnet was a 1588cc, B-Series-based, 108bhp, twin-overhead-camshaft engine.

Twin Cams were briefly raced by MG in 1958, before a corporate ban on competition put a stop to such activities. However, the road cars, unusually for an Abingdon product, suffered from niggling faults. These were progressively resolved but they had damaged the model's sales prospects and production ceased in 1960 after just 2111 Twin Cams had been completed. They are, consequently, much sought after today by collectors.

Above: One of the few giveaways of what lurked beneath the bonnet, these badges adorned the top of each front wing.

Left: A Twin Cam roadster shod with the distinctive centre-lock Dunlop wheels. Disc brakes were fitted all round. It was also available in coupé form.

Below left: The BMC-based twin-overhead-camshaft engine, which developed some 30bhp more than the pushrod version. Reliable – if sensitively maintained!

Specification	**MGA** Twin Cam
Engine location	Front, in-line
Configuration	Four-cylinder
Bore and stroke	75 x 89mm
Capacity	1588cc
Valve operation	Twin overhead camshaft
Horsepower	108bhp @ 6700rpm
Transmission	Manual four-speed
Drive	Rear
Chassis	Box section
Suspension – front	Wishbones and coil spring
Suspension – rear	Half-elliptic spring
Brakes	Disc
Top speed	113mph (182km/h)
Acceleration	0-60mph (0-96km/h): 13.3 seconds

Ferrari 410 Superamerica

**Top speed
165mph**
266km/h

*Below: Rare and rapid, this
style of Pinin Farina body
was only applied in 1959 to
10 or 12 Superamericas.
About half had cowled
headlights while the final
four or five, of which this
car is one, featured exposed
units. These so-called
Series 3 cars were produced
in 1958 and 1959 and their
4.9-litre V12 engines
developed an impressive
400bhp.*

It did not take Enzo Ferrari long to recognize the potential of the transatlantic market. In 1951 he launched his potent, costly and exclusive America models, a line which led to the 410 Superamerica of 1955.

In those early years there was a close relationship between Ferrari's racing and road cars and this particularly applied to the America series. Formula 1 regulations of the 1946-1951 era specified that race cars should either have 1.5-litre supercharged engines or 4.5-litre uncharged ones. Prior to 1950, Ferrari, like most manufacturers, opted for the latter configuration. However, in that year his chief engineer Aurelio Lampredi created the Type 375 Formula 1 car which was powered by the larger V12 and the success it enjoyed effectively spelt the end of the supercharger in grand prix racing.

The first example of the line, the 340 America, was unveiled at the 1950 Paris Motor Show with a 4.1-litre V12 'Lampredi' engine mated to a five-speed all synchromesh gearbox. The cars which followed were variously bodied by Vignale and, in particular, Ghia. Most were sports racers – of the 22 completed, only about eight were road cars.

For 1953 came the 342 America, a more civilized road car, mostly bodied by Pininfarina. Only six were built. Its 375 America successor was produced in rather larger numbers. It had a 4.5-litre engine and the 350bhp it developed meant a top speed of some 130mph (209km/h).

Faster replacement

Its 410 Superamerica replacement for the 1956 season had a 340bhp 5-litre engine. It was even faster, being capable of between 137mph and 162mph (220km/h and 260km/h), depending on the rear axle ratio chosen by the owner. Again production was limited, only 15 were completed, and most were Pinin Farina coupés.

In 1957 the 410 received the longer 8ft 6in (2600mm) chassis of its Superfast stablemate; these were designated the Series 2 cars but only about seven were completed. However, the Series 3 of 1958-59 was, by contrast, almost mass produced because 15 were built. While this retained its predecessor's 4.1-litre V12 engine, changes to the cylinder head design saw its output soar to 400bhp.

As befitted their name, most of these cars were sold in America; tellingly the US *Road & Track* magazine recorded a top speed of 165mph (266km/h) in a three-year-old example with a slipping clutch!

For the record, the 410 Superamerica of 1960 was the last of the line and one of the fastest road cars in the world being able to hit the 180mph (290km/h) mark. It was a car with few rivals, with the possible exception of the Maserati 5000 GT.

Left: The vented side panels adjoining the rear windows of these Series 3 cars revived a feature that had appeared on Ferrari's 4.9 Superfast of 1957 and replaced the glass of the earlier cars. Note the Pinin Farina badge mounted on the door panel which has moved from its customary location on the wing because of the presence of hot air outlets.

Left: The Superamerica's dashboard is unusual because, instead of being covered in the customary leather, Ferrari instead opted for a black crackle paint finish that had previously been reserved for its sports-racing cars. Practically every example was left-hand drive.

Specification	Ferrari 410 Superamerica Series 3
Engine location	Front, in-line
Configuration	V12
Bore and stroke	88 x 68mm
Capacity	4962cc
Valve operation	Single overhead camshaft per cylinder bank
Horsepower	340bhp @ 6000rpm
Transmission	Manual four-speed
Drive	Rear
Chassis	Oval tubular
Suspension – front	Wishbones and coil spring
Suspension – rear	Half-elliptic spring
Brakes	Drum
Top speed	165mph (266km/h); see text
Acceleration	0-60mph (0-96km/h): N/A

BMW 507

**Top speed
125mph**
201km/h

*Right: The 507's engine
was not only Germany's
first V8 but also, in 1954,
the first in the world to be
mass-produced in alloy.
The twin carburettors are
Zenith units.*

*Below: A modern classic, a
507 with the hardtop in
place. Although it is
detachable, it looks an
integral part of the body.
Paradoxically, sales were
slow although today it is a
much sought-after car.*

 Capable of nearly 125mph (201km/h),
BMW's graceful but expensive 507 did
not, alas, attract customers in great
numbers; only 250 examples were produced
between 1956 and 1959. BMW cars had been built
before the Second World War at Eisenach in what
subsequently became East Germany. Production of
a 2-litre 501 saloon, based on the pre-war 326, did
not restart at the company's former aero-engine
factory in Munich until 1951.

The 507's origins can be traced to this model. It
was much improved by the fitting, in 1954, of a
new 2.5-litre aluminium V8 engine. This was a first
in Germany – the car was designated the 502. It
was designed by Fritz Fiedler, who had returned to
BMW after a spell in England, where he had been
responsible for the design of Frazer Nash's High
Speed model (page 24).

With its engine enlarged to 3168cc in 1955, the
502 was renamed the 3.2 and survived in this form
until 1961. At that year's Frankfurt Motor Show
BMW introduced the 503 which was based on the
3.2 chassis. This was endowed with a new coupé
body by the German-born freelance stylist Count

Albert Goertz, who had opened a design studio in
New York in 1951. He had been encouraged to bid
for the BMW assignment by importer Max
Hoffman, who specialized in the sale of European
cars and who had played a catalytic part in the
creation of the race-bred and fabulous Mercedes-
Benz 300SL gullwing coupé.

The 507, a short wheelbase derivative which
had 16in (400mm) taken out of its chassis, was
even more attractive. Goertz's flawless roadster
body is rightly regarded today as styling of the

Specification	BMW 507
Engine location	Front, in-line
Configuration	V8
Bore and stroke	82 x 75mm
Capacity	3168cc
Valve operation	Pushrod
Horsepower	150bhp @ 5000rpm
Transmission	Manual four-speed
Drive	Rear
Chassis	Box section and tubular
Suspension – front	Wishbone and torsion bar
Suspension – rear	Torsion bar with live axle
Brakes	Drum
Top speed	125mph (201km/h)
Acceleration	0-60mph (0-96km/h): 8.8 seconds

highest order. However, it differed from its predecessors by being the first BMW not to feature the marque's famous and distinctive kidney-shaped vertical twin radiator grilles. Instead he opted for a horizontal rendering of the familiar theme.

Inside, the car was compact – only two people could be accommodated. An optional substantial hardtop transformed the 507 into a coupé. The result was a very real rival to Mercedes-Benz's 300SL coupé, but without the latter's mechanical complexity and its challenging accommodation.

Sensational appearance

The engine was a 150bhp version of the V8 and performance matched the sensational looks. But the 507 was expensive. It was only available in left-hand-drive form and its price in Britain was £5251, a sum which would have bought two and a half Jaguar XK150s.

Sadly production only built up very slowly and America, which should have proved a strong

market for the model, did not receive its first 507 until two years after the 1955 Frankfurt launch. In consequence production only ran from November 1956 until May 1959. But the 507 concept survives, in spirit, in the form of BMW's current Z8 sports car of 2000 (see page 258).

Above left: The four-speed gearbox was an all-synchromesh unit and, unusually, was separate from the engine, being located under the front seat.

Above: Looking just as good without the hardtop, the 507 in more sporting mode. Echoes of its hot air outlet are to be found in BMW's current Z8.

Left: Nice lines, the 507's styling shown to good effect. For aerodynamic reasons an undershield was fitted, a feature that also applied to some Ferraris.

Jaguar XK SS

Top speed 145mph +
233km/h

Right: Essentially a D-Type but with revised dashboard and lacking the sports racers' central rib and cowl. The doors are small and hinge downwards; the windscreen is high enough to provide ample protection from the weather.

Below: The presence of a full-width windscreen, bumpers, shielded exhaust system and luggage rack identifies the XK SS. The side windows do not wind. This car, chassis no 757, was dispatched in July 1957 and exported to Hong Kong.

A sports racer for the road, the XK SS was a mildly detuned version of Jaguar's Le Mans-winning D-Type. Able to attain over 145mph (233km/h), this rare and now highly collectible model was both expensive, at £3878, and impractical. As a consequence, only 16 examples were completed.

The Coventry company's first purpose-designed sports racer was the C-Type of 1951. Following a win that year at Le Mans and again in 1953, chief engineer William Heynes recognized that a new car would be necessary if Jaguar was to maintain its pre-eminent position.

The result in 1954 was the legendary D-Type, the most famous Jaguar sports racer of all time. Heynes' intention had been to reduce weight, improve aerodynamics and increase the power of the 3.4-litre engine. To these ends the C-Type's tubular chassis was replaced by a monocoque tub with the engine and front suspension mounted on an extended framework of square section magnesium tubing. This was cloaked in a beautifully styled open two-seater body, with a distinctive fin behind the driver. This was the work of the company's aerodynamicist Malcolm Sayer.

Victory at Le Mans

Although the cars failed to win Le Mans in 1954, they proved victorious in 1955 and 1956, at which point Jaguar announced its withdrawal from racing. However, a D-Type entered by the Scottish Ecurie Ecosse racing stable was victorious in 1957.

Having withdrawn from racing, the firm retained a number of unsold D-Types and it decided to convert these to road use and market them as the XK SS. The lines remained essentially the same, but the fin was dispensed with. There was a

rudimentary hood and a full-width windscreen. A passenger's seat and door were introduced while the exhaust, which emitted much heat and noise, emerged directly below it!

There was no room for a boot. The space where one should have been was occupied by the spare wheel and twin flexible aircraft-style 36-gallon (164lit) petrol tanks. So a luggage rack was attached to the tail to which could be secured a solitary suitcase.

Ravaged by fire

The 250bhp, dry sump, triple-Weber-carburettored, XK twin-cam engine was essentially the same as that fitted to the racers. However, sales, unlike acceleration, were sluggish. Then the production line was damaged by a fire that ravaged Jaguar's Browns Lane factory in February 1956.

Production restarted in March, but then stopped entirely in November. Of the 16 examples completed, a total of 12 were exported across the Atlantic, the car being eligible for Sports Car Club of America events. Despite its poor sales record, the seeds had been sown for the greatest of all Jaguar sports cars. The D-inspired E-Type appeared in 1961. This proved, unlike the XK SS, to be a stunning sales success.

Above: With its D-Type ancestry clearly apparent, in 1957 the Jaguar XK SS was one of the fastest cars on the road.

Left: With a forward-hingeing bonnet inherited by its legendary successor, the XK SS's engine is readily accessible.

Specification	Jaguar XK SS
Engine location	Front, in-line
Configuration	Six-cylinder
Bore and stroke	83 x 106mm
Capacity	3442cc
Valve operation	Twin overhead camshaft
Horsepower	250bhp @ 6000rpm
Transmission	Manual four-speed
Drive	Rear
Chassis	Monocoque/squared tubular front sub-frame
Suspension – front	Wishbones and torsion bar
Suspension – rear	Trailing arms and torsion bar
Brakes	Disc
Top speed	Over 145mph (233km/h)
Acceleration	0-60mph (0-96km/h): 5.2 seconds

Lotus Elite

**Top speed
115mph**
185km/h

*Right: A Stage II version of
the Coventry Climax FWE
engine with twin SUs, high-
lift cam and four-branch
exhaust.*

*Below: The Elite, still
looking good, was a
triumph for its amateur
stylist, accountant Peter
Kirwan-Taylor. This is a
1962 example.*

 Lotus's first significant road car, the
visually stunning 115mph (185km/h) Elite
coupé of 1958, also had the distinction of
being the world's first glass-fibre monocoque. It
was undeniably noisy but it was light and it offered
its owners, in the best traditions of the marque,
outstanding handling.

Colin Chapman's North London-based Lotus
concern had produced its first kit car in 1953 and
initially offered club racers multi-tubular chassis
which were then powered by a variety engines,
mostly side-valve Ford units. The Elite, coded
Lotus 14 in the corporate design register, made its
appearance at the 1957 London Motor Show.
Endowed with a magnificent coupé body, the work
of Chapman's accountant friend Peter Kirwan-
Taylor, it was powered by a 1.2-litre, 75bhp, FWE
single-overhead-camshaft, Coventry Climax engine
derived from a fire pump unit!

Chapman strut

Suspension was all-independent with coil springs and wishbones at the front and a so-called Chapman strut, named after Lotus's founder, at the rear. Because of the pioneering construction, the Elite lacked a conventional chassis and accordingly weighed just 1484lb (673kg). Acceleration was impressive for a 1.2-litre car, 60mph (0-96km/h) arriving in a little over 12 seconds. A downside of the monocoque concept was that noise levels were unacceptably high, although this did not appear to adversely affect sales, initially at least.

The Elite was strictly a two-seater and the spare wheel lived on a shelf behind the occupants. There were roomy storage bins in the doors – these were for the windows which did not wind down, but which could be removed and stored in pockets behind the seats. This was regarded as a disadvantage by some potential buyers.

Production did not begin until December 1958, when the first customer was band leader, Chris Barber. In June 1959 Lotus moved from its cramped North London premises to a new, larger factory at Cheshunt, Hertfordshire. The overwhelming majority of cars were produced there although the bodies were made by Bristol.

Improvements were incorporated into the Series 2 Elite that arrived for the 1961 season – the principal alterations were suspension changes and the fitment of a ZF five-speed gearbox. In its original form the Elite had been fitted with a single carburettor, but the Special Equipment model, that also arrived for the 1961 model year, had a 83bhp engine fitted with twin SUs and a four branch tuned exhaust system.

Specification	Lotus Elite
Engine location	Front, in-line
Configuration	Four-cylinder
Bore and stroke	76 x 66mm
Capacity	1220cc
Valve operation	Single overhead camshaft
Horsepower	75bhp @ 6100rpm
Transmission	Manual four-speed
Drive	Rear
Chassis	Unitary
Suspension – front	Coil springs
Suspension – rear	Strut, coil spring and radius arm
Brakes	Disc
Top speed	115mph (185km/h)
Acceleration	0-60mph (0-96km/h): 12.2 seconds

In 1962 the Elite became available in kit form. By the time that production ceased in 1963 about 1000 examples had been completed. However, Colin Chapman did not persist with the innovative construction – the new offering, called the Elan, had a separate chassis and was an open car, something the Elite, because of its ingenious design, could never have been.

Below: The Elite name was revived by Lotus in 1974 for this four-seater sports hatchback with the glass-fibre bodywork the only common denominator. This latter-day Elite survived until 1983.

Left: Access to the Elite's interior was reasonably good, thanks to the fact that the window opening extended into the roof structure. The wood-rimmed steering wheel was considered to be large in its day, being over 16in (406mm) in diameter. It was later reduced in size. Ingeniously the contours of the metal instrument panel echo the car's profile.

Aston Martin DB4, DB5, DB6

**Top speed
140mph**
225km/h

*Below: The sought-after GT
version of the DB4.
Identifiable by its shorter
wheelbase, enlarged bonnet
scoop, lightweight Borrani
wheels and aerodynamically
cowled headlamps, just 75
examples were completed
between 1959 and 1963.
The more potent engine
differed from the standard
DB4 in being fitted with
twin sparking plugs and
developed 272bhp, even if
Aston Martin claimed 302!*

 The fastest British GT of its day, the
magnificently Italian-styled DB4 of 1958
could attain 140mph (225km/h). It was
the first model of a line that endured until 1971.

There were no legacies from the previous DB2
generation of road cars. Chief engineer Harold
Beech was made responsible for the mechanicals
while the 240bhp, 3.6-litre, twin-overhead-
camshaft, alloy engine was the work of the
company's Tadek Marek. However, there the home-
grown influence ended. General manager John
Wyer was determined that the body should be
designed in Italy rather than being entrusted to a
British stylist. The resulting coupé was the work of
the famous Milan-based Carrozzeria Touring. Built
to its superleggera principles, which featured a sub-
structure of small diameter load-bearing tubes, the
bodies were made under licence at Aston Martin's
Newport Pagnell factory.

Announced at the 1958 Paris Motor Show, the
DB4 was destined to survive until 1963. However,
in truth, it entered production too soon and early
examples were plagued with engine and gearbox

problems. These shortcomings had been largely
resolved by the time that the 260bhp Vantage
engine arrived in 1962. When production ceased in
the following year, a total of 1110 examples had
been completed. This made the DB4 the best-
selling model to date in Aston Martin's history.

The DB5 of 1964 was its much improved
successor. Outwardly identifiably by its cowled
headlamps that had featured on the last of the
DB4s, the engine's capacity was increased to 4
litres and a ZF gearbox replaced the original four-
speed unit. Once again there was a Vantage option
which developed 314bhp.

Film star looks

The model was destined to gain immortality when
James Bond drove an imaginatively enhanced
example in the 1964 film *Goldfinger*. World
demand for the model was instantaneous but,
tantalizingly, the small factory could not cope with
the demand.

Only destined for a two-year production life,
the DB5 was replaced for the 1966 season by the

DB6. Instantly identifiable by its distinctive right angular Kamm tail and with its wheelbase lengthened by 3.75in (95mm), it was destined to survive until 1969. A Mark II version with flared wheel arches followed and this was built until 1971. By then the top-of-the-range Vantage version could attain 148mph (238km/h).

An open model had always been a feature of the Aston Martin line and accordingly the DB4 drophead coupé appeared in 1961. The concept was perpetuated with the DB5, and the open DB6 of 1967 was dubbed the Volante. This name has been applied ever since to all its open successors. The DB6 was destined to be the last six-cylinder Aston Martin. Therafter, until 1999, all its cars would be V8 powered.

Above: The drophead coupé version of the DB5 looked just as good as the coupé; it is considerably rarer.

Left: The longer wheelbase DB6, immediately identifiable by its truncated Kamm tail. Unlike its predecessors, most DB6s were not built to Touring's superleggera principles.

Below left: One of three DB5s built to James Bond's demanding requirements for the film Goldfinger *with overriders extended and machine guns armed!*

Specification	Aston Martin DB4
Engine location	Front, in-line
Configuration	Six-cylinder
Bore and stroke	92 x 92mm
Capacity	3670cc
Valve operation	Twin overhead camshafts
Horsepower	240bhp @ 5500rpm
Transmission	Manual four-speed
Drive	Rear
Chassis	Platform
Suspension – front	Wishbones and coil spring
Suspension – rear	Trailing link/Watts linkage coil spring
Brakes	Disc
Top speed	140mph (225km/h)
Acceleration	0-60mph (0-96km/h): 9.3 seconds

Maserati 5000 GT

**Top speed
170mph**
274km/h

*Right: Allemano was
responsible for bodying
most 5000 GTs, with 20
examples to his credit. Its
distinctive badge proudly
proclaims the coachwork's
design and construction.*

*Below: Costly coupé, a
'stock' 5000 GT. Allemano
bodied his first example in
1961, introducing
rectangular headlamps to
the body which thereafter
featured on all his work for
Maserati. This is a 1964 car.*

It was rare, raucous and rapid. Maserati's
5000 GT was effectively a roadgoing
version of its 350S sports racer of 1957.
Little wonder that it was capable of 170mph
(274km/h) even if refinement was another matter!

Maserati had withdrawn from its costly racing
programme in 1958 to concentrate on more
lucrative road cars. However, the 5000 GT was
never intended for series production. It seems more
likely that its creation was prompted by the fact
that the works had a number of racing V8 engines
surplus to its requirements.

Introduced at the 1959 Turin Motor Show for
the following year's season, under the bonnet of the
Touring-bodied coupé was a 4935cc V8, courtesy
of Maserati's competition car. Initially its four
overhead camshafts were gear-driven although,
happily, wiser counsels prevailed after the first
three 5000 GTs had been completed, and they were
replaced by quieter chains. Initially four Weber
carburettors were fitted, although later examples
used Lucas fuel injection.

The engine was installed in an appropriately
modified tubular chassis, courtesy of the company's
3500 GT of 1958. A four-speed manual gearbox
was an option, although most examples were fitted
with five-cog ZF units. Like Ferrari, Maserati relied
on a conventionally sprung live rear axle.

Production versions were fitted with handsome

and well appointed coupé bodies by Allemano, which was the only version to be catalogued by the factory, and it was responsible for bodying some 20 of them. Other versions were produced by Pinin Farina, Ghia, Frua and Bertone, these variations no doubt being produced at the request of the model's very select clientele.

Affluent customers

These were expensive cars and Maserati ordered its retail outlets not accept an order for the 5000 GT without a significant deposit. It was acquired by some of the world's most affluent people, such as the Shah of Persia, the Aga Khan and the head of Fiat, Giovanni Agnelli.

In 1962 the American *Sports Car Graphic* magazine published a road test on a 5000 GT which had attained a top speed of 152mph (245km/h). However, motoring journalist Hans Tanner had enjoyed trips on the Italian *autostradas* with Maserati's chief test driver when he had personally observed a top speed in excess of 170mph (274km/h).

Although only produced in small numbers, this exclusive Maserati's specifications were updated in 1961 when the engine was modestly enlarged to 4941cc and disc brakes were extended to the rear wheels. By the time that the last example had been completed in October 1964, total production amounted to just 34 cars.

Above: The Maserati's cockpit with handsome Nardi wood-rimmed steering wheel and featuring a clock located between the speedometer and rev counter.

Specification	Maserati 5000 GT
Engine location	Front, in-line
Configuration	V8
Bore and stroke	98 x 81mm
Capacity	4935cc
Valve operation	Twin overhead camshafts per cylinder bank
Horsepower	340bhp @ 6000rpm
Transmission	Manual four-speed
Drive	Rear
Chassis	Twin tubular
Suspension – front	Wishbones and coil spring
Suspension – rear	Half-elliptic spring
Brakes	Front disc, rear drum
Top speed	170mph (274km/h)
Acceleration	0-60mph (0-96km/h): N/A

Jaguar Mark II

**Top speed
125mph**
201km/h

*Right: Walnut veneer and
leather upholstery in the
British coachbuilding
tradition survived in the
mass-produced Mark II.*

*Below: A 1963 top-of-the-
range 3.8-litre version with
optional wire wheels. A
great visual improvement
on its 2.4-litre predecessor,
it could not be mistaken for
anything other than a
Jaguar.*

Jaguar's best-selling car of the 1960s, this
stylish and distinctive saloon was
comfortable, well equipped and, in its 3.8-
litre form, a fast and competitively priced model.

The Mark II sprang from the 2.4-litre Mark I
saloon of 1956 which was Jaguar's first unitary
construction car. As its name suggested, it was
powered by a new 2483cc version of the XK
engine, which was the first variation on the 3.4-litre
theme. Capable of speeds approaching 120mph
(193km/h), a supplementary 3.4-litre version
became available in 1957.

The model attained a new lease of life for the
1960 season with the arrival of the much improved
Mark II version. Chairman and stylist in chief, Sir
William Lyons, (knighted 1956), slimmed down the
window and door pillars which increased the glass
area. Rear vision was also improved by the fitment
of a wraparound rear window. All these changes
combined to transform the model's looks.

Improved handling

Improvements were not only cosmetic – handling
also benefited from a slightly wider rear axle. All-
round race-proven disc brakes, an option since
1958, were standardized.

Wire wheels had been available as an option on
the 2.4 and they particularly suited the Mark II for

which they could also be specified as a desirable extra. Not only did they greatly improve the model's looks but they also helped to keep the brake discs cool. The model proved to be particularly popular on the American market where the Mark II for several years topped the vote for the country's 'Best Imported Car'.

The existing 2.4 and 3.4-litre engine options were maintained but they were joined by a top-of-the-range 3.8-litre version. This was the engine already fitted in the XK150 sports car and the commodious Mark IX saloon. However, the version used in the passenger cars was the less powerful 220bhp unit, as opposed to the fiercer 265bhp one. Inevitably, the 3.8 proved to be the fastest of the Mark II range being capable of 125mph (201km/h). Inside the model was enhanced by a walnut veneer dashboard and comfortable leather upholstered seats, a feature of the marque to this day.

The 3.8-litre version was discontinued in 1967 when the engine was transferred to Jaguar's acclaimed XJ6 that appeared in 1968. However, the 2.4 and 3.4 lines were perpetuated in 240 and 340 guises with less opulent interiors and synthetic Ambla replacing the leather seats. These had ceased production by 1969 – by then Jaguar was concentrating its resources on the increasingly popular XJ6.

Specification	**Jaguar** Mark II (3.8 litres)
Engine location	Front, in-line
Configuration	Six-cylinder
Bore and stroke	87 x 106mm
Capacity	3781cc
Valve operation	Twin overhead camshafts
Horsepower	220bhp @ 5500rpm
Transmission	Manual four-speed
Drive	Rear
Chassis	Unitary
Suspension – front	Wishbones and coil spring
Suspension – rear	Cantilever sprung live axle
Brakes	Disc
Top speed	125mph (201km/h)
Acceleration	0-60mph (0-96km/h): 8.6 seconds

Left: The model's elegant tail. The enlarged wrap-around rear window which greatly improved driver visibility is just visible. The rear axle was 3.5in (89mm) wider than previously, which improved roadholding. The rear lights were also larger than those fitted to the Mark I and the below-bumper skirt deeper.

Left: Jaguar's famous mascot was designed by The Autocar's *celebrated artist, Frederick Gordon Crosby, and was offered from the 1939 season as an optional extra on the SS Jaguar range. This revised version appeared in 1955, and was offered as a factory accessory on the 2.4. It was designed for the bonnet rather than the radiator cap.*

Daimler SP250

**Top speed
120mph**
193km/h

*Right: The Daimler's
functional cockpit featured
comfortable bucket seats.
This a 1964 B specification
car with automatic
transmission.*

*Below: Looking like
nothing else on the road,
the glass-fibre-bodied
SP250 was a relatively
small car to be powered by
a 2.5-litre engine.*

 After more than 50 years of producing
luxurious and dignified saloons and
limousines, in 1959 Daimler experienced
a personality change when it introduced a 120mph
(193km/h) glass-fibre-bodied sports car. Announced
at the 1959 New York Motor Show, it was initially
known as the Dart, but was renamed the SP250
after protests from Chrysler, whose Dodge marque
owned the Dart name.

The model's arrival reflected a change in the
top management of Daimler's BSA parent. In 1956
the profligate 12-year reign of Sir Bernard Docker
came to an end. His replacement was motorcycle
magnate Jack Sangster and he promoted Edward
Turner from his Triumph motorcycle concern to the
post of Daimler's chief engineer. He was
accordingly responsible for the SP250 which was
intended to give Daimler a slice of the lucrative
American sports car market.

The lines of the glass-fibre bodywork were
unusually distinctive and dominated by twin rear
fins that were all the rage in America at the time.
The use of this material contributed to the model
turning the scales at a respectable 2218lb (1006kg).

Left: A 1964 SP250 with its distinctive V radiator motif, intended to underline the presence of a V8 engine under the bonnet. This was an unusual configuration in Britain, but popular in America which was where the model was targeted.

Below: Edward Turner's fine 2.5-litre V8 engine with cast iron block, alloy head and, unusually, short alloy pushrods to help keep weight to a minimum to allow the revs to rise. The crankshaft was a five-bearing counterbalanced unit.

Beautifully flexible V8 engine

Because this was a wholly new concept, there were no components carried over from Daimler's traditional closed cars. A conventional box-section chassis was employed and the SP250 was powered by a beautifully flexible and economical 2.5-litre V8 engine, an unusual configuration for the British motor industry, although it would have struck a chord with transatlantic customers.

Daimler had a long tradition of producing cars with semi-automatic transmission and the SP250 was its first model since the late 1920s to be fitted with a manual gearbox. However, automatic transmission was available at extra cost.

Then in 1960 Daimler was acquired by Jaguar and there could clearly be no long-term future for the SP250 as it was now competing with the in-house E-Type. Despite this, in April 1961 the B specification cars made their appearance. These possessed stronger sills to prevent body flexing and resultant cracking. The bodywork was also strengthened. The final variant, the C spec cars of 1963, were better equipped but production ceased in January 1964 after a total of 2650 examples had been completed.

However, in 1963 Jaguar had united its Mark II saloon body with the SP250's engine and the resulting V8 250 survived until 1968, the year in which the medium-sized Jaguar was discontinued. With its demise, all traces of Daimler's brief excursion into the performance sector had been firmly extinguished.

Specification	Daimler SP250
Engine location	Front, in-line
Configuration	V8
Bore and stroke	76 x 69mm
Capacity	2548cc
Valve operation	Pushrod
Horsepower	140bhp @ 5800rpm
Transmission	Manual four-speed
Drive	Rear
Chassis	Box section
Suspension – front	Wishbones and coil spring
Suspension – rear	Half-elliptic spring
Brakes	Disc
Top speed	120mph (193km/h)
Acceleration	0-60mph (0-96km/h): 10.4 seconds

Austin-Healey 3000

**Top speed
114mph**
183km/h

*Right: A Mark III 3000
produced for the 1964
model year – this was a
more civilized offering with
a revised dashboard with
wood veneer, central console
complete with cubby box,
and wind-up windows. The
seats were also improved,
including the smaller
occasional rear ones.*

*Below right: A Mark II car
with factory hardtop and
the sliding side screens in
place. This example has
non-standard vents cut into
the front wings to permit
hot air to escape from the
engine compartment. The
wire wheels were also a
desirable optional extra,
but usually disc wheels
were fitted as standard.*

*Opposite: A Mark II car of
1961. Produced between
1961 and 1963, it is instantly
identifiable by the radiator
grille's vertical bars; its
Mark I predecessor's were
horizontal. There is also a
small Mk II badge placed
beneath the winged Austin-
Healey motif.*

The rugged Big Healey of the 1960s, with
no-nonsense specifications and a
consistent rallying record, owed its
origins to the Healey 100 of 1952 which was the
brainchild of successful pre-war rally driver Donald
Healey. He had initially produced, in Warwick
between 1946 and 1952, a range of Riley-engined
models that were costly, heavy but potent.

The single-minded Cornishman soon realized
that he ought to create a smaller, cheaper, open
sports car of a type that was introducing America to
the delights of two-seater motoring. The 1.8-litre
Austin-engined Healey 100 accordingly made its
debut at the 1952 London Motor Show. It was
immediately commandeered by Leonard Lord,
chairman of the newly formed British Motor
Corporation that was a merger of the Austin and
Morris motor businesses.

Overnight Donald's roadster became the Austin-
Healey 100, so styled to reflect the fact that it was
capable of 100mph (161km/h) and was BMC's
corporate sports car. It was produced in this form
until 1956 when the four-cylinder engine was
replaced by a 2.6-litre six. Renamed the 100/6 and
available in two- and more popular two-plus-two
seater guises, it was, if anything, slower than the
model it replaced! Fortunately this shortcoming
was rectified by the adoption, from the 1958
season, of a six-port cylinder head.

In 1957 production was transferred from
Austin's Longbridge factory to MG's Abingdon
works and two years later the engine's capacity was
increased to 3 litres. Arriving for 1960, the
appropriately renamed 3000 greatly benefited from
the bigger-bored 132bhp engine. It was capable, in
overdrive top, of speeds approaching the 115mph
(185km/h) mark. This speed required the fitment of
front disc brakes.

Although raced and rallied by BMC on both
sides of the Atlantic, in the event these rugged,
reliable but pushrod-engined cars were invariably
outpaced by the consistently faster 3-litre Ferraris
with overhead camshafts.

The last of the line

The Mark II 3000 of 1961 was briefly offered with triple carburettors although it reverted to twins in 1962. The last of the line, the Mark III of 1963, was only produced in two-plus-two form – by then the engine was boosted to 150bhp.

The Big Healey died in 1968, following the absorption of BMC by the Leyland Corporation. The new owner was reluctant to continue paying royalties to an outside contractor who built what had become an outdated design.

Although Donald Healey attempted to fill the gap left in America by the 3000's demise with the smaller Jensen-Healey of 1972/76, it proved to be a pale shadow of the original.

Specification	Austin-Healey 3000 Mark I
Engine location	Front, in-line
Configuration	Six-cylinder
Bore and stroke	83 x 88mm
Capacity	2912cc
Valve operation	Pushrod
Horsepower	124bhp @ 4600rpm
Transmission	Manual four-speed with overdrive
Drive	Rear
Chassis	Platform
Suspension – front	Wishbones and coil spring
Suspension – rear	Half-elliptic spring
Brakes	Front disc, rear drum
Top speed	114mph (183km/h)
Acceleration	0-60mph (0-96km/h): 11.5 seconds

1961–1970
The Coupé Comes of Age

Sales of fast cars boomed in the 1960s as a new post-war generation of young buyers came of age. Although Britain continued successfully to export its open two-seaters, the growing popularity of the high speed aerodynamically refined coupé was exemplified by Porsche's 911, along with Ferrari's exclusive V12-engined berlinettas and the delectable products of its new Lamborghini rival.

Datsun's popular 240Z, significantly also a closed car, highlighted the growing strength of Japan's motor industry. And America gave birth to the muscle car which harnessed V8s of growing capacity and power. But how long could the boom last?

Jaguar E-Type

**Top speed
150mph**
241km/h

Below: The Series III E-Type, introduced in 1971, was the first recipient of Jaguar's long-awaited 5.3-litre V12 engine. Identifiable by its enlarged radiator grille and flared wheel arches, this example has been fitted with optional wire wheels – usually discs were used. It was similarly produced in coupé form.

 Without question one of the world's outstanding sports cars, the 3.8-litre E-Type sprang from Jaguar's Le Mans-winning D-Type and caused a sensation on its announcement at the 1961 Geneva Motor Show.

Appearing first in hardtop coupé form with a useful rear opening door, a roadster soon followed. Certainly the E-Type's looks were sufficient to ensure immortality. Jaguar claimed a top speed of 150mph (241km/h) but, in truth, only a few carefully assembled examples were capable of this figure. The £2000 price tag ensured that the model was destined for a long production run, and in fact it survived in this form until 1971.

Independent rear suspension, created for the impending Mark X saloon, featured for the first time on a Jaguar sports car, while all-round disc brakes, honed on the motor racing circuits, were fitted front and rear.

Triumph of styling

Stylistically the E-Type's lines were a triumph for Jaguar's aerodynamicist Malcolm Sayer, who also had the bodies of the sports racing C- and D-Types to his credit. For once Jaguar's chairman, William Lyons, who usually styled the company's products, took a back seat.

Like the E-Type's XK120 predecessor, the new model found immediate favour in America, where it was known as the XK-E, and no less than 80 per cent of production was exported there.

For 1966 the E-Type was fitted with a 4.2-litre engine which did not push up the top speed but improved bottom end torque. An all-synchromesh gearbox replaced the unrefined Moss unit, which lacked synchromesh on the bottom cog.

The original version was strictly a two-seater but 1966 saw the arrival of a 2+2 E-Type coupé, which offered rear seating for two small children.

This extended the model's appeal. On the debit side, the redesign caused a dilution of those impeccable lines and an increased weight.

The American market

A Series II E-Type arrived for 1969. It was revised to take account of American safety and emissions regulations. It was outwardly identifiable by its forward-mounted open headlamps, which dispensed with the previous perspex covers, and an enlarged radiator intake. The interior was also revised with tumbler switches replacing the more attractive but projecting lever-type units. But under the bonnet detoxing the engine for the US market meant 171 rather than 265bhp and a top speed of 'only' 125mph (201km/h).

The Series II was discontinued in 1971, when the Series III version appeared on the 2+2 chassis powered by Jaguar's long-awaited 5.3-litre V12 engine. Less of sports car, more of a grand tourer, it survived until 1975. By then the twin effects of soaring petrol prices and advancing age spelt the end of what had become a motoring legend in its own lifetime.

Below: The superlative lines of a 1962 E-Type coupé are shown to good effect. Unusually, this particular example raced at Le Mans.

Bottom left: The 'office' of a 4.2-litre E-Type with the original flick switches that survived until 1969.

Specification	**Jaguar** E-Type (3.8 litres)
Engine location	Front, in-line
Configuration	Six-cylinder
Bore and stroke	87 x 106mm
Capacity	3781cc
Valve operation	Twin overhead camshafts
Horsepower	265bhp @ 5500rpm
Transmission	Manual four-speed
Drive	Rear
Chassis	Monocoque/squared tubular front sub-frame
Suspension – front	Wishbones and torsion bar
Suspension – rear	Wishbone and coil spring
Brakes	Disc
Top speed	150mph (241km/h) but see text
Acceleration	0-60mph (0-96km/h): 7 seconds

Above: One of the rare and desirable 'Lightweights', this very original example, delivered in December 1963, was used by Dick Wilkins as a road car, no doubt to the consternation of his fellow motorists! It was later sold to Tony Harrison, who hill-climbed it. It has clocked up very few miles since new.

Right: Something special, the 3.8-litre engine of car number 11 above with alloy block, wide angle cylinder head and Lucas fuel injection. The latter system was renowned for the noise it generated! Those cars that are run in current historic races have been converted to Weber carburettors. Dry sump lubrication featured.

Although the E-Type had sprung from the sports racing D-Type, it was first and foremost a road car. However, this did not deter a number of owners from campaigning the new Jaguar on the racetrack, the most successful of whom was American millionaire Briggs Cunningham. In 1962 he entered an E-Type coupé for the Le Mans 24 hour race and, sharing the driving with Roy Salvadori, they attained a creditable third placing.

Introduction of the 'Lightweight'

The factory responded by producing what it described as the 'Special GT E-Type' which has since been known as the 'Lightweight', although this was never an official designation. They were capable of speeds approaching 170mph (274km/h), some 35mph (56km/h) faster than the production models and very much quicker off the mark.

In all 18 examples were completed and, at about 2220lb (1007kg), they weighed some 500lb (227kg) less than the road car. This was because, where practical, steel elements were replaced by aluminium ones. For instance, the monocoque tub and body panels were made of aluminium. Under the bonnet the 3.8-litre XK engine had an aluminium block in place of the cast iron original, although this was not a wholly satisfactory arrangement as it lacked rigidity. This meant that reliability, a key tenet of the Jaguar racing philosophy, was compromised.

Alterations to the camshafts, a special cylinder head and the provision of fuel injection meant that the Lightweight's engine developed 296bhp, some 35bhp more than the norm.

Although these were sports racers, they could also be used as road cars. Only roadsters were built, and the cars were run in GT class events with their hardtops in place which improved their aerodynamic efficiency. The Lightweights were supplied to Jaguar distributors and private owners who had a good track racing record. They were run in European events and as far afield as America. But the result of the 1963 Sebring 12 hour race foretold the future when the two Lightweights were decisively outclassed by the V12-engined GTO Ferraris, which took the first six places, leaving the racing E-Types to occupy a lowly seventh and eighth positions. They were, nevertheless, the first British cars home.

The last of these potent E-Types was delivered to its owner in January 1964 and thus Jaguar's involvement with the car ceased. But they continued to be raced enthusiastically on British circuits and in club events. Of the 12 cars completed, all but one survive and these rare E-Types are now widely sought by Jaguar enthusiasts around the world.

Above: Cockpit of the Low Drag Coupé illustrated at the bottom of this page. Created for racing, it was never campaigned by the factory, but it was when acquired in 1963 by Dick Protheroe who registered it, memorably, CUT 7.

Left: This is one of three Lightweights owned by American millionaire racing driver Briggs Cunningham. He ran at Le Mans in 1963 but had to retire. He also owned another car which for a time used this registration number, so there is some doubt regarding its history.

Left: Jaguar's Low Drag Coupé. Four were planned but only this one was built for the World GT Championship. Work began in 1962 and the lines were the design of aerodynamicist Malcolm Sayer.

Triumph TR4, TR5, TR6

**Top speed
121mph**
195km/h

*Below: Triumph sports cars
with a 1966 TR4A,
complete with Michelotti's
ingenious 'Surrey-top', in
the foreground with a
similarly enhanced 1965
TR4 behind and a 1972 TR6
in the background.*

Triumph met the fresh challenges of the 1960s with the TR4 which benefited from an impressive new Michelotti body that survived, in essence, until its ultimate descendant, the TR6, was discontinued in 1976.

In 1959 Triumph had launched its Herald saloon and much of its success was credited to the styling, which was the work of the Italian Giovanni Michelotti. So when the TR3A, whose lines dated back to the TR2 of 1953, was updated, it was not surprising that he was commissioned to undertake the work.

Launched at the 1961 London Motor Show, the TR4's mechanicals were essentially the same as those of its predecessors, although an all-

synchromesh gearbox was employed. This meant essentially the same 2138cc engine, although the car was 12in (305mm) longer and had a wider track. Top speed remained at 102mph (164km/h).

Engine boosted

The TR4 sold a respectable 40,000 examples before the TR4A arrived for the 1965 season. Although outwardly similar, mechanically there was a radical change with the arrival of semi-trailing arm independent rear suspension, as pioneered on Triumph's 2000 saloon of 1962. The long running engine was boosted by changes to the profile of the camshaft to increase top speed to 110mph (177km/h) but at the expense of petrol consumption.

Specification	**Triumph** TR5
Engine location	Front, in-line
Configuration	Six-cylinder
Bore and stroke	74 x 95mm
Capacity	2498cc
Valve operation	Pushrod
Horsepower	150bhp @ 5500rpm
Transmission	Manual four-speed
Drive	Rear
Chassis	Box section
Suspension – front	Wishbones and coil spring
Suspension – rear	Semi-trailing arm and coil spring
Brakes	Front disc, rear drum
Top speed	121mph (195km/h)
Acceleration	0-60mph (0-96km/h): 8.9 seconds

Even more radical, its TR5 successor of 1968 was fitted with a 150bhp, fuel-injected, 2.5-litre, six-cylinder engine and was capable of over 120mph (193km/h). And a 0-60mph (0-96km/h) figure of 8.9 seconds made it noticeably quicker off the mark.

Unfortunately the fuel injection system proved to be unreliable and those cars sold on the American market were fitted with carburettors. Even though it was rooted in the 1950s, there was still some mileage in this sports car, and in 1969 the TR6 appeared – it looked like a new model. In fact the TR4 sub-structure survived but it was enhanced with new front and rear ends essayed by the German Karmann company.

The TR6, which was destined to remain in production until 1976, was the most popular TR to date and 94,619 were produced. While top speed remained about the same, acceleration was improved thanks to a more highly tuned engine.

Sadly the 2-litre TR7 coupé which replaced it in 1976 was some 10mph (16km/h) slower! Intended as British Leyland's corporate sports car, it proved to be ill conceived, visually uninspiring and unreliable. A better-looking convertible version followed in 1979 and there was the short-lived 3.5-litre V8-engined TR8 of 1980. But although some 112,000 TR7s were built, the once highly regarded initials had lost much of their lustre.

Above left: Cockpit of a TR6 with a new steering wheel introduced for the 1973 season. Detail changes were also made to the instruments at the same time. In truth this layout was essentially the same as that created by Michelotti when he designed the TR4's body back in 1961 and it was only mildly modified over the years.

Left: The driving compartment of the 1966 TR4A opposite with a new wood-veneered dashboard introduced in the spring of 1965 for European customers. It had already been offered in the American market. The layout of its TR4 predecessor was retained. Triumph also took the opportunity to relocate the handbrake to the top of the transmission tunnel – it had previously been mounted alongside it.

AC Cobra

**Top speed
138mph**
222km/h

*Below: An AC 289 of 1966,
this example has been in the
same ownership since new.
Produced for the European
market, this was AC's
version of the Cobra, but
under a different name. The
lines of the Ace, on which it
was based, are readily
apparent in the styling.*

One hundred miles an hour (161km/h)
coming up in 14 seconds is still a very
respectable acceleration figure today – in
the 1960s it was truly sensational. The AC Cobra,
in which a lusty American V8 engine replaced a
British power unit of a mere 2-litres capacity, was
one of the truly great performance cars of the post-
war years.

The Cobra was rooted in AC's Ace of 1954, an
open two-seater sports cars with a tubular chassis
and all-independent transverse leaf suspension.
This behaved best when powered by a 2-litre
Bristol engine, which was an alternative to the
Thames Ditton's company's own 2-litre six,
although the last of the line used a 2.5-litre Ford
Zephyr unit.

Then American racing driver Carroll Shelby
approached AC with a view to extending the Ace's
life with a 260cid (4.2-litre) V8, courtesy of Ford
of America. He proposed that left-hand-drive cars
should be built without engines at AC's factory and
then shipped to California where he would install
their power units. The resulting car would be called
the AC Shelby-Cobra, the name having come to
him in a dream!

AC Shelby-Cobra in production

The British company agreed to this proposal and
the car was announced in the autumn of 1962. After
the first 75 had been completed, the original engine
was replaced by a 289cid (4.7-litre) unit.
Performance of this Mark II was excellent for its
day, top speed being 138mph (222km/h).

But the engine transplant displayed the
limitations of the 1954 vintage suspension and
Shelby initiated, with Ford input, the uprated Mark

Left: All beef and muscle: a 427 Mark III Cobra, shod with the appropriate Halibrand alloy wheels. Left-hand-drive, of course.

Below left: The Mark III engine with the Shelby-fitted rocker covers which replaced the original pressed steel ones.

Below: UK Cobra guru Rod Leach at the wheel of the impressivly powerful 427. The front wing vent permits hot air to escape from the engine compartment.

III Cobra of 1965 with a wider chassis and all-round wishbones and coil spring suspension. A 427cid (6.9-litre) V8 was now employed and the Halibrand alloy wheels required even wider wheel arches. In this form what was now called the Shelby-Cobra was capable of 165mph (265km/h). It continued to be sold until 1968.

Right-hand-drive Cobras had been available on the British market since 1964. The Mark III, though fitted with the 4.7-litre V8, was marketed as the AC 289 in Britain between 1966 and 1968 because AC did not own the rights to the Cobra name.

After a hiatus, in 1983 the Cobra concept was revived in Britain. Initially the 4.9-litre AC Mark IV could not be called a Cobra but in 1986 permission for use of the name was forthcoming from Ford, which by then owned it. The car remains in limited production at the time of writing, no less than 40 years since this ingenious Anglo-American sports car was first conceived.

Specification	**AC** Shelby-Cobra Mark II
Engine location	Front, in-line
Configuration	V8
Bore and stroke	4.0 x 2.87in (101 x 72mm)
Capacity	289cid (4735cc)
Valve operation	Pushrod
Horsepower	300bhp @ 5700rpm
Transmission	Manual four-speed
Drive	Rear
Chassis	Tubular steel
Suspension – front	Transverse leaf spring and wishbones
Suspension – rear	Transverse leaf spring and wishbones
Brakes	Disc
Top speed	138mph (222km/h)
Acceleration	0-60mph (0-96km/h): 5.6 seconds

Above: Chunky, muscular and a direct descendant of AC Cobra of the 1960s, the CRS, announced for the 2000 season, differed from its predecessors in using a carbon-fibre body in place of the aluminium previously employed. The 5-litre Ford V8 engine developed 225bhp. The CRS was available in road-ready form or in tuned and tautened racing guise.

The AC company acquired a new owner in 1996, South African businessman Alan Lubinsky, and he was determined that the company would not rest on its laurels. In 1998 it unveiled the Mark IV-based Superblower which, as the name suggested, was powered by a supercharged version of the Ford 4.9-litre V8. With a top speed of 165mph (266km/h), acceleration was electrifying with 60mph (96km/h) arriving in 4.2 seconds. The price, however, was some £70,000.

Carbon fibre body

The 2000 season saw the arrival of the Cobra CRS. This retained the model's traditional chunky and purposeful look, but it differed from its predecessors in that instead of having the usual open two-seater aluminium body, it was made of light but immensely strong carbon fibre. In consequence the CRS turned the scales at 2380lb (1080kg) and it cost some £20,000 less than the metal-bodied car. The Ford V8 produced a healthy 225bhp which resulted in a 0 to 60mph (96km/h) time of 5.3 seconds. Both racing and roadgoing versions were on offer.

The 2001 season saw the appearance of a further variation of the evergreen classic in the shape of the 212 S/C. Launched at the 2000 British Motor Show, it was essentially a re-engined CRS. Although the traditional open two-seater lines were retained, AC forsook the usual Ford V8 for the twin turbocharged 3.5-litre Lotus unit of a similar specification to that used in the Lotus Turbo. The model's name reflected the power unit's 3506cc capacity expressed in cubic inches.

It is no coincidence that John Owen, AC's chief engineer, previously worked for Lotus where he headed the design team that conceived the V8. He was, therefore, no stranger to the engine, its performance capabilities and potential.

Drive is taken through a six-speed Tremec manual gearbox. Power steering is a refinement, but the 212 remains at heart a near 50-year-old concept with its twin tubular chassis and all-round wishbone suspension which dates from the Cobra 427 of 1965.

In addition AC also produces a more luxurious variation on the open two-seater theme in the shape of the Ace that was launched for the 1998 season.

Similarly powered by a Ford V8, it is also available in twin-cam 4.6-litre form, courtesy of the Mustang. The '4.9' is also used in the Aceca coupé unveiled at the 1998 British Motor Show. This is a genuine four-seater with 9.8in (250mm) added to its wheelbase. AC thus offers a quartet of distinctive, fast cars for the enthusiast who wants to combined tradition with out-and-out performance.

Above: A change of emphasis; the well-appointed, refined Aceca coupé arrived for the 1999 model year.

Left: Despite its state-of-the-art body material, the dashboard of the CRS is pure 1960s.

Below left: Lotus's twin turbocharged 3.5-litre V8 used in its Esprit is employed by AC in the 212 S/C.

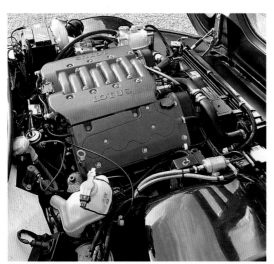

Specification	AC 212 S/C
Engine location	Front, in-line
Configuration	V8
Bore and stroke	83 x 81mm
Capacity	3506cc
Valve operation	Twin overhead camshafts per cylinder bank
Horsepower	350bhp @ 6500rpm
Transmission	Manual six-speed
Drive	Rear
Chassis	Twin tubular
Suspension – front	Wishbones and coil spring
Suspension – rear	Wishbones and coil spring
Brakes	Disc, ventilated at front
Top speed	155mph (249km/h)
Acceleration	0-60mph (0-96km/h): 3.9 seconds

Mini Cooper S

**Top speed
98mph**
158km/h

Right: The immaculate but crowded underbonnet of the 1275 Cooper S shown below. The component to the left of the engine is the brake servo.

Below: This Austin 1969 Cooper S MkII can be identified by the enlarged radiator grille which was also shared with the Morris versions.

The lion-hearted little car that scored a resounding three wins in 1960s Monte Carlo Rallies, the Cooper S was the competition version of Alec Issigonis's legendary Mini. Created for the British Motor Corporation, the Mini bristled with ingenuity. Its 848cc engine was transversely mounted and the gearbox was ingeniously located in the sump from where it drove the front wheels.

A small car in which every inch of interior space was used to the maximum effect, Issigonis never envisaged that the roadholding advantages of front-wheel drive could be successfully harnessed for use on the racetrack and rally course. But he had not reckoned with John Cooper of the Cooper Formula 1 team which had won the World Manufacturers Championship in 1959 and 1960. He proposed a faster version and the Mini Cooper was born in 1961 powered by a 55bhp, 997cc, twin-carb version of BMC's versatile A Series engine.

This was enlarged to 998cc in 1963 and it paved the way for the even more potent Mini Cooper S of 1963 with a 1071cc engine. Initially developing 70bhp, this was a 90mph (145km/h) car although it became progressively faster as it evolved. Outwardly similar to the standard Cooper, it retained the white roof by which that variant was usually distinguished.

Definitive Cooper S

In March 1964 this was replaced by a choice of 970cc (although it only lasted for 11 months) and 1275cc versions, the latter being regarded as the definitive Cooper S. These all used the Mini's rubber-based suspension, although this was replaced by the interconnected Hydrolastic system for the 1965 season.

By then the S had already attained international recognition. Skilfully prepared by BMC's Competition Department based at MG's Abingdon factory, in 1964 Paddy Hopkirk won the Monte Carlo Rally outright and BMC took the team prize. Timo Makkinen repeated the feat in 1965 and these triumphs were consolidated when the car achieved a one, two, three victory in 1966, although this was overturned by the organizers on a technicality. However, there were no mistakes in 1967 when the Cooper S was again victorious.

But Minis were beginning to feel the effect of sure-footed opposition from Ford. Then in 1968 BMC was taken over by Leyland and the famous Competitions Department was closed down. The 1275cc Cooper S ceased production in 1971, two years after the Cooper had been discontinued.

However, the 1275cc Mini Cooper concept was revived in 1990 by the Rover Group, BMC's latter-day descendant, and the new BMW-built Mini of 2001 also includes a Cooper version in tribute to its now legendary forebear.

Specification	Mini Cooper S (1275cc)
Engine location	Transverse
Configuration	Four-cylinder
Bore and stroke	70 x 81mm
Capacity	1275cc
Valve operation	Pushrod
Horsepower	76bhp @ 5800rpm
Transmission	Manual four-speed
Drive	Front
Chassis	Unitary
Suspension – front	Wishbone and rubber
Suspension – rear	Trailing arm and rubber
Brakes	Front disc, drum rear
Top speed	98mph (158km/h)
Acceleration	0-60mph (0-96km/h): 10.9 seconds

Left: Interior of the 1965 Monte Carlo-winning 1275cc Morris Mini Cooper S with enhanced instrumentation and more supportive seats than usual.

Below: The 1965 Monte Carlo Rally-winning Cooper S. The car was subsequently extensively rebuilt and won the 1982 Lombard-RAC Golden 50 rally.

Aston Martin DB4 GT Zagato

**Top speed
152mph**
244km/h

In October 1958 Aston Martin unveiled its acclaimed Touring-styled DB4 and a lighter, shortened, faster GT version followed a year later. Then, at the 1960 London Motor Show, the memorable and even more potent DB4 GT Zagato appeared. It was so named because it was bodied in Italy by the Zagato styling house of Milan.

Visually stunning

The work of the talented young Ercole Spada, 'the Zagato', as it was invariably known, was a visually stunning competition car although it was also available in roadgoing form.

Under the bonnet was a high specification version of the DB4's twin-overhead-camshaft 3.6-litre engine. Originally developing 240bhp, the GT version was boosted to a claimed 302bhp, actually 267, thanks to 9:1 rather than 8.2 compression ratio, special high lift camshafts, twin sparking plugs per cylinder and triple Weber carburettors in place of the original twin SUs. Running on a 9.7:1 compression, the Zagatos' engines were further boosted to 285bhp.

At 2800lb (1270kg), the tubular-framed, purposeful, alloy coupés were about 100lb (45kg) lighter than the factory GTs and could attain over 150mph (241km/h). Once completed, the cars were returned to Aston Martin's Newport Pagnell works for trimming, although a few examples were completed by Zagato.

Like the factory DB4 GTs, there were only two seats in the front. The space usually occupied by the rear seat was occupied by a platform for the storage of luggage.

Above: A 1962 right-hand-drive Zagato, arguably the best and most original of the cars as it was purchased new in October of that year by J.E. Beck of Cheshire, who kept it for many years. Note the absence of a rear bumper.

Right: The Zagato's lines shown to advantage. The transparent headlamp covers were fitted in the interests of aerodynamic efficiency. All the cars differ slightly in details and, of the 19 cars built, all survive. The only 'missing' car was discovered in Italy in 1974.

Over the next three years a total of 19 cars was completed, each one differing slightly from the others. Production was almost evenly split with ten right-hand-drive examples built while the remainder were left hookers. Perversely, one chassis was bodied by Bertone.

Essex Racing Stables

Aston Martin had withdrawn from sports-car racing in 1959 so the Zagatos were campaigned on the racing circuits during 1961 and 1962 by privateers, most significantly John Ogier's Essex Racing Stables which ran two of them memorably registered 1 VEV and 2 VEV. While the cars invariably finished in GT races in Britain and on the Continent, they were unable to hold their own against the might of Ferrari's GTOs.

Although production ceased in 1963, this was not quite the end of the story. In 1991 Aston Martin decided to utilize four unused chassis numbers that had been allocated to the original series. Zagato

Specification	Aston Martin DB4 GT Zagato
Engine location	Front, in-line
Configuration	Six-cylinder
Bore and stroke	92 x 92mm
Capacity	3670cc
Valve operation	Twin overhead camshafts
Horsepower	285bhp @ 6000rpm
Transmission	Manual four-speed
Drive	Rear
Chassis	Platform
Suspension – front	Wishbones and coil spring
Suspension – rear	Trailing link, Watt's linkage/coil spring
Brakes	Disc
Top speed	152mph (244km/h)
Acceleration	0-60mph (0-96km/h:) 6.2 seconds

produced a further four cars under the Sanction II designation, outwardly almost identical to the originals and with only detail differences to their specifications. Otherwise they remained true to the 1960 classic design.

Above left: Cockpit of a left-hand-drive Zagato. The seven instruments can be clearly seen through the wood-rimmed steering wheel. The seats, which are adjustable for rake, are supportive while the pedals are well positioned.

Above right: The Zagato's engine with the DB4 GT's twin-plug cylinder head serviced by distributors driven off the bulkhead end of each camshaft. The triple Weber carburettors on the far side of the engine use a cool air intake box.

Left: Strictly a two-seater, the Zagato still looks good some 50 years after its first appearance. Made of light alloy, it is vulnerable to damage. Note the Z monogram ahead of the air intake on the front wing, so there can be no doubt of the body's origins!

Ferrari 250 GTO

**Top speed
185mph**
298km/h

*Right: The GTO's engine
with the 12 stacks of the
inlet ports for the six Weber
carburettors readily
apparent. With weight an
ever-present consideration,
the cam covers were made
of magnesium.*

*Below: The semi-circular
air intakes could be covered
and were opened to increase
air flow to the engine at
slow speeds. The apertures
below the headlamps direct
air to the brakes.*

One of the rarest (just 39 were built) and today the most collectible and expensive of Ferraris, the legendary GTO was created for the newly introduced GT World Championship of 1962. A sports racer that could also be used as a road car, it was capable of a blistering 185mph (298km/h).

The car was engineered by Giotto Bizzarrini, who was later to be responsible for Lamborghini's enduring V12 engine. Unusually he not only laid out the chassis but also the sensational lines of the Ferrari's berlinetta body, a task usually undertaken by Pininfarina.

The resulting design was not only supremely elegant but utterly distinctive, for Bizzarrini also recognized the importance of improving a car's performance by aerodynamic refinement and he accordingly undertook airflow experiments in Pisa University's wind tunnel. The results were confirmed during testing at the Modena and Monza circuits and even on the Italian *autostradas*, no doubt to the delight of other motorists.

Distinctive rear spoiler

The Scaglietti-built body's distinctive rear spoiler helped to kept the wheels of the 295bhp 3-litre V12 on the road. This proven and reliable power unit was inherited from the GTO's open sports-racing Testa Rossa predecessor.

The car was the ultimate development of Ferrari's 250 GT of 1955, which was produced in short wheelbase form for the racetrack from 1959.

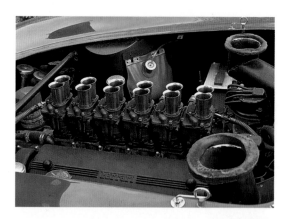

The GTO title stood for *Gran Turismo Omologato* – in other words homologated, a racing stipulation which required that 100 examples of a particular car be constructed. After some controversy with the authorities, Enzo Ferrari got around the problem by proclaiming that he had been producing 3-litre GTs since 1955!

Although the overwhelming majority of GTOs were 3-litre powered, there was a trio of 4-litre models. It was typical of Ferrrari that while much attention was lavished on the engine and body, the tubular chassis featured conventional wishbones and coil springs and the essentials of a cart-sprung rear which had not been much updated since 1947.

Created for the new 3-litre GT World Championship, the GTO not only gave Ferrari victory in 1962 but also in 1963 and 1964. The latter year proved to be the last for this potent and, it should be said, beautiful and purposeful car.

Success on the racing circuits

The GTO had proved itself invincible on the GT racing circuits and an example was placed second at Le Mans in 1962. It was only displaced in the mid-1960s when rear-engined sports racers, following in the wheeltracks of Formula 1 cars, gained the upper hand.

In 1965 the Maranello company decided to concentrate all its efforts on Formula 1 and prototype sports car racing. Ferrari therefore bowed out from GT competition after a highly successful decade, mostly spent on top.

Above: The GTO looks just as good from the rear. The large air outlet positioned on the rear wing allowed hot air generated by the back tyres and brakes to escape more quickly.

Below left: The instrument panel was dominated by a revolution counter; all the dials can be easily seen through the spokes of the lovely Nardi aluminium and wood steering wheel.

Specification	Ferrari GTO
Engine location	Front, in-line
Configuration	V12
Bore and stroke	73 x 58mm
Capacity	2953cc
Valve operation	Twin overhead camshafts per bank
Horsepower	295bhp @ 7400rpm
Transmission	Manual five-speed
Drive	Rear
Chassis	Tubular steel
Suspension – front	Wishbones and coil spring
Suspension – rear	Half-elliptic springs, radius arms and Watts linkage
Brakes	Disc
Top speed	185mph (298km/h)
Acceleration	N/A

Porsche 911

**Top speed
130mph**
209km/h

*Right: A 911S shod with the
distinctive Fuchs five-spoke
forged alloy wheels
introduced to the model in
1967 – they were an option
on the standard version.
They had the virtue of being
5lb (2.2kg) lighter than the
usual steel variety.*

*Below: A Targa top on a
1973 911, a halfway house
between a convertible and
fixed-head coupé. It had
proved to be a popular
option ever since 1969.
Introduced in 1965, it
originally featured a
removal rear window.*

One of the world's greatest sports cars,
Porsche's legendary, unconventional, yet
utterly distinctive 911 was introduced at
the 1963 Frankfurt Motor Show. Today, some 40
years on, it remains in production and the current
model is recognizably a descendant of the original.
However, its top speed of 174mph (280km/h) is
some 40mph (64km/h) faster than the first of the
line. Acceleration has been similarly enhanced.

The 911 has been produced in countless
variations for both road and track, and is the
descendent of a line that began with a single model
which entered production back in September 1964.

Work on the project had begun in 1958 and
followed the theme established with the 356. It was
an aerodynamically refined coupé powered by a
rear-mounted, air-cooled, horizontally opposed
engine. But there the resemblance ended because
the 911's power unit did not possess a trace of its
predecessor's Volkswagen ancestry. The purpose-
designed 2-litre six-cylinder engine, which
developed 130bhp, employed chain-driven single-
overhead camshafts in place of pushrods. However,
torsion bar suspension was inherited from the 356,
although it was used at the front in conjunction
with struts.

Arrival of the Targa

Until the 1967 season there was only one model in
the 911 family but then came the more powerful
160bhp 911S which was shod with distinctive
Fuchs alloy wheels. No convertible was offered at
this stage, but the 911T, for Targa, arrived for the
1969 season. This had a fixed rear window and
detachable roof panel, an initiative which was
widely copied by other sports car manufacturers.
Powered by a detuned 110bhp engine, it was
offered with semi-automatic transmission.

In the 1969 model year fuel injection arrived on
the 911S and the newly introduced 911E. The 911's
first increase in engine capacity, to 2.2-litres, came

Above left: The Carrera RS's engine had its capacity enlarged to 2687cc by increasing the bore of the existing 2.3-litre unit to 90mm. It developed 210bhp.

Above right: The sought-after Carrera RS of 1973 which could reach 60mph (96km/h) in under six seconds. A mere 1600 examples were built.

Left: A 1984 Carrera Cabriolet. The hood can be raised and lowered single-handed. Later, for 1986, came similarly equipped open Turbos.

in 1970. There was another rise, to 2.4-litres, for the 1972 season and the following model year saw the return of the Carrera. This RS version had a 210bhp engine and was capable of a spirited 150mph (241km/h).

The 1974 models were distinguished by another rise in engine capacity, to 2.7-litres, although the Carrera broke ranks and sported a 2.9-litre power unit which developed 230bhp.

A turbocharged 911 with a 3-litre engine followed for the 1975 model year and this variant can be found on page 166. This engine, although in unblown form, was extended to the Carrera for the 1976 season and was fitted in detuned 180bhp form in the mainstream cars of the 1978/79 model years.

Specification	Porsche 911 (2 litres)
Engine location	Rear, in-line
Configuration	Six-cylinder
Bore and stroke	80 x 66mm
Capacity	1991cc
Valve operation	Single overhead camshaft
Horsepower	130bhp @ 6100rpm
Transmission	Manual five-speed
Drive	Rear
Chassis	Unitary
Suspension – front	MacPherson strut and torsion bar
Suspension – rear	Semi-trailing arms and torsion bar
Brakes	Disc
Top speed	130mph (209km/h)
Acceleration	0-60mph (0-96km/h): 8.9 seconds

Above: A Carrera 2 of 1993, identifiable by its five-spoked alloy wheels which appeared in 1992 and which replaced the seven-spoked units of the 1990-91 era. The so-called 964 series of the 911, introduced for 1989, were powered by a 3.6-litre 250bhp engine. It was replaced for the 1994 season by the radically revised 993 series.

Right: A 1995 Carrera 2 cabriolet with Tiptronic automatic transmission. This 993 series interior is identifiable by its redesigned steering wheel which incorporated an airbag – one was also added for the passenger. The dashboard has not really changed significantly since the 911's arrival in 1963.

The next increase in engine capacity came with the Carrera for the 1984 season, the 3.2-litre unit, a very 'torquey' engine, developed 231bhp and was destined to endure until 1989.

Unlike the 356 that had been available in cabriolet (open) form since its inception, the 911 had only been produced, the Targa excepted, in coupé guise. It was not until 1982, no less than 19 years since the 911's announcement, that the Cabriolet made its appearance, and it has been an integral part of the model line ever since. Originally designated the 911SC, it continued as a Carrera for 1984 and the option was extended from the 1986 season to the Turbo.

Four-wheel drive joined the Carrera line for 1989, a model year in which its engine capacity was increased to 3600cc. Yet another mechanical change was the replacement of the torsion bars, a feature of the 911 since its inception, by all-round coil springs.

The body underwent further revision for the 1994 model year with newly contoured bumpers and flared wheel arches. The cars were powered by 3.6-litre engines, but there were further changes in the offing prompted by the arrival of Porsche's cheaper, mid-engined, 2.4-litre Boxster convertible for 1997.

Radical re-design

When the current version of the 911 arrived for the 1998 season it shared no less than 36 per cent of its components with its smaller capacity stablemate. This was nothing short of a root and branch re-design of the famous model.

The new shell is 45 per cent more rigid than its predecessor which means more interior room. Its distinctive headlamp covers extend to incorporate the side lamps and flashing indicators are also shared with the Boxster. Quarterlights, a body feature that the 911 had inherited from the 356, have been deleted.

An even more radical departure is the engine

Specification	**Porsche** 911 Carrera 2
Engine location	Rear, in-line
Configuration	Horizontally opposed six-cylinder
Bore and stroke	96 x 78mm
Capacity	3387cc
Valve operation	Twin overhead camshafts
Horsepower	300bhp @ 6800rpm
Transmission	Manual six-speed
Drive	Rear
Chassis	Unitary
Suspension – front	MacPherson strut
Suspension – rear	Wishbone and strut
Brakes	Disc
Top speed	174mph (280km/h)
Acceleration	0-60mph (0-96km/h): 5.1 seconds

which is of a slightly smaller capacity than its predecessor. The 3.4-litre 'flat' six is water-cooled, so dispensing with air cooling that dated back to the 356. It similarly shares the Boxster's layout of twin overhead camshafts, four valves per cylinder and twin front-wing-located indicators.

Suspension is common to both models and is mounted front and rear on aluminium sub-frames to reduce noise levels. There are MacPhersont struts at the front with strut-sprung wishbones at the rear.

The mainstream model is the Carrera 2 and, like other variations on the contemporary 911 theme, it is a far more refined product that its predecessors, although Porsche has succeeded in retaining its sports car credentials. It is also available in four-wheel-drive form as the Carerra 4 while a Cabriolet and Turbo complete the range. The 911 will celebrate its 50th birthday in 2003, making it the world's most enduring and celebrated performance car.

Above left: The 911 was radically revised for the 1998 season and the resulting 996 series was developed in conjunction with Porsche's cheaper, mid-engined Boxster. It shared many components with the new two-seater, most obviously the headlamp units. It was also a quieter car than previously because the 3.4-litre engine was water- rather than air-cooled.

Left: A second-generation Targa arrived with 993 series 911 Carrera for 1996. Unlike its predecessor, which featured a manually removable roof panel, this version used an electrically controlled roof, which contained an ultra-violet filter to protect the occupants from the sun's glare. At the touch of a button the panel retracted beneath the fixed rear window, so leaving the roof completely open.

Chevrolet Corvette Sting Ray

**Top speed
142mph**
228km/h

*Right: The 'Ray's engine
was a 327cid V8, introduced
in 1962. Developing
250bhp, a more powerful
365bhp unit was available
at extra cost.*

*Below: Well proportioned
and distinctive, a 1963
Corvette roadster. The
dummy hot air outlets were
opened up in 1965 to duct
heat away from the engine.*

 The Corvette Sting Ray with its glass-fibre body, finely chiselled lines and concealed headlights came of age in the 1963 season. For, apart from its V8 engine, there were no legacies from earlier 'Vettes, and the car was based on a new all-independent suspension chassis to the benefit of roadholding.

Its memorable and distinctive aerodynamically-honed styling was the work of William Mitchell, General Motors' head of styling, who was much more susceptible to European influences than his predecessor Harley Earl. And while the Sting Ray possessed its own distinctive personality, the stylistic subtleties of Jaguar's superlative E-Type were readily apparent (Mitchell was an enthusiastic owner/driver of one).

Further visual input came from two of Mitchell's experimental cars, the 1958 Stingray two-seater racer and XP-720 coupé of 1959. The latter was significant because the '63 Corvette was

to be offered in coupé form in the Continental European manner and the style has been an enduring feature of the line ever since.

'Father of the Corvette', Belgian-born engineer Zora Arkus-Duntov, was intent that the Sting Ray would offer better interior accommodation than its predecessor, along with better handling. This was

achieved, despite the fact that the car had a shorter wheelbase, at 98in (2489 mm), than the 1953-62 generation's 102in (2590mm). To allow for this, there was a new box-section chassis and rear transverse leaf spring/radius rod independent suspension demanded by the body's design.

Speed in excess of 140mph

The engine was the previous year's 327cid (5.3-litre) V8 which was to be available in 250 and 365hp guises during the Sting Ray's production life. The latter powered the model to over 140mph (225km/h). Fuel injection, introduced in 1957, remained as an option until 1966.

There were further engine enhancements in the pipeline and in 1965 a 396cid (6.5-litre) V8 appeared. This was the year in which the Corvette was also provided with all-round disc brakes. Yet a further engine option arrived for 1966, in the form of a 427cid (7-litre) V8; however, less desirably, the model's increased weight dropped its top speed to 135mph (217km/h).

Outwardly the classic lines remained essentially unchanged during the 'Ray's six-year production life, although the coupé underwent a small but

significant modification from the 1964 season. Mitchell had initially insisted on a divided rear window but this was deleted on the grounds that it restricted visibility. But he has had the last word because today collectors are queuing up to buy pre-1964 examples...

The line was discontinued in 1967 after some 180,000 Sting Rays had been completed. A legend was in the making.

Above: The Corvette acquired a coupé body with the Sting Ray. This 1963 car is identifiable by its now highly desirable divided rear window which was deleted in 1964. The fact that the doors intrude into the roof is a nice touch.

Specification	**Chevrolet** Corvette Sting Ray (327cid)
Engine location	Front, in-line
Configuration	V8
Bore and stroke	4.0 x 3.25in (101 x 82mm)
Capacity	327cid (5358cc)
Valve operation	Pushrod
Horsepower	250bhp @ 4400rpm
Transmission	Manual three-speed
Drive	Rear
Chassis	Perimeter
Suspension – front	Wishbones and transverse leaf spring
Suspension – rear	Radius rod and transverse leaf spring
Brakes	Drum
Top speed	142mph (228km/h)
Acceleration	0-60mph (0-96km/h): 5.9 seconds

Ford GT40

**Top speed
160mph**
257km/h

*Right: The mid-located
Ford V8 engine, this
example exhibiting Cobra-
related Shelby origins.*

*Below: A desirable race-
bred road car. Note the
scuttle-mounted petrol tank
and single windscreen wiper.*

 Created by Ford with the express aim of winning the Le Mans 24 hour race, the Anglo/American GT40 did precisely that and took the chequered flag there in four successive years from 1966 to 1969.

However, Ford's Le Mans triumphs were not lightly won and it took no less than three years to develop a winning car. Ford was a company used to producing value-for-money, mass-produced saloons, and it lacked any experience of creating such a racer. So it acquired the rights to the innovative Lola GT, which had run, albeit unsuccessfully, at the 1963 Le Mans race. Radically its 4.2-litre Ford V8 engine was mounted longitudinally behind the driver in the manner of contemporary Formula 1 cars.

Using this ingenious concept as a starting point, Ford proceeded to develop the design at Slough, Berkshire in a facility managed by John Wyer, formerly of Aston Martin. The trio of cars that

Left: Because the GT40 is such a desirable car, its numbers have increased over the years! However, this is a 1966 example converted for road use. It was destined for Shelby American but was returned to Ford Advanced Vehicles because of troubles relating to its documentation.

Below: The original chassis for this car was scrapped when it was damaged during testing at Silverstone and it was rebuilt around a Mark III one. Note the coupé's low lines, it is just 40in (1016mm) high.

appeared at the 1964 Le Mans event were thus closely related to the Lola, although they were powered by an alloy version of Ford's V8. The GT40 name was adopted because on the road the coupés stood a mere 40in (1016mm) high.

Although spectacularly fast, one was timed at 187mph (301km/h), all the cars suffered from teething troubles, after which Ford transferred the GT40's development to America and placed the project under the control of Carroll Shelby, creator of the AC Cobra.

The original V8 was replaced by a 7-litre unit. Six examples of what was designated the Mark II were run at the 1965 Le Mans event but all succumbed to mechanical failures.

Radical modifications

Further radical modifications followed and in 1966 Ford was triumphant and took the first three places in the 24 hour classic. The following year the Mark IV, with a lighter stronger chassis made of an aluminium honeycomb sandwich material, was also victorious. At this point Ford decided to quit while it was ahead. However, GT40s prepared by John Wyer took the chequered flag at Le Mans for the next two years under the sponsorship of Gulf Oil.

In the meantime Wyer had produced a roadgoing version of the Mark III powered by a 4.7-litre V8. Introduced in December 1965, it cost £6647 and closely resembled the sports racer, apart from a reprofiled nose, twin headlamps which

replaced the single units, and a taller tail that incorporated overheated luggage compartments located either side of the gearbox. Even this tamed version could attain 160mph (257km/h).

Production ceased in 1968, by which time just 31 examples of these fabulous street machines had been completed.

Specification	Ford GT40 Mark III (4.7 litres)
Engine location	Mid, in-line
Configuration	V8
Bore and stroke	101 x 72mm
Capacity	4736cc
Valve operation	Pushrod
Horsepower	306bhp @ 6000rpm
Transmission	Manual four-speed
Drive	Rear
Chassis	Steel semi-monocoque
Suspension – front	Wishbone and coil spring
Suspension – rear	Trailing arm, wishbones and coil spring
Brakes	Disc
Top speed	160mph (257km/h)
Acceleration	0-60mph (0-96km/h): 5.3 seconds

Sunbeam Tiger

**Top speed
120mph**
193km/h

*Right: One of the few
outward giveaways, the two
badges on the front wings
indicate that this is not a
standard four-cylinder
Alpine.*

*Below: Although it went on
sale in Europe from the
1965 season, inevitably
most Tigers crossed the
Atlantic as it was created
with the American market
in mind. Otherwise this
Sunbeam was pure Alpine IV.*

 The AC Cobra was the inspiration for the
Sunbeam Tiger that transformed the open
two-seater Alpine into a 120mph
(193km/h) sports car. In its original form the Alpine
of 1959 was powered by a 1.5-litre engine which
endowed it with 90mph plus (145km/h+)
performance. Created for the American sports car
market, it had to compete with the likes of MG and
Triumph. It also suffered commercially from the
dawning of the muscle car era and the increased
performance that came in its wake.

The outcome, in April 1964, was the Sunbeam
Tiger, inspired by the company's 1925 land speed
record car of that name. The man behind it was Ian
Gerrad, who was Rootes West Coast sales manager.
He enlisted Carroll Shelby's assistance and Shelby
shoe-horned Ford's 260cid (4.2-litre) V8, which
had just been fitted to the first of the Cobras, under
the Series II Alpine's bonnet. A second prototype
was built by Ken Miles who was Rootes' chief
development engineer in America.

Results were sufficiently encouraging for
Rootes to proceed with the project and the Tiger's
assembly was entrusted to Jensen. Outwardly the
car appeared little different from its Alpine Series
IV stablemate, which remained in production, the
substitution having been effected with remarkably
little modification.

Specification	**Sunbeam** Tiger
Engine location	Front, in-line
Configuration	V8
Bore and stroke	3.8 x 2.87in (96 x 73mm)
Capacity	260cid (4261cc)
Valve operation	Pushrod
Horsepower	141bhp @ 4400rpm
Transmission	Manual four-speed
Drive	Rear
Chassis	Unitary
Suspension – front	Wishbones and coil spring
Suspension – rear	Half-elliptic spring
Brakes	Front disc, rear drum
Top speed	120mph (193km/h)
Acceleration	0-60mph (0-96km/h): 9.4 seconds

Revised steering gear

A rack and pinion steering gear replaced the original recirculating ball unit, and there was a cross-flow radiator and a new Salisbury rear axle. Changes were also made to the spring rates and a Borg-Warner manual four-speed gearbox was fitted, although it was soon replaced by a Ford all-synchromesh unit.

Petrol consumption was in the region of 18mpg (15lit/100km) but this was not a problem because the Alpine III had already been fitted with twin fuel tanks to increase its range. The V8 transformed the Alpine's performance – it was capable of about

120mph (193km/h) and 60mph (96km/h) arrived from standstill in under 10 seconds. Initially only available for export, right-hand-drive versions were introduced in March 1965.

In 1967 came the 125mph (201km/h) export only Tiger II powered by the Mustang's 289cid (4.7-litre) V8 complete with an egg-crate radiator grille and side stripes. However, in that year Chrysler obtained control of Rootes and it did not wish to continue producing a car powered a rival engine. Production therefore ceased in mid-1967. By then 6495 examples of the Tiger I and just 571 examples of its successor had been completed.

Above left: The 260 badge on the boot lid of this 1965 car describes the capacity, in cubic inches, of the Ford V8 engine which powered the Tiger. The two exhaust pipes were another giveaway although the twin fuel tanks were shared with the Alpine IV. Steel wheels were fitted as standard with wires available at extra cost.

Left: The Tiger's smart wood-veneered dashboard which was fitted to most of the cars; originally PVC had sufficed. Note the length of the gear lever. Originally a short control, similar to that used on the AC Cobra, was fitted, but this made engaging first and third gears uncomfortable for Tiger drivers. So Ford introduced this more ergonomically acceptable lengthened stick.

Gordon-Keeble

**Top speed
137mph**
220km/h

*Right: The crowded
underbonnet of a 1965
Gordon-Keeble, which, in
addition to the 5.3-litre
Corvette V8 engine, had to
accommodate twin brake
servos and two cooling fans.*

*Below: Bertone styling,
Chevrolet power and
British craftsmanship
combined in this acclaimed,
fast, glass-fibre-bodied
grand tourer. The badge
featured a tongue-in-cheek
tortoise emblem.*

Although the Gordon-Keeble of 1964
experienced a somewhat protracted
gestation period, when it appeared the
137mph (220km/h) grand tourer looked like a sure-
fire winner. This was thanks to its assured Italian
styling and reliable, guaranteed performance from a
5.4-litre V8, which came courtesy of its Chevrolet
Corvette contemporary.

The marque took its first name from John
Gordon, who ran Slough-based Peerless Motors. In
1957 the company launched the glass-fibre-bodied,
Triumph TR3-engined Peerless GT which survived
until 1960. It was subsequently produced, until
1962, under the Warwick name.

In the meantime Jim Keeble, an Ipswich garage
proprietor, was asked by an American customer to
install a 4.6-litre Chevrolet V8 engine into a
Peerless. As a result of the ensuing dialogue,
Gordon and Keeble decided to market the reworked
concept, which was named the Gordon GT.
Ambitiously, it was displayed at the 1960 Geneva
Motor Show.

Its understated, well-proportioned, two-door,
four-seater Bertone body was the work of Giorgetto
Giugiaro. Later, in 1968, he created the renowned
Ital Design styling house. The body concealed a
space-frame chassis with a de Dion rear axle; under
the Gordon's bonnet was the Corvette's V8.

Although there were plans for the car to enter
production in September 1960, unfortunately there
was a four-year hiatus before the Gordon-Keeble

Left: The deep framed windows and slender pillars ensured excellent visibility. Note the twin petrol tanks, with fillers on each rear wing – each one contained 11 gallons (50lit) of petrol.

Below: The well equipped cockpit with rev counter, speedometer, oil pressure and water temperature gauges in front of the driver. Buttons for the electric windows adjoin the gear lever on the central console.

GK1 was launched in March 1964. It was outwardly similar to the show car, but the original metal body had been replaced by a glass-fibre one. The car was built in Eastleigh, Hampshire at a factory located at Southampton Airport.

By this time the capacity of the Corvette V8 had increased to 5.3-litres. The result was a reliable, flexible GT with excellent traction, handling and brakes. Quiet, yet rapid, it was able to reach 60mph (96km/h) in a mere 7.5 seconds.

Breaking the mould

Weighing 3164lb (1435kg), thanks to its choice of body material and tubular chassis, its build quality was commended by commentators. Williams and Pritchard of London made the moulds and the first 12 hulls. But there were many who believed that the body was constructed of steel or aluminium, which also reflected well on the factory that was responsible for the shell's manufacture.

The only fly in the ointment was that the fact that the Gordon-Keeble sold for just £2798. It was seriously underpriced and the original company only survived until March 1965, by which time 93 examples had been completed. Although it was revived later that year as Keeble Cars and the price was raised to £4058, the opportunity that had existed in 1960 had all but disappeared. The production of these now Southampton-built cars only continued until 1967. Although the rights to the design were acquired by American John De Bruyne and two rebadged examples were duly exhibited at the 1968 New York Motor Show, the promised cars never entered production. In all just 99 Gordon-Keebles were built.

Specification	Gordon-Keeble
Engine location	Front, in-line
Configuration	V8
Bore and stroke	101 x 82mm
Capacity	5355cc
Valve operation	Pushrod
Horsepower	300bhp @ 5000rpm
Transmission	Manual four-speed
Drive	Rear
Chassis	Space-frame
Suspension – front	Wishbones and coil springs
Suspension – rear	De Dion axle and coil springs
Brakes	Disc
Top speed	137mph (220km/h)
Acceleration	0-60mph (0-96km/h): 7.5 seconds

Pontiac GTO

**Top speed
110mph**
177km/h

The GTO was the car that ushered in America's muscle car era. Destined to revitalize Pontiac's sales in the booming youth market of the 1960s, such was the success of this outwardly deceptive model that the rest of the American motor industry wasted little time in following suit.

It was in January 1963 that Pontiac advertising executive Jim Wagners (or engineers John DeLorean and Bill Collins depending on who was telling the story) decided to insert a 389cid (6.4-litre) V8 under the bonnet of Pontiac's newly minted Tempest line.

Development undertaken in secret

The only trouble was that Pontiac was a division of General Motors and there was a corporate ban on engines larger than 330cid (5.4-litres) powering an intermediate model such as the two-door Tempest. Development work was consequently undertaken in secrecy with prototypes fitted with '326' V8s although, in reality, they carried the larger capacity 389 unit.

Pontiac got around the corporate diktat by making what it named the GTO. The appellation was filched from the Ferrari of the same name, the initials standing for *Gran Turismo Omologato*, an option in the Tempest Le Mans series.

The model, introduced for 1964, was available in sports coupé, hardtop and convertible forms. It used the 389 unit with distinctive chromed valve covers, enhanced by a 'hotter' camshaft and High Output cylinder heads which were crowned by a Carter four barrel carburettor. Available in two states of tune, the standard was 325hp and there was an optional 348 version.

Selling for a highly competitive $3400, the GTO could reach 60mph (96km/h) in around 4.5 seconds and top speed was in excess of 110mph (177km/h). Such performance had not previously been available at this price.

The following year's GTO underwent a reskin and was easily identifiable by its vertically

Above: The Pontiac GTO was reskinned for the 1965 season, and was better looking than the rather angular original. It is easily identifiable by the stacked headlamps that were taken from larger Pontiacs.

Right: The GTO name lingered on until 1974, its performance image being a victim of the depression fuelled by the oil price rise. This is the GTO 400 version of the two-door Pontiac Le Mans. Note its curious bonnet scoops.

Specification	**Pontiac** GTO
Engine location	Front, in-line
Configuration	V8
Bore and stroke	4.06 x 3.75in (103 x 95mm)
Capacity	389cid (6374cc)
Valve operation	Pushrod
Horsepower	325bhp @ 4800rpm
Transmission	Manual three-speed
Drive	Rear
Chassis	Box section
Suspension – front	Wishbones and coil spring
Suspension – rear	Trailing links and coil spring
Brakes	Drum
Top speed	110mph (177km/h)
Acceleration	0-60mph (0-96km/h): 6.9 seconds

Above left: An optional bonnet-mounted revolution counter appeared on the GTO 400 during the 1967 model year.

Left: The GTO convertible for the 1967 season was essentially the same as the previous year's cars, apart from more visible rear lights.

Below: The impressive cockpit with bucket seats, floor gear change and GTO initials proudly emblazoned on the dash.

mounted twin headlamps which replaced the horizontal ones. Otherwise the mechanicals remained the same although the 389's outputs were modestly increased to 335 and 360hp.

There was an impressive and distinctive new GTO for 1966 and demand was such that Pontiac built no less than 96,946 of them in a single year which was a production record for any muscle car. Similarly powered by a 389 engine, this was a 120mph (193km/h) model. The second generation GTO was uprated for the 1967 season with the V8 enlarged to 400cid (6.5-litres). Top speed was now 125mph (201km/h).

The last of the line, the GTO of the 1968-72 era, retained the 400 V8 but also offered an optional 455cid (7.4-litre) unit. But by then Pontiac was concentrating resources on its increasingly potent and popular Firebird line.

Shelby Mustang GT-350

**Top speed
119mph**
191km/h

The sporty Mustang of 1964, the fastest-selling model in Ford's post-war history, spawned a rare and successful track-ready derivative in 1965 in the form of the GT-350.

Commissioned by the company and prepared by Carroll Shelby, creator of the AC Cobra, it was built to challenge the rival Chevrolet Corvette in Sports Car Club of America events and simultaneously to hone Ford's performance image.

Power was boosted to 306bhp

Taking the 2 + 2 GT Mustang coupé as his starting point, Shelby retained the 271bhp 289cid (4.7-litre) V8 but power was boosted to 306bhp by the fitment of a bespoke Holley carburettor, a high rise aluminium inlet manifold and new exhaust system. A Borg-Warner aluminium four-speed close-ratio manual gearbox was employed.

Suspension was uprated and adjustable Koni shock absorbers added. Perversely, the unassisted steering box was removed and replaced by a higher geared powered unit. Inside the trim was discarded and replaced by two competition front seats with the spare tyre taking the place of the rear squab.

As for the name of the conversion, legend has it that this was born during a meeting held at Shelby American's modest factory at Venice, California. When he asked about the distance to a nearby engineering shop, a colleague paced out the gap and declared it to be some 350 feet. So the GT-350 was born...

Shorn of its corporate badges, the Shelby Mustang was unveiled in January 1965 and was offered in two guises. There was a potent 360bhp GT-350R which was intended for racing, but the overwhelming majority of cars were the more tractable GT-350S street machine.

Above: A 1965 Shelby Mustang in obligatory white. The interior is black. Based on the fastback model, the cars were delivered from Ford minus bonnet, exhaust system and back seat, the conversion work being undertaken at Shelby's factory in Venice, California.

Right: The 1965 GT-350 bore a closer resemblance to the production Mustang than 1966 cars. They had plastic rear quarter windows and scoops behind the doors to cool the rear brakes. In both cases the Ford badges were removed.

There was just one exterior finish specified, white, which is America's racing colour, with blue striping that ran along the cars' sills and proclaimed the *GT-350* designation. There were also extra matching 'Le Mans' stripes added to a car's centre-line. Other identifying features were side air scoops introduced ahead of the rear wheel arches while small triangular rear side windows replaced the original louvres.

Racing success

Some 680,000 standard Mustangs were built in 1965 and Shelby's production accounted for a mere 562 examples, of which perhaps 30 were racers. But they did everything expected of them and won that year's SSCA's B-Production National Championship and repeated the success over the next two years.

1966's cars were rather tamer than the originals and the colour range was expanded to embrace red, blue, green and black which were complemented by black or gold racing stripes. Just 2380 were built in 1966 and this included 936 which were rented that year to lucky customers by Hertz. They were invariably returned with telltale signs of racing activity in evidence!

Specification	**Shelby** Mustang GT-350
Engine location	Front, in-line
Configuration	V8
Bore and stroke	4.0 x 2.87in (101 x 73mm)
Capacity	289cid (4735cc)
Valve operation	Pushrod
Horsepower	306bhp @ 6000rpm
Transmission	Manual four-speed
Drive	Rear
Chassis	Unitary
Suspension – front	Wishbones and coil spring
Suspension – rear	Half-elliptic springs
Brakes	Front disc, rear drum
Top speed	119mph (191km/h)
Acceleration	0-60mph (0-96km/h): 6.5 seconds

Below: A distinctive plain grille with the famous Mustang motif moved from its customary central position to the side.

Iso Grifo

**Top speed
171mph**
275km/h

*Right: The heart of the
Grifo, an American V8
which provided plenty of
performance at a reasonable
price. This is a 7-litre
Chevrolet Corvette unit, but
this was later replaced by a
smaller capacity Ford one.*

*Below: The fine lines of the
Grifo's Bertone body helped
to sell a model that was one
of the fastest cars in the
world. The hot air vents
helped keep the engine and
rear brakes cool.*

 Seizing on the concept of a potent
American V8 shoe-horned into a stylish
coupé body, in 1963 the Italian Iso
concern produced the Grifo which was one of the
fastest GTs of its day and could attain speeds in
excess of 180mph (290km/h).

Milan-based motorcycle manufacturer Iso was
the creator of the Isetta bubble car; in 1955 it sold
the design to BMW and there was to be a seven-
year hiatus before it produced another vehicle. In
1960 founder Renzo Rivolta attended the London
Motor Show and he was influenced there by the
Bertone-styled, Corvette-V8 engined Gordon-
Keeble. The result was the 1962 Rivolta GT with
body lines similarly essayed by Bertone and
powered by a 5.4-litre 300bhp Chevrolet V8. Its
chassis was engineered by Giotto Bizzarrani,
formerly of Alfa Romeo and Ferrari, and the
transmission was of transatlantic origin, being Borg
Warner or, later, Powerglide automatics. A five-
speed ZF manual gearbox was also available.

This paved the way the following year for the
lighter and faster two-seater Grifo which used a
shortened version of the Rivolta's chassis. It was,

once again, Bertone-bodied although it was far
more stylish that its rather soberly styled
predecessor. In addition to the mainstream coupé, it
was also available with a sun roof, a Targa-type top
and as a full roadster.

7-litre version introduced

This initially used the Chevvy V8; the 365bhp
version was capable of 158mph (254km/h).
However, it was also successively available in 350,

300 and 340hp states of tune. A top-line muscular 7-litre version followed in 1969 which used the Corvette 427 engine, and a 7.4-litre unit followed in 1970. The latter version was fitted with modified bodywork, developed no less than 460bhp and could attain 186mph (299km/h) flat out. Later, in 1973 and 1974, 'smaller' 5.7-litre Ford V8s replaced the Chevvy units.

There was also a sports-racing Grifo A3/C which Bizzarrini produced at his own plant at Livorno. When Iso ceased its racing activities at the end of 1965, he continued to produce the car, which was variously named the Bizzarrini GT Strada or GT America, until 1969.

The Grifo proper ceased production in 1974, by which time 412 examples had been completed. But in 1998 Pietro Rivolta, the founder's son, announced plans for a new Grifo with Zagato-styled composite body and a Ford 4.5-litre V8. Sadly this latter-day car has failed to materialize.

Above: Looking as good from the rear, the twin exhaust pipes reveal the presence of V8 power…

Below left: The Grifo's left-hand-drive interior was very light, thanks to the large rear window.

Specification	Iso Grifo (7 litres)
Engine location	Front, in-line
Configuration	V8
Bore and stroke	108 x 95mm
Capacity	6998cc
Valve operation	Pushrod
Horsepower	390bhp @ 5200rpm
Transmission	Manual four-speed
Drive	Rear
Chassis	Unitary
Suspension – front	Wishbones and coil spring
Suspension – rear	De Dion axle, radius arm and coil spring
Brakes	Disc
Top speed	171mph (275km/h)
Acceleration	0-60mph (0-96km/h): 7.1 seconds

Lamborghini Miura

**Top speed
171mph**
274km/h

Below: Often hailed as the world's first supercar, the Miura's Bertone body was as stunning as its mid-engined mechanicals that were inspired by Ford's sports-racing GT40. The cabin was of monocoque construction while the bonnet and engine cover were made of aluminium and, accordingly, unstressed. Note the cooling ducts for the transversely mounted V12 engine.

In 1966 the Miura supercar, in which a sensational body was united with innovative mid-engined mechanicals, set the seal on the credibility of the three-year-old Lamborghini marque.

It was the only make to challenge Ferrari's pre-eminent position as Italy's foremost supercar builder. Tractor manufacturer Ferruccio Lamborghini's first model, the 350GT for 1963, was powered by a magnificent 3.5-litre quad-cam V12 engine, designed by former Ferrari engineer Giotto Bizzarrani. Yet although the Touring-designed body was elegant, it lacked that special elusive quality that Lamborghini was seeking.

It arrived in abundance with the Miura. Daringly, Lamborghini's young chief engineer Giampaolo Dallara transferred the 350bhp V12, by then extended to 3.9-litres, from the front of the car to the middle of it. But rather than positioning it longitudinally, Ford GT40-style, he adventurously opted for a transverse configuration in the manner of the British Mini. The five-speed gearbox was similarly located in the engine's sump.

Stunning styling by Bertone

These revolutionary mechanicals were cloaked in a stunning Bertone coupé body, the work of 26-year-old Marcello Gandini. The resulting car was displayed at the 1966 Geneva Motor Show where its name was revealed as the Miura. This was in tribute to Don Eduardo Miura, a breeder of fighting bulls – Ferruccio Lamborghini, who was born under the Zodiac sign of Taurus the bull, being drawn to names with taurine associations.

Entering production early in 1967, the Miura was a mere 41in (1041mm) high, and was utterly distinctive and beautifully proportioned with a tail that could be mistaken for no other on account of the innovative engine location.

If you can't stand the heat...

The heat generated by the V12 was a major problem, however, so a series of louvres, that were likened to the slats of a venetian blind, were introduced to permit some rear visibility and, principally, to allow the hot air to escape. However, this meant inserting a window between the cockpit

WPA 43F

and engine compartment to separate the occupants from the twin bugbears of high temperature levels and noise.

At the front, the swivelling headlamps were set in what looked suspiciously like eyelashes but which were in fact disguised ducts that directed cooling air to the front brakes.

Top speed was over 170mph (274km/h) and the Miura combined out and out performance with the handling expected from a mid-engined machines.

In 1969 the even more powerful Miura S with 375bhp on tap was unveiled but the ultimate version was the SV of 1971 with 385bhp, wider track and rear wheels and, in consequence, back wings. The original 'eyelashes' were also banished. Destined for a relatively short life, the last SV was built late in 1972. There would be a two-year hiatus before the Miura was replaced by the equally spectacular Countach.

Left above: The Miura's headlights rapidly elevated when they were switched on. The colour of the 'eyelashes' changed with the paint colour.

Left below: The only way in which the V12 could be transversely mounted was to locate the gearbox Mini-style in the sump.

Below: The cockpit was well equipped, but it was a little on the small side and noisy because of the close proximity of the engine.

Specification	Lamborghini Miura
Engine location	Mid, transverse
Configuration	V12
Bore and stroke	82 x 62mm
Capacity	3929cc
Valve operation	Twin overhead camshafts per bank
Horsepower	350bhp @ 7000rpm
Transmission	Manual five-speed
Drive	Rear
Chassis	Steel box section
Suspension – front	Wishbones and coil spring
Suspension – rear	Wishbones and coil spring
Brakes	Disc
Top speed	171mph (274km/h)
Acceleration	0-60mph (0-96km/h): 6 seconds

Above: The lines of a 1969 Miura S shown to good effect. This example lacks the headlamp 'eyelashes' which were also deleted on its SV successor. The right-hand bonnet grille conceals the petrol filler cap.

Below: The Miura was only 3ft 5in (1041mm) high. This is a 1972 SV model. While the driving position was fine for drivers of average height, it was not so good for taller people.

In all only 150 examples of the SV were built. Apart from the modifications already mentioned, the factory took this opportunity to correct many of the shortcomings owners had experienced with the earlier Miuras. As a consequence the SV is the best of the breed and, in retrospect, it seems unfortunate that its manufacture was halted early, particularly as its Countach successor did not enter production until 1974.

The SV's chassis was notably stronger than those of its predecessors. While the Miura's sensational lines remained essentially the same, beneath the surface heavier gauge sheet steel was used in the unitary hull because the original had a tendency to flex, particularly when the driver was hard down on the accelerator.

Improved handling

The design of the suspension remained essentially the same, but it was subtly improved and refined. Handling improved as a consequence. At the front the car was slightly lower than before which improved the aerodynamics and countered a tendency for the SV's nose to lift at high speeds.

The magnificent V12 engine was also an improvement on the original. Its S predecessor had reshaped combustion chambers, high lift camshafts and larger carburettors. This improved output to 370bhp. Yet further changes were made to the SV's valve timing with different valves and further changes to the carburettors. Another difference was a new sump to correct excessive oil surge on fast cornering. Previously Miuras had occasionally suffered from this problem which resulted in bearing failure.

While every Miura sold was a coupé, a single open version was made but, alas, it never entered production because the company lacked the necessary capital. In 1968 Bertone produced a single car as a design study which, although it used many of the original body panels, featured changes to the cockpit and its tail.

However, this car did not disappear, as is the fate of many such design exercises. It was acquired by the International Lead Zinc Research Organisation. Assisted by Bertone, many original metal parts, such as inlet and exhaust manifolds, sump, bumpers and door handles, were replaced with zinc ones.

Although the last Miura was delivered to Italian industrialist Luigi Innocenti on 15 January 1973, this was not quite the end of the story. One further example was completed in 1975 from existing parts for dedicated Canadian Lamborghini enthusiast Walter Woolf. He took the car over in April and that really was the end of the line.

In all 765 Miuras were completed during six years of production. There were 475 examples of the original car, 140 Miura Ss and 150 SVs. But in the meantime, Ferruccio Lamborghini had lost control in 1972 of his company, having sold his tractor business to Fiat. Such is the vulnerability of the supercar manufacturer.

Below: The Miura's lines are extraordinarily impressive and remained essentially the same on the SV. Lamborghini's famous badge displaying a fighting bull is prominent.

Chevrolet Camaro Z-28

**Top speed
126mph**
203km/h

Below: There were no Z-28 emblems on the 1967 version – these arrived in 1968 – but the racing stripes were a distinctive feature. The rear spoiler was an optional extra.

The success of the Shelby-prepared Ford Mustangs in Sports Car Club of America events had not escaped the attention of rival General Motors. Its response was the Z-28 version of the Chevrolet's newly introduced Camaro coupé of 1967, which was capable of speeds nudging the 130mph (209km/h) mark.

But the SCCA's rules specified that for TransAm races the engines of competing cars could not exceed 305cid (5-litres) – the Mustang had been eligible because it was powered by a 289cid (4.7-litre) unit. Unfortunately Chevrolet's smallest V8 was of 327cid (5.3-litre) displacement. The answer was to rework its internals so reducing the engine's capacity to 302cid (4.9-litres).

Corvette cylinder heads

Corvette parts were incorporated, namely its big port cylinder heads. There was a special camshaft and the hydraulic tappets were replaced by solid lifters. There was a baffled sump and high pressure oil pump. A Holley four-barrel carburettor, complete with a special manifold, was fitted.

At this time General Motors – Chevrolet's parent – did not permit its divisions to be directly involved in racing, so the development of the car was placed in the hands of front-line drivers Roger Penske and Mark Donohue who would also race it.

The regulations required that 1000 examples of a street-ready model needed to be sold before it could be certified to compete. The Z-28 was based on the mainline Camaro but fitted with the new 302cid (4.9-litre) V8. Other enhancements included uprated suspension, wider wheels and higher ratio steering, all for an extra $400. It was only available with a four-speed Munci manual gearbox; this was a no-nonsense specification, automatics and air conditioning options were not listed.

The Z-28 was soon proving its worth in the SCCA events for which it had been created. After a faltering 1967 season, it wrested the title from Mustang in 1968, winning 10 out of 11 races in the series. It was the same story in 1969 when Donahue again took the championship.

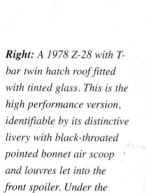

Right: A 1978 Z-28 with T-bar twin hatch roof fitted with tinted glass. This is the high performance version, identifiable by its distinctive livery with black-throated pointed bonnet air scoop and louvres let into the front spoiler. Under the bonnet was a 350cid (5.7-litre) V8 which developed 170 or 185 horsepower.

Specification	**Chevrolet** Camaro Z-28 (350cid)
Engine location	Front, in-line
Configuration	V8
Bore and stroke	4 x 3.50in (102 x 89mm)
Capacity	350cid (5735cc)
Valve operation	Pushrod
Horsepower	360bhp @ 6000rpm
Transmission	Manual four-speed
Drive	Rear
Chassis	Unitary
Suspension – front	Wishbones and coil spring
Suspension – rear	Half-elliptic spring
Brakes	Front disc, rear drum
Top speed	126mph (203km/h)
Acceleration	0-60mph (0-96km/h): 5.9 seconds

The model was reskinned and its lines sharpened up that year, but its replacement in 1970 had a new coupé body that looked mean, purposeful and distinctive. A change in the TransAm rules meant that 350cid (5.7-litre) units could be used and Chevrolet promptly installed the 350 engine from its Corvette stablemate.

Best-selling Camaro

Although the winning Penkse/Donohue duo had departed for America Motors and the championship that year went to Ford, this Z-28 proved to be the fastest and best-handling of the line. And the regular Camaro became one of Chevrolet's best-sellers, surviving in this form until 1981.

Above left: The cockpit of a comprehensively instrumented 1993 model.

Below: A purposeful-looking 1985 European Version Camaro Z-28.

Ferrari Daytona

**Top speed
174mph**
280km/h

*Below: Last of the great
front-engined Ferrari
berlinettas, for the time
being at least, the Daytona's
Pininfarina-styled body is
regarded as one of the
design house's finest
creations. The sense of
balance between the long
bonnet, its lines
uninterrupted by projecting
headlights, and the
relatively small passenger
area is outstanding.*

Ferrari's first generation of fabled V12-engined berlinettas came to an end in 1973 with the demise of the big and memorable Daytona which was capable of no less than 174mph (280km/h). When the prototype was unveiled at the 1968 Paris Salon, what was then described at the 365 GTB/4 was hailed as the fastest road car in Ferrari's history.

Interestingly, the Daytona name was not an official one but the car was so christened by the press following Ferrari's victory in the 1967 Daytona 24 hour race.

Pininfarina had produced a magnificent and distinctive coupé body in which the headlamps, for aerodynamic considerations, were located behind clear plastic covers within the finely chiselled nose. However, they were subsequently found not to conform to regulations in the all-important American market so retractable units were introduced above the originals.

The seat of power

The long bonnet concealed an all-alloy, 4.4-litre, four-cam, V12 engine; although this followed the layout of Ferrari's earlier power units, it was essentially new in execution. The dry sump unit came complete with six Weber carburettors and it developed an impressive 352bhp. The five-speed ZF gearbox was in unit with the transaxle.

There was the usual tubular chassis with all-independent suspension and disc brakes but this was a heavy car with a long wheelbase and it turned the scales at 3600lb (1633kg).

Although Pininfarina had been responsible for the design and construction of the prototype, the bodies of the production cars, which appeared a year after the model's Paris debut, were built in Modena by Scaglietti. Audaciously, there was only room for two occupants.

Performance and handling was up to Maranello's usual demanding standards. And while

the brakes were sufficient for road use, they displayed their limitations on racing versions that were capable of speeds approaching 200mph (321km/h). Examples ran at Le Mans in 1971 and 1972 when Daytonas attained creditable fifth placings on both occasions, and in the latter year also occupied sixth to ninth positions.

A convertible (spider) version of the model was unveiled at the 1969 Frankfurt Motor Show and it also displayed sensational lines. Although the berlinettas inevitably predominated, about 150 open cars were built.

When Daytona production ceased in 1973, some 1350 examples had been completed. It was replaced by the mid-engined 365 GT4BB, the legendary Boxer. But if the public thought that it had seen the last front-engined Ferrari, it was very much mistaken…

Above: Despite the Daytona's size, there is only room for two people; the view down that long bonnet is memorable.

Left: Although the great majority of Daytonas were coupés, there were some convertibles which are greatly sought after.

Below left: Beneath that substantial air cleaner are six Weber carburettors. The twin oil filters are remarkably accessible.

Specification	Ferrari 365 GTB/4 Daytona
Engine location	Front, in-line
Configuration	V12
Bore and stroke	81 x 71mm
Capacity	4390cc
Valve operation	Twin overhead camshafts per bank
Horsepower	352bhp @ 7500rpm
Transmission	Manual five-speed
Drive	Rear
Chassis	Tubular steel
Suspension – front	Wishbones and coil spring
Suspension – rear	Wishbones and coil spring
Brakes	Disc
Top speed	174mph (280km/h)
Acceleration	0-60mph (0-96km/h): 5.4 seconds

Above: Ferrari prepared this right-hand-drive Daytona for UK Ferrari importers Maranello Concessionaires to race in 1972.

Below: A NART Daytona in the paddock; it dramatically raised the model's profile in the American market.

Although the Daytona had particularly proved its worth at Le Mans, it was also successfully campaigned in America, which was appropriate in view of its (unofficial) model name. In truth, Ferrari seemed a little reluctant to lend support to owners who wanted to race what was essentially a road car. But its hand was forced to some extent by the fact that, in late August 1971, no less than 500 examples had been completed. This meant that the Daytona became eligible for Group 4 racing in the Special Grand Tourer series.

Competition versions

At this point Ferrari's importers in Britain, France, Belgium and Switzerland pressed Maranello to produce competition versions of the car. But it was American importer Luigi Chinetti, who in 1972 was appointed the company's East Coast representative, who was in the forefront of racing the model.

The reality was that the America-designated Daytonas became available well after the European specification cars had been marketed. Sales began modestly in 1971 but it was only the following year that they began to gather any momentum.

Unlike Europe's Daytonas, which had optional air conditioning, this feature was standard, if not overly efficient, on those cars sold on the American market. They were also distinguished by the fitting of every conceivable option, from leather upholstery to electrically operated radio antennas.

It was against this background that in 1971 the factory began to support, albeit reluctantly, the racing effort. Back-up was not provided by Ferrari's racing workshop but by the company's separate 'customer facility' in Modena and its 'competition Daytona' did not become a reality until 1972.

Chinetti's North America Racing Team (NART) had already run at the Daytona 24 hour and the Sebring 12 hour races, in 1970, but without success. But works involvement from 1971 saw a 12th placing at Sebring, and Chinetti co-drove a Daytona to eighth position at the circuit in 1972. A NART-entered example also won its class at Watkins Glen.

Five special cars were prepared for the 1973 season with 450bhp engines, and uprated brakes and suspension. Chinetti achieved a second place and first in class at the 1973 Daytona event, paradoxically in NART's non-works enhanced car, and another example was placed fifth and second in class. In addition there was a class win at Le Mans and a sixth overall placing.

However, with the arrival in 1973 of the mid-engined Boxer, the works turned its attention away from front-engined cars like the Daytona. Of course, private individuals continued to campaign Daytonas on the track, so providing another strand in the history of this fabulous Ferrari.

Above: A notable feature of the production Daytona was that its twin headlamps were concealed behind transparent cowlings. However, in the Daytona, chassis 15681, that Maranello entered for Le Mans in 1972 (the only occasion it was raced by the company), the lights were exposed to view.

Left: The cockpit of the Maranello Daytona prepared for the 1972 Le Mans race where it was driven by Peter Westbury and John Hine. Noise levels in the cockpit were high because the twin pipes of the unsilenced exhaust emerged just below the driver's door! The Ferrari only survived until the eighth hour, when it was withdrawn when lying in 29th position because of a blown cylinder head gasket.

Morgan Plus 8

**Top speed
125mph**
201km/h

Right: The magnesium alloy wheels which were fitted to the Plus 8 right from its introduction in 1968 were still doing sterling service 20 years later.

Below: Ancient and modern – the Plus 8's lines were firmly rooted in the 1930s but an alloy V8 engine resided under the bonnet.

It has the looks of a pre-war sports car but the performance of a 21st century one. Production of the Morgan Plus 8 began in 1968 and continued until 2004. Essentially the same car, with a more modern V6 engine, is still in production today.

It comes as no surprise to find that the Plus 8's origins stretch back to 1935, which was when Morgan recognized that the days of its famous three-wheeler line, introduced back in 1910, were numbered. So it introduced the 4/4 which in turn spawned the Plus 4 of 1951. Initially this used a 2-litre Standard engine, but it was subsequently powered by the closely related Triumph TR 2.2-litre unit which endured until the TR4A was discontinued in 1967.

However, the impending arrival of the six-cylinder TR5 placed Morgan in a predicament because the longer straight-six engine could not be squeezed into the Plus 4 without major surgery. Salvation came in the shape of Rover, which in

1965 had acquired the rights to an ex-Buick alloy 3.5-litre V8 engine and successfully reworked it for its own use. Although the unit's compact configuration meant that it could have been shoe-horned into the Morgan's original underbonnet space, the Plus 8, which made its debut at the 1968

London Motor Show, actually had a 2in (50mm) longer wheelbase. It was also slightly wider than its predecessor, to the benefit of roadholding, because of its new alloy wheels and tyres.

Otherwise it was the same mixture as before: hand-built ash-framed steel-panelled bodywork mounted on a Z-frame chassis with Morgan's famous sliding pillar independent front suspension and a conventional half-elliptic sprung rear axle endowed with a limited slip differential.

With a sparsely furnished but comfortable cockpit, the two-seater Plus 8 was capable of 125mph (201km/h), a significant 30mph (48km/h) faster than the Plus 4 it replaced.

Sports Lightweight

An alloy-bodied Sports Lightweight appeared for 1976 and the following year the original separate Moss gearbox was replaced by Rover's unit-construction five-speed unit. The V8 engine itself was extensively revised in 1982, and fuel injection became available as an option from 1984 later beoming standardized. In 1990 the power unit's capacity was increased to 4-litres.

Further radical changes were made for 1998.

The body panels were now aluminium, the cockpit was enlarged and the doors lengthened. A top-of-the-range model appeared with a 4.6-litre V8 engine.

Production of the Plus 8 finally came to an end in 2004, but the classic Morgan style lives on. The company's current range includes the four-cylinder 4/4, the BMW V8-engined Aero 8 and the Ford V6-engined Roadster, an indication of the ongoing vitality of this British family-owned concern.

Below left: An example of a 1970 Plus 8. Its exposed spare wheel is another pre-war inheritance.

Below right: The 1970 model also boasted this revised, functional dashboard.

Specification	Morgan Plus 8 (3.5 litres)
Engine location	Front, in-line
Configuration	V8
Bore and stroke	89 x 71mm
Capacity	3529cc
Valve operation	Pushrod
Horsepower	160bhp @ 5200rpm
Transmission	Manual four-speed
Drive	Rear
Chassis	Z section
Suspension – front	Sliding pillar
Suspension – rear	Half-elliptic spring
Brakes	Front disc, rear drum
Top speed	125mph (201km/h)
Acceleration	0-60mph (0-96km/h): 6.8 seconds

Datsun 240Z

**Top speed
125mph**
201km/h

*Right: The 240Z's 2.4-litre
engine, a strong, reliable
power unit with seven-
bearing crankshaft, cast
iron block and alloy
cylinder head. The twin
carburettors are SU units.*

*Below: A British-
specification 240Z
distinguished by the rubber
spoilers front and rear. The
indicator lights have been
awkwardly positioned
above the bumper to meet
UK regulations. This
example dates from 1973.*

Datsun successfully shrugged off its
image as a mass-producer of well
equipped but dull saloons when, in 1969,
it launched the 125mph (201km/h) 240Z that was
destined to become the world's most popular sports
car, snatching the crown from the MGB.

Conceived to occupy the void left by Britain's
ageing sports car lines in America, the project's
starting point was a sports coupé designed for
Datsun in 1963 by German-born US-domiciled
freelance stylist Albert Goertz, who was
responsible for the acclaimed lines of BMW's 507
roadster of the 1950s.

Using the Jaguar E-Type coupé as his starting
point, he reduced its dimensions to those
approximating the Porsche 911. It was
provisionally powered, like the Jaguar, by a twin-
overhead-camshaft engine but, when this proved
troublesome, work on the project was suspended.

And there the story might have ended, had it
not been for Datsun's rival Toyota which in 1965
produced its not dissimilar 2000GT. The appearance
of this car prompted Datsun to reactivate the sports

car concept. The essentials of Goertz's styling were
retained, but the complex twin-cam power unit was
replaced by an engine that was uniquely conceived
for the emerging Z car.

This was a 2.4-litre six-cylinder version of the
overhead-camshaft four which had powered the
company's 1967 510 saloon. Interestingly, ohc
engines were still relatively scarce at this time and
were usually reserved for more expensive models.

Left: The Z's well-equipped interior. Instrumentation was good, as was leg room, but the degree of seat recline was limited by the luggage shelf. The seats were nicely shaped but rather thinly padded. Note the 'dead pedal' rest for the driver's left foot.

Below: The 240Z was replaced in 1978 by the 280ZX, bigger, broader and heavier, but outwardly less attractive, than the original. Surviving until 1983, there was a choice of 2 and 2.7-litre engines. But somehow the magic of the original had been lost.

A four-speed gearbox was fitted to those 240Zs sold in America but in other markets, including Britain, a five-cog unit was employed.

The all-independent suspension was similarly adventurous and took the form of all-round struts. A further progressive feature was rack and pinion steering which was a well established feature of European cars of the day, but not Japanese ones.

Only available as a coupé

The 240Z, so named to reflect its engine capacity, differed from most British sports cars in that it was only produced in closed form. Strictly a two-seater, like the E-Type it had an opening tailgate. And there was also plenty of luggage space.

On the road the model performed best on long straight roads and was able to cover mile after mile at 100mph (161km/h). And 60mph (96km/h) from a standing start was attainable in just 8 seconds which made it quicker than a Porsche 911 or Triumph TR6.

The 240Z remained in production until 1973; of the 156,000 or so built, some 85 per cent were sold in the United States. It was replaced by the 260Z and, later, the 280Z which were better equipped but heavier and, consequently, slower.

In short the first of the Z cars did everything expected of it and underlined to the motoring world that Japan was able produce well-engineered, marketable cars at a price the public could afford.

Specification	Datsun 240Z
Engine location	Front, in-line
Configuration	Six-cylinder
Bore and stroke	83 x 73mm
Capacity	2393cc
Valve operation	Single overhead camshaft
Horsepower	151bhp @ 5600rpm
Transmission	Manual five-speed, see text
Drive	Rear
Chassis	Unitary
Suspension – front	MacPherson strut with lower link
Suspension – rear	MacPherson strut with lower wishbone
Brakes	Front disc, rear drum
Top speed	125mph (201km/h)
Acceleration	0-60mph (0-96km/h): 8 seconds

Aston Martin V8

**Top speed
170mph**
274km/h

*Right: The top-of-the-range
Vantage, a 1978 car. The
model is immediately
identifiable by its closed
radiator grille. Its
impressive top speed of
170mph (274km/h) made it
one the world's fastest cars.*

*Below: This DBS V8 dates
from 1970 and is easily
distinguished by its twin
headlamps. They were
replaced by single units in
1972. Styled by William
Towns, the lines were
destined to survive for
20 years.*

Mainstay of the marque for no less than
20 years, the V8 was one of Britain's
great performance cars, able to attain
170mph (274km/h). It was magnificently styled and
carefully handbuilt at Aston Martin's famous
Newport Pagnell factory.

Launched in 1969 and successor to the DB6,
which remained in production until 1971, what was
initially named the DBS appeared in 1967. It was
no less than 4in (102mm) wider than the DB6.
Styled by William Towns, it had been designed to
accommodate a new 5.3-litre alloy V8 engine but
this was not completed in time, so it continued to
be powered by the existing 4-litre twin-cam six.

What was named the DBS V8 saloon, although
it was clearly a coupé, duly arrived two years later,
and it was powered by the long-awaited engine.
This was fuel-injected but, like Rolls-Royce, Aston
Martin did not disclose the brake horsepower it
developed. Capable of 160mph (257km/h), there
was the option of a manual five-speed ZF gearbox
or three-speed automatic transmission. However,
the latter was far and away the most popular choice
with customers.

New owners

Then in 1972 Sir David Brown (knighted 1968),
who had owned Aston Martin since 1947, sold the
firm to Company Developments, a property
business. In consequence the model was shorn of
its DB prefix and was renamed the V8. The original
twin headlamps were replaced by a single lamp
design and this new nose was to endure for the rest
of the car's production life. A Volante (open)
version appeared in 1978.

In 1977 a more powerful Vantage version
arrived with a disclosed 380bhp on tap, capable of

a creditable 170mph (274km/h) and identifiable by a rear spoiler and a blanked-off radiator intake.

But Company Developments had succumbed to bankruptcy in 1974 and there were to be no less than three changes of ownership before Aston Martin was acquired by Ford in 1987. Both the V8 and Vantage continued to undergo development. In 1982 the company was forced to disclose the horsepower generated by the basic V8 engine because it became a requirement of German import regulations. It proved to be 305bhp, which was probably rather less than most owners had imagined.

Zagato tribute

In 1986 came a version bodied in Milan by Zagato in tribute to the legendary DB4 GT Zagato of 1960. There were 75 in total, 50 coupés and 25 convertibles. A top speed of over 180mph (290km/h) was attainable. The last V8 was completed in

December 1989, although its Virage successor had made its debut at the previous year's British Motor Show. This entered production in 1990, and ultimately sired the awesome, supercharged Vantage of 1993.

Above: A V8 Volante of 1979, introduced in the previous year. A power-operated hood and air conditioning were fitted.

Left: The luxurious interior of a 1978 V8 automatic. The instrumentation was comprehensive and included an oil temperature gauge and an ammeter.

Below left: The engine of the Volante shown above. Although the compartment appears rather congested, access to components is reasonably good.

Specification	Aston Martin V8 Vantage
Engine location	Front, in-line
Configuration	V8
Bore and stroke	85 x 100mm
Capacity	5340cc
Valve operation	Twin overhead camshafts per cylinder bank
Horsepower	380bhp @ 5000rpm
Transmission	Three-speed automatic
Drive	Rear
Chassis	Platform
Suspension – front	Wishbones and coil springs
Suspension – rear	Radius arms, De Dion rear axle and coil springs
Brakes	Disc
Top speed	170mph (274km/h)
Acceleration	0-60mph (0-96km/h): 5.5 seconds

Jensen Interceptor FF

**Top speed
130mph**
209km/h

*Right: A bonnetful of
engine, the Chrysler V8 was
dominated by the air filter
of the four-barrel Carter
carburettor.*

*Below: A 1968 Interceptor
FF, with identifying twin air
outlets. All models were
enhanced by stainless steel
trim. The alloy wheels were
later extended to the Mark
III cars.*

 The 133mph (214km/h) Interceptor of
1967 was the last and most popular of the
West Bromwich-built Jensens. Also
produced in four-wheel-drive form, this FF variant
appeared 11 years before the Audi Quattro made
the configuration a marketing reality.

The Interceptor's origins are to be found in
Jensen's glass-fibre-bodied, Chrysler V8-engined
CV8 of 1962. Although capable of 130mph
(209km/h), its styling was controversial and its
appeal limited.

The Interceptor, announced at the 1966 London
Motor Show, replaced the CV8. From a visual
standpoint it differed radically from it. Not only did
the new car have a metal body, its styling, instead
of being undertaken in-house, was the work of the
Italian Touring concern.

A distinctive grand tourer with a large and
useful opening tailgate, the Interceptor's twin

tubular chassis was based on those of its CV8
predecessor, while its 6.2-litre Chrysler V8 hailed
from the same source. Automatic transmission was
fitted, although a four-speed manual 'box could be
specified for more sporting owners.

New alloy wheels

A Mark II version arrived for 1970 with a modified nose and interior changes; its Mark III successor for the 1972 season was identifiable by its new alloy wheels. These were also shared with the more expensive and larger 7.2-litre engined SP Interceptor. This was capable of 143mph (230km/h), but it only remained in production for a year.

The Interceptor FF, for Ferguson Formula, was a four-wheel-drive version which incorporated that company's long nurtured 4WD system. A further refinement was the pioneering use of Dunlop Maxaret anti-lock brakes.

Advertised as 'the world's most advanced car', it was outwardly similar to the original, apart from an imperceptible 2in (51mm) that was added to its wheelbase. It was easily identifiable by the second cooling duct introduced in the front wings. Traction was excellent and, as might be excepted, roadholding sensational.

But on the debit side was greater weight and mechanical complication, which reduced the FF's top speed to 130mph (209km/h), and caused some teething troubles. And at £6018, it was a significant £1543 more than the conventionally driven car.

The FF shared the updates applied to the mainstream Mark II and, briefly, Mark III before production ceased at the end of 1971. Only 224 had been completed. However, the conventionally driven Interceptor continued to sell strongly, and in 1972 the 7.2-litre engine, already being used in the SP, replaced the 6.2-litre unit.

Unfortunately the oil price rise of 1973 spelt disaster for the big, thirsty Jensen. Although the

Specification	**Jensen** Interceptor FF
Engine location	Front, in-line
Configuration	V8
Bore and stroke	108 x 86mm
Capacity	6276cc
Valve operation	Pushrod
Horsepower	325bhp @ 4600rpm
Transmission	Automatic three-speed
Drive	Four-wheel
Chassis	Twin tubular
Suspension – front	Wishbones and twin coil springs
Suspension – rear	Half-elliptic leaf spring
Brakes	Disc
Top speed	130mph (209km/h)
Acceleration	0-60mph (0-96km/h): 8.5 seconds

Left: The interior with its comfortable seats, distinctive central console and lockable compartment behind the automatic transmission lever.

Below: The FF in profile with the large rear window readily apparent. When this hatch was opened in conjunction with the spring-loaded parcel shelf, access could be gained to the luggage compartment. Fittingly for a grand tourer, the Interceptor could carry plenty of suitcases.

business struggled on, car production finally ceased in 1976, after 4112 Interceptors had been completed. Some further examples were built in the 1983-92 era but that really was the end of this ingenious, well conceived grand tourer.

Citroën SM

**Top speed
135mph**
217km/h

*Below: Bristling with
hydraulic refinement,
Citroën declared the front-
wheel-drive SM the safest
and most comfortable grand
tourer of its day. The
suspension maintained a
constant height, regardless
of load, and could be set for
four different cruising
positions depending on the
state and type of road. The
distinctive body lines
reflected the results of
aerodynamic testing.*

Capable of 135mph (217km/h), the SM of
1970 – an extravagantly conceived
Maserati-engined grand tourer – was
destined to be the last flowering of the Citroën
company, a business that was taken over in 1974 by
its Peugeot rival.

The SM was a child of the buoyant 1960s.
When Citroën planned a grand touring flagship for
the following decade, it soon recognized that it did
not possess a sufficiently large capacity engine to
power such a prestigious model.

Instead of designing one, Citroën decided in
1968 to acquire the struggling Maserati concern
and it wasted little time in adapting its 4.1/4.7-litre
V8 for its special needs. Because French taxation
penalized cars of over 15CV, the equivalent of 2.8-
litres, the result was a V6 unit of 2.6-litres capacity.
A purpose-designed five-speed manual gearbox
was employed.

Announced at the 1970 Geneva Motor Show,
the SM (S had been the project code and M stood
for Maserati) was – by French standards – a large,
complicated car that was clearly intended to place

Citroën head and shoulders above its rivals and
contemporaries.

The styling was distinctive rather than attractive
and, as ever, it was aerodynamically refined. The
mechanicals were based on those of Citroën's
enduring DS saloon. This meant, of course, front-
wheel-drive and hydraulically charged self-
levelling pneumatic suspension. Much else was
hydraulically assisted with sophisticated power
steering that also self-centred; cleverly, the inner
pair of six headlights, concealed behind a
transparent cover, turned with the wheels.

Left-hand-drive only

The intention was to build about 20 SMs a day.
Although only made in left-hand-drive form, the
model was available in Britain from 1972 where it
sold for a pricey £5342. But drivers took some time
to adapt to the steering and the Maserati engine,
typically, provided good performance but without
much refinement. In consequence it was found to
be unduly noisy. And petrol consumption was an
unhealthy 16mpg (17lit/100km).

Left: Parisian coachbuilder Henri Chapron produced this four-door version of the SM which was exhibited at the 1972 Paris Motor Show. Only produced in prototype form, it was over 16ft (4877mm) in length.

Below: The Chapron SM convertible was named the Mylord. Previously the company had produced an open four-door car reserved for use by the French president. It remained in service long after the model had ceased production.

Although there was sufficient space for the driver and front passenger, rear seat accommodation was found to be unduly cramped. Despite these shortcomings, the SM sold well enough for the first two years of production, but the oil price rise of 1973 and the consequent increase in petrol costs spelt the end for the SM. Sales slumped and Citroën also succumbed to a take-over by Peugeot.

This was despite the addition, in 1972, of fuel injection, and the appearance in 1973 of a 3-litre version with automatic transmission.

It was all over by 1975 when SM production ceased and support was withdrawn from Maserati which was left to its own fate. Just 12,920 examples of the SM had been built in five years.

Specification	Citroën SM
Engine location	Front, in-line
Configuration	V6
Bore and stroke	87 x 75mm
Capacity	2670cc
Valve operation	Twin overhead camshafts per cylinder bank
Horsepower	180bhp @ 6250rpm
Transmission	Manual five-speed
Drive	Front
Chassis	Unitary
Suspension – front	Twin transverse arms with hydropneumatic struts
Suspension – rear	Trailing arm with hydropneumatic struts
Brakes	Disc
Top speed	135mph (217km/h)
Acceleration	0-60mph (0-96km/h): 9.1 seconds

Plymouth Road Runner Superbird

**Top speed
140mph**
225km/h

Right: The Superbird was fitted with a 440cid V8 as standard, but there was an optional and even more powerful 426 'hemi' available.

Below: You couldn't mistake it for anything else! The black vinyl roof was a standard fitment, along with the unmissable fixed rear stabilizer, the presence of which did not significantly affect the car's behaviour.

OK, it looks as though it has just landed! But in 1970 this zany be-winged coupé was one of the fastest cars on America's roads and racetracks, being capable, in its most potent form, of 190mph (306km/h).

In 1968 Plymouth, Chrysler's bargain-basement car division, introduced the two-door, no-frills Road Runner coupé, the car being named after the Warner Brothers cartoon character of that name. It even possessed a distinctive beeb-beeb horn in tribute to its inspiration.

In what was to be dubbed the Muscle Car era, the 'Runner was based on Plymouth's new Belvedere model, and powered by the company's proven 383cid (6.3-litre) V8, enhanced to produce 325bhp. Aimed at the young driver to take to the racetrack, the 'Runner was progressively up-engined, surviving in this form until 1970. In that year its most extreme manifestation was unveiled in the form of the Superbird.

Created to meet NASCAR (National Association for Stock Car Auto Racing) homologation track

requirements, the authorities required that no less than 1000 Road Runner Superbirds had to be sold commercially to meet qualification regulations. Plymouth responded that it had orders for 2000 and, in due course, 1971 machines found owners.

As such small numbers were involved, aftermarket specialist Creative Industries was responsible for the aerodynamic modifications.

This required extending the front of the car by 18in (457mm) – the resulting chiselled nose incorporated pop-up headlamps behind glass-fibre flaps. The original recessed rear window was replaced by flush-fitting glass but, to hide evidence of this modification, all 'Birds were fitted with a black vinyl roof.

Outlandish spoiler

Much more apparent was a large spoiler mounted some 24in (610mm) above the car's boot with the Road Runner decal featuring on the supports. But despite the 'Bird's outlandish looks, this aerodynamic extension did not prove to be wholly satisfactory. The modifications added weight and didn't really kick in until the Plymouth was travelling at 80 to 90mph (129 to 145km/h).

Most Superbirds were powered by a 375bhp version of the 440cid (7.2-litre) Super Commando V8 with either four-speed manual or TorqueFlite automatic transmission. There was an optional 390hp version and a top line 'hemi' 426cid (7-litre) with 425hp in harness.

While the street cars were good for 140mph (225km/m), those created for the racing circuits only used hemi power and were capable of about 50mph (80km/h) more.

Solely produced for 1970, revised legislation rendered the Superbird obsolete and Plymouth introduced a new Road Runner shape for 1971. Sales of the old line were slow although today they are much sought after by collectors.

Specification	Plymouth Road Runner Superbird
Engine location	Front, in-line
Configuration	V8
Bore and stroke	4.32 x 3.75in (110 x 95mm)
Capacity	440cid (7210cc)
Valve operation	Overhead valve
Horsepower	375bhp @ 4600rpm
Transmission	Manual four-speed
Drive	Rear
Chassis	Unitary
Suspension – front	Wishbones and torsion bar
Suspension – rear	Half-elliptic spring
Brakes	Drum
Top speed	140mph (225km/h)
Acceleration	0-60mph (0-96km/h): 4.9 seconds

Left: The Road Runner cartoon character from which the mainstream model took its name was a 'fun feature' of the car. This cheerful emblem appeared on the spoiler mounts and was repeated on the left-hand headlight flap.

Below: The Superbird's aerodynamically refined nose was made of glass fibre and also incorporated pop-up headlamps.

1971–1980
Down but Not Out

The post-war boom came to an abrupt halt with the outbreak, in 1973, of the Arab-Israeli war. The result was a hike in oil prices with predictable consequences for the cost of petrol at the pumps.

The economic downturn that followed wrought havoc within Britain's uncompetitive motor industry and its rapid contraction effectively spelt an end to its increasingly dated range of sports cars.

In Germany rising fuel prices killed off BMW's pioneering 2002 Turbo saloon but the turbocharger was here to stay. A further technological milestone arrived in the form of a viable four-wheel-drive system, thanks to Audi's innovative, impressive and influential quattro coupé.

De Tomaso Pantera

**Top speed
150mph**
241km/h

*Below: The outstanding
lines of the Pantera's Ghia-
styled body were one of its
most enduring attributes, as
this 1974 GTS bears
witness. Note the recessed
rear window.*

On paper the Pantera which in its most
potent GTS form was capable of over
170mph (273km/h), was the ideal grand
tourer, stylish, fast and not overly expensive.
Unfortunately, early examples were hopelessly
unreliable but this Italian car proved to be
remarkably enduring and survived for no less than
25 years.

Argentinian-born Alejandro De Tomaso left his
native country and in 1955 arrived in Italy, home of
his paternal grandfather. Establishing a business at
Modena in 1959, he progressed from building
racing cars to roadgoing GTs – the Pantera of 1970
was his first series production model.

Style guru

By this time De Tomaso had acquired the Ghia and
Vignale styling houses and in 1969 Ford, wishing
to maintain its performance credentials and
underpin its Le Mans triumphs both at home and
abroad, took a majority shareholding in all these
disparate businesses.

Outwardly the mid-engined Pantera looked
impressive, having been styled by American-born
John Taajara, who had joined Ghia in 1958 and
consequently found himself in De Tomaso's
employ. Engineering was the responsibility of
Giampaolo Dallara, latterly of Lamborghini, where
he had responsibility for the celebrated Miura.

The Pantera, the name is Italian for Panther,
was based on a steel sub-structure with a 5.7-litre
Ford 310bhp V8 mounted in line, driving the
wheels via a ZF five-speed gearbox. The latter unit
reputedly cost more to produce than the engine!

Capable of 150mph (241km/h), European
versions of the model could reach 60mph (96km/h)
in an impressive 6.5 seconds although the US cars
were half a second slower on account of the
engine's de-toxing equipment.

The model was well received on its
announcement at the 1970 New York Motor Show.
But the cars, which were sold in America through
Ford's Lincoln-Mercury dealers, were plagued with
reliability problems which remained largely

*Right: Frontal view of the
left-hand-drive GTS shown
above. Unusually for the
day the rear tyres were
wider than those at the
front. What look like air
intakes behind the rear
windows are fakes; the
radiator was front-mounted
and the carburettors drew
their air through an
opening on the rear deck
near to the back window.*

unresolved. As a result Ford cut its losses in 1973, although it retained the Ghia business and its respected name.

That year a more powerful version of the Pantera, named the GTS, was introduced. With its V8 boosted to 350bhp, top speed was a reputed 175mph (282km/h) and the 0-60mph (96km/h) acceleration figure for the US models was shaved to 5.6 seconds.

The rupture with Ford saw De Tomaso move to smaller premises in Modena and for the next 20 or so years a trickle of Panteras continued to be built there. This seemingly indestructible model was given a modest stylistic facelift in 1991 and a 4.9-litre Ford V8 replaced the long-running 5.7-litre unit. It continued to be listed until 1996, by which time it had been replaced by the equally shadowy Guara GT!

Above: Still looking good, a 1984 GTS which has acquired a rear wing, a popular Pantera extra.

Below left: Interior of the car shown above, a right-hand-drive example built for the UK market.

Specification	De Tomaso Pantera
Engine location	Mid, in-line
Configuration	V8
Bore and stroke	101 x 88mm
Capacity	5763cc
Valve operation	Pushrod
Horsepower	310bhp @ 5400rpm
Transmission	Manual, five-speed
Drive	Rear
Chassis	Unitary
Suspension – front	Wishbones and coil spring
Suspension – rear	Wishbones and coil spring
Brakes	Disc
Top speed	150mph (241km/h)
Acceleration	0-60mph (0-96km/h): 6.5 seconds

Panther J72

**Top speed
122mph**
196km/h

Created for the worldwide playboy fraternity, the Panther J72 was one of the fastest accelerating cars of its day, the V12 version being able to sprint to 60mph (96km/h) in a mere 6.6 seconds. The car was the brainchild of Robert Jankel, who had begun his motoring career with the SuperSpeed Conversions Ford tuning concern, prior to moving into the fashion industry. The resulting cars thus incorporated these rather eclectic ingredients.

Initially Jankel produced replica cars on a one-off basis and before long orders began to mount. The outcome, in 1971, was the creation of Panther West Winds and the first Panther appeared in the following year.

'The best replica yet' declared *Autocar* after testing the J2, the first of the line, that had been announced in June 1972. Inspired by the SS Jaguar 100 sports car of 1935, the reason behind the choice of the big-cat Panther name was now apparent. It was well designed and carefully built with a hand-crafted aluminium body resplendent in gleaming paint work. It sold for £4380, or about the price of two E-Type Jaguars.

Built up around a chassis of square-section tubing, beam axles were fitted rear *and* front with all-round coil springs – each was located by a five link system. Under the heavily louvred bonnet was a Jaguar XK 3.8-litre engine which developed 240bhp in twin carburettored guise. This was essentially the same unit that had powered the Mark II saloon rather than the E-Type. It was mated to an XJ6 all-synchromesh gearbox with overdrive on top gear.

Connolly upholstery

The finish of the cockpit was very much in keeping with the rest of the car, the seats being upholstered in the best Connolly hides, with the material also extended to the door panels and steering wheel. The tastefully veneered dashboard was replete with Jaguar instruments.

In this form the J2 was capable of 115mph (185km/h). Generally the Panther lived up to expectations, being easy to drive, comfortable and ideal for motorways, even if on country roads the limitations of the all-too-basic non-independent suspension became apparent.

Below: Unashamedly based on the pre-war SS Jaguar 100, the build quality of the J72 attracted many admirers. Available in 3.8 and 4.2-litre six-cylinder form, as well as in 5.3-litre V12 guise, this example is powered by the smallest capacity engine. It is identifiable by the absence of a bonnet bulge on the nearside.

Improved acceleration

Subsequently the 3.8 engine was replaced by Jaguar's 4.2 unit and, best of all, the 5.3-litre V12 for 1974, which could be enhanced by fitting triple Weber carburettors. This not only pushed the top speed to about 122mph (196km/h), acceleration was also dramatically improved although, inevitably, at the cost of fuel consumption which was an overall 11mpg (25.6lit/100km). The price was £9745. By the time production ceased in 1981 a total of 430 cars had been completed.

Unfortunately an over-extended Jankel succumbed to liquidation in 1979, although the Panther name continued until 1996, cars being latterly manufactured in South Korea.

Specification	Panther J2 (V12)
Engine location	Front, in-line
Configuration	V12
Bore and stroke	90 x 70mm
Capacity	5343cc
Valve operation	Single overhead camshaft per cylinder bank
Horsepower	250bhp @ 6000rpm
Transmission	Manual four-speed
Drive	Rear
Chassis	Twin rectangular steel tube
Suspension – front	Leading arm, Panhard rod and coil spring
Suspension – rear	Leading arm, Panhard rod and coil spring
Brakes	Disc
Top speed	122mph (196km/h)
Acceleration	0-60mph (0-96km/h): 6.6 seconds

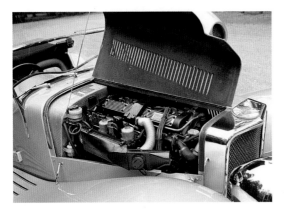

Far left: The 3.8-litre Jaguar XK engine.

Left: The ultra traditional walnut-veneered instrument panel and leather-bound steering wheel.

Below: The bonnet pod followed the contours of the air filter to service the twin SU carburettors.

Lancia Stratos

**Top speed
140mph**
225km/h

*Right: Heart of the matter –
the Stratos' 2.4-litre Fiat-
built Ferrari engine.*

*Below: A mid-located
engine meant that the nose
could be aerodynamically
efficient. The pop-up
headlamps helped too.*

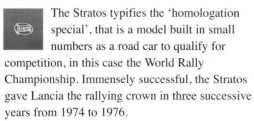

The Stratos typifies the 'homologation
special', that is a model built in small
numbers as a road car to qualify for
competition, in this case the World Rally
Championship. Immensely successful, the Stratos
gave Lancia the rallying crown in three successive
years from 1974 to 1976.

This is a car that began life as a Bertone styling
exercise that appeared at the 1970 Turin Motor
Show. The work of Marcello Gandini, who is better
known for having styled the bodies of the
Lamborghini Miura and Countach, it was based on
the Lancia HF coupé sub-structure with its 1.6-litre
V4 engine relocated behind the driver. Futuristic,
wedge-shaped and doorless, access to what its
maker named the Stratos was by a single opening
front flap.

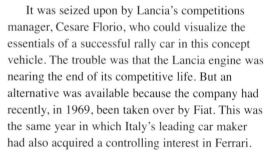

It was seized upon by Lancia's competitions
manager, Cesare Florio, who could visualize the
essentials of a successful rally car in this concept
vehicle. The trouble was that the Lancia engine was
nearing the end of its competitive life. But an
alternative was available because the company had
recently, in 1969, been taken over by Fiat. This was
the same year in which Italy's leading car maker
had also acquired a controlling interest in Ferrari.

Ferrari power

Another 1969 initiative was Ferrari's mid-engined
Dino coupé. Powered by a Fiat-built 2.4-litre V6
engine, it was also used in a Fiat of the same name.
And this was the power unit that Florio chose for
the Stratos.

The project took a further leap forward with a
car displayed at the 1971 Turin show. Unlike the
previous year's offering, it had orthodox doors and
was based on a steel sub-structure with glass-fibre
body panels. But the definitive Stratos had to wait
until the 1972 event.

This version was a stubby, purposeful Bertone-
refined wedge with a wheelbase of a mere 7ft 2in
(2184mm). The Ferrari engine was mounted
transversely behind the driver, and the car was able
to attain a spirited and reliable 140mph (225km/h).
The Stratos was first blooded in the 1972 Turin de
Corse event, although suspension failure forced its
retirement. However, it soon found its form.

Left: A Stratos in rallying guise. It gave the Lancia works team considerable success and the model also proved its worth in the hands of private teams. Strong and versatile, it had the virtue of being exceptionally fast, while also having excellent traction. Between 1974 and 1977 the Stratos were regularly fitted with four-valve cylinder heads which increased power to 285bhp.

Left: A 1975 Stratos in roadgoing mode. Although performance was guaranteed, on the debit side was unpredictable handling while the interior was somewhat cramped. But in the hands of a professional this did not matter, as was underlined by a victory in the 1979 Monte Carlo Rally when Darniche, a privateer, trounced Ford and other factory teams.

Its first victory came in the 1973 Spanish Firestone rally but production did not begin in earnest until 1974, so the cars ran in the prototype class because homologation was not achieved until that autumn. From there on and for the next three years this Lancia proved to be virtually invincible.

When detuned for road use the Ferrari V6 produced a subdued 190bhp but it was perfectly tractable. The seating was rather cramped and, while forward visibility was fine, side views were restricted. Luggage space was minimal although the doors contained storage bins.

Stratos production ceased in 1975 by which time 492 had been completed, eight short of the required 500!

Specification	Lancia Stratos
Engine location	Mid, transverse
Configuration	V6
Bore and stroke	92 x 60mm
Capacity	2418cc
Valve operation	Twin overhead camshafts per cylinder bank
Horsepower	190bhp @ 7000rpm
Transmission	Manual five-speed
Drive	Rear
Chassis	Unitary
Suspension – front	Coil springs and wishbones
Suspension – rear	Coil springs and wishbones
Brakes	Disc
Top speed	140mph (225km/h)
Acceleration	0-60mph (0-96km/h): 5.9 seconds

Jaguar XJ12

**Top speed
140mph**
225km/h

*Right: Interior of the
coupé, marketed as the
XJ12C, pictured opposite.
Automatic transmission was
obligatory, a pity because a
manual box would have
been desirable on this
rather 'sporty' model.*

*Below: This saloon dates
from 1973 and is a Series 2
car, identifiable by the
raised bumper which
necessitated repositioning
the sidelights underneath.*

Smooth, turbine-like acceleration is the principal characteristic of the V12 engine and in 1972 Jaguar extended this power unit to its acclaimed XJ6 saloon. The result was an extraordinarily impressive car; the world's most popular 12 cylinder-powered four-seater.

The 250bhp 5.3-litre unit with single cam heads made its debut in the Series III E-Type of 1971. It was extended to the hull of the XJ6 four-door saloon which had been accorded the Car of the Year title on its 1968 launch. It was a model which set new levels of silent running and refinement for the motor industry.

Able to attain 120mph (193km/h) in 4.2-litre six-cylinder form, the XJ12 outwardly resembled the six-cylinder car but was identifiable by a vertically slatted radiator grille in place of the original latticework one. This was enhanced by the presence of a discreet centrally located V symbol.

Automatic transmission came as standard, but this contributed to a prodigal average petrol consumption figure of 12mpg (23.5lit/100km). The

figure was even worse on a long-wheelbase version, the XJ12L, which arrived for the 1973 model year. This was also produced in Daimler Double Six guise.

Able to cruise at 140mph (225km/h), this well appointed Jaguar could reach 100mph (161km/h) in under 20 seconds. Sadly sales of the model suffered in the wake of the energy crisis of 1973-74. The entire XJ range received a facelift in 1975. These

Series II XJ12s were only built in long wheelbase form and were identifiable by a squatter radiator grille and higher bumper line.

The V12 engine was uprated to 285bhp with the arrival of fuel injection and later in 1975 the model's name was changed to XJ5.3, diplomatically expunging the notion of 12 thirsty cylinders!

Pininfarina styling

The range received a further stylistic update, the work of Pininfarina, in 1979 with the Mark III XJs. Jaguar addressed the fuel consumption bugbear with the arrival, in 1981, of the HE, for High Efficiency, version. This employed new, more efficient cylinder heads, the work of Swiss engineer Michael May. Fuel consumption was now a more respectable 16mpg (17.6lit/100km).

The 1984 season saw the Sovereign name replace the XJ initials, and the model became the Jaguar V12 for 1990. Although a new version, coded XJ40, of the XJ6 was introduced in 1986, the V12 continued to be the sole engine fitted in the Series III body and this remained in production until 1993. The engine, enlarged to 6-litres, was then carried over to the XJ40 line. It was built until 1996 when the 12 finally made way for Jaguar's new V8.

Above: A 1974 coupé with its distinctive vinyl roof, fitted at the behest of the marketing department, not engineering!

Left: Broadspeed prepared XJ12Cs for Group 2 racing. Campaigned in 1976 and 1977, they did not achieve any measure of success.

Specification	Jaguar XJ12
Engine location	Front, in-line
Configuration	V12
Bore and stroke	90 x 70mm
Capacity	5343cc
Valve operation	Single overhead camshaft per cylinder bank
Horsepower	250bhp @ 6000rpm
Transmission	Automatic three-speed
Drive	Rear
Chassis	Unitary
Suspension – front	Wishbones and coil spring
Suspension – rear	Wishbone, drive shaft and coil springs
Brakes	Disc
Top speed	140mph (225km/h)
Acceleration	0-60mph (0-96km/h): 7.4 seconds

Maserati Bora

**Top speed
162mph**
261km/h

*Right: The Italian/French
Bora, Maserati's first
production mid-engined car,
with styling by Giorgetto
Giugiaro. This is a 1975
example. Power was
courtesy of Maserati's
proven V8 engine.*

*Below: The Bora possessed
the virtues of being a quiet,
powerful car with plenty of
room for its two occupants.
But on the debit side was a
poor heating and
ventilation system.*

 It was quite unlike any previous Maserati.
The mid-engined Bora coupé, capable of
over 160mph (257km/h), combined
outstanding roadholding with remarkable
refinement, the latter attribute not a characteristic
always associated with the marque!

The model was conceived during Citroën's
ownership of Maserati and it was for this reason
that the Bora used hydraulically pressurized brakes.
The pop-up headlamps were also hydraulically
activated and the same went for the driver's seat
and even the steering column.

The coupé body, commissioned in 1969, was
the work of Ital Design and was visually enhanced
by a stainless steel roof. The lines were both
distinctive and attractive, but rear visibility was,
alas, far from perfect because of the location of
Maserati's 4.7-litre V8 engine. This was already
being used in the conventional forward position in
the two-seater Ghibli coupé. Longitudinally located
in the Bora, it drove the rear wheels through a five-
speed ZF gearbox.

Designated Maserati's Type 117, the car was
announced at the 1971 Geneva Motor Show,
although it was to be a further year before
production got underway. An uncompromising two-
seater, the model was found to be comfortable with
excellent handling, as befitted the engine location,
and it was surprisingly quiet. Criticisms were
confined to the brakes which were thought to be
too sensitive, and poor heating and ventilation. And

the lusty 310bhp V8 was thirsty, consuming fuel at the prodigious rate of a mere 11 miles per gallon (25.6lit/100km).

Increased top speed

The upheavals of the 1970s saw a hefty rise in petrol prices and Citroën disposing of its Maserati asset. Bora production slumped from 56 cars produced in 1975 to a mere half dozen in 1976. Consideration was given to discontinuing the model, but instead the engine was enlarged to 4.9 litres which increased the top speed to 165mph (265km/h). It was destined to remain in production until 1978 by which time 571 examples had been completed.

The Bora lived on in the shape of its Merak derivative of 1972 which shared its body but was powered by a 2-litre version of the Citroën SM's V6 unit. This was a 127mph (204km/h) car, and in 1975 the lighter, faster Merak SS appeared with engine capacity upped to 3 litres. This was capable of 153mph (246km/h).

Much more popular than the Bora, some 1500 Meraks had been completed by the time that production ceased in 1983, making it the most popular Maserati of its day.

Specification	**Maserati** Bora (4.7 litres)
Engine location	Mid, in-line
Configuration	V6
Bore and stroke	91 x 75mm
Capacity	4719cc
Valve operation	Twin overhead camshafts per cylinder bank
Horsepower	310bhp @ 6000rpm
Transmission	Manual five-speed
Drive	Rear
Chassis	Unitary
Suspension – front	Hydraulic and coil spring
Suspension – rear	Hydraulic and coil spring
Brakes	Disc
Top speed	162mph (261km/h)
Acceleration	0-60mph (0-96km/h): 6.5 seconds

Above: While having a distinctive tail, driver visibility was poor at the rear because of the mid-located engine. The simple rear bumper meant that the car was not allowed to be sold in America.

Left: A right-hand-drive Bora. Although the steering wheel was correctly positioned, the handbrake was not relocated and so was somewhat inaccessible.

BMW 2002 Turbo

**Top speed
130mph**
209km/h

*Below: The Turbo with its
unmistakable front spoiler,
distinctive livery and
decals, lowered suspension
and wider wheels and tyres.
It was only produced in left-
hand-drive form.*

Europe's first turbocharged road car, the
performance of BMW's two-door 2002
saloon was a revelation with a top speed
(compared to the normally aspirated version)
increased by some 12mph (19km/h) to 130mph
(209km/h). Acceleration was similarly enhanced.

The starting point, certainly as far as the public
was concerned, for this exciting project was an
'experimental safety vehicle' that BMW unveiled in
1972. Although not intended for production, this
glass-fibre-bodied coupé had a theoretical top speed
of 155mph (249km/h). Powered by a turbocharged
version of the 2002's 2-litre engine, it developed
some 200bhp, about 70bhp more than the normally

aspirated unit. Its origins are to be found in a racing
engine which powered a BMW 2002 that won its
class in the 1969 European Touring Car
Championship. This was the first appearance of a
turbocharged engine in this event and, having
proved its reliability, BMW embarked on a
programme to produce a roadgoing version.

Fortunes of war

Unfortunately the 2002 Turbo's launch at the 1973
Frankfurt Motor Show coincided with the outbreak
of the Arab-Israeli war. As a consequence oil and
petrol prices soared and the car only remained in
production for 10 months.

Invariably finished in white, there could be no doubt that it was something out of the ordinary because of its lowered suspension, wider wheels and tyres which required arch extensions. There was no front bumper, in its place was a deep spoiler which was embellished with the word *turbo* in mirror writing so that other drivers would be in little doubt of what was about to overtake them! However, this feature came in for serious criticism from the usually sympathetic German press and BMW quickly dropped the idea. However, colourful and distinctive striping along the car's flanks was retained.

The KKK turbocharger installation differed from that of the 1972 mid-engined coupé in being mounted low down below the exhaust manifold, rather than above it. The result of this location meant that the model could only be produced in left-hand-drive form.

On the road, the turbocharger's presence only became noticeable above 4000rpm when the extra power seemed to arrive all at once. And because this was a pioneering installation, the Turbo also lacked flexibility.

A rapidly deteriorating world economy meant that when production ceased in 1974 only 1672 examples had been completed. BMW would not revive the concept until 1978, by which time the turbocharged road car was a proven concept, thanks to the Munich company's pioneering efforts.

Above: The rear spoiler and front and rear flared wheel arches were further Turbo features. Unlike the front of the car which lacked one, a bumper was fitted at the rear.

Left: A smaller padded steering wheel and extra instruments were just some of the Turbo's interior refinements. The fuel tank was also larger than usual.

Specification	**BMW** 2002 Turbo
Engine location	Front, in-line
Configuration	Turbocharged four-cylinder
Bore and stroke	89 x 80mm
Capacity	1990cc
Valve operation	Single overhead camshaft
Horsepower	170bhp @ 5800rpm
Transmission	Manual four- or five-speed
Drive	Rear
Chassis	Unitary
Suspension – front	MacPherson strut
Suspension – rear	Semi trailing arm, coil spring
Brakes	Front disc, rear drum
Top speed	130mph (209km/h)
Acceleration	0-60mph (0-96km/h): 6.8 seconds

Lamborghini Countach

**Top speed
175mph**
282km/h

*Right: Lamborghini's V12
was mounted longitudinally
in the Countach, and in its
Diablo successor. However,
it was less accessible than
the transversely mounted
engine in the Miura.*

*Below: The Countach's
wedge-shaped profile was
made possible by the mid-
position of the engine. This
is an LP400S model of
1981. What appear to be
the headlamps are in fact
flashing indicators. The real
headlamps are of the pop-
up variety.*

Replacing a model of the stature of the
Miura should have represented a daunting
prospect for any car company, but then
Lamborghini is no run-of-the-mill motor
manufacturer. The new supercar made its debut in
1971 and was named the Countach, a regional
North Italian slang word which echoed the
appreciative exclamation of a worker when viewing
the new car for the first time.

Mid-engined like the Miura, the V12 unit was
enlarged to 5 litres, and positioned longitudinally
rather than transversely. Chief engineer Paolo
Stanzani also dispensed with its predecessor's sump
in gearbox design and instead decided to position
the five-speed unit in the centre of the car,
alongside the driver. But with the drive at the rear it
was conveyed, via a sealed tube, within the
engine's sump.

Lamborghini once again turned to Bertone's
Marcello Gandini to design an appropriate body for
these unconventional mechanicals and he did not
disappoint. The result was a piece of automotive
sculpture of the highest quality, an audacious
wedge-shaped coupé with concealed headlamps
and memorable upward-opening doors.

Enthusiastic reception at launch

The first Countach was completed just in time to be
launched at the 1971 Geneva Motor Show where its
enthusiastic reception convinced Lamborghini that
this was the Miura's true successor. But it was to be
a further three years before the first production
Countach left the Saint' Agata Bolognese factory in
mid-1974. The enlarged V12 had disintegrated
during testing so the original 375bhp 3.9-litre unit
was reinstated.

Left: Rear view of the 400S. Although the rear spoiler makes a visual contribution to the car, contrary to appearances the Countach does not suffer from aerodynamic lift, and the spoiler adds drag, weight and expense. Note the four exhaust pipes.

Below: A 5000QV bereft of a rear wing and probably the better for it. Outwardly identical to its predecessors, its performance was enhanced by a redesign of the V12 engine which was not only enlarged in capacity but featured four valves per cylinder.

The model was, nevertheless, faster than its predecessor; it could be wound up to about 175mph (282km/h) with 100mph (161km/h) arriving in a little over 13 seconds. And if the driver and passenger found some difficulty in entering or leaving the cockpit, no matter!

The original version survived until 1978 when it was replaced by the Countach S with wider Campagnolo alloy wheels – the arches were flared to accommodate them. A rear wing, which added to the car's aerodynamic aura, became a popular (if not a wholly necessary) extra.

More powerful engine

In 1982 the capacity of the V12 was upped to 4.7 litres and the car was now known as the LP5000S. Further changes were in hand and in 1985 the V12 was not only again increased in capacity, to 5.2 litres, but was also the beneficiary of twin-cam four-valve cylinder heads. Now producing 455bhp, the resulting 5000QV (for *quattrovalvole*) was faster, at 178mph (286km/h), and owners found it easier to drive than its predecessor on account of its torquier engine.

The QV was destined to have a four-year production life. In 1988 Lamborghini released the Anniversary model with mildly revised bodywork which celebrated 25 years as a motor manufacturer. Countach production ceased in July 1990, after a total of 1549 examples had been completed.

Specification	Lamborghini Countach (3.9 litres)
Engine location	Mid, in-line
Configuration	V12
Bore and stroke	82 x 62mm
Capacity	3929cc
Valve operation	Twin overhead camshafts per bank
Horsepower	375bhp @ 8000rpm
Transmission	Manual five-speed
Drive	Rear
Chassis	Tubular steel
Suspension – front	Wishbones and coil spring
Suspension – rear	Wishbones and coil spring
Brakes	Ventilated disc
Top speed	175mph (282km/h)
Acceleration	0-60mph (0-96km/h): 5.7 seconds

*Above: A right-hand-drive
Anniversary Countach,
some 30 of which were sold
in Britain. It is easily
identifiable by its softer,
smoother lines.*

*Below: Significant changes
were made at the rear –
stylist Marcello Gandini
was particularly pleased
with this aspect of his work.*

Although the 5-litre V12 engine originally
developed for the Countach was sidelined, there
was a second example built and the story behind
this provides yet another fascinating strand of the
Countach story.

Lamborghini aficionado Walter Woolf, owner of
the very last Miura, also played a significant role in
the development of the much improved Countach S
of 1978. A Canadian of Austrian birth and an oil
equipment mogul, his commitment to motor sport
was underlined by the formation, in 1976, of his
own Formula 1 racing team.

In 1974 he had taken delivery of a red
Countach, reputedly the first car off the line. Woolf
was able to get the Sant' Agata factory to
manufacture a second 5-litre engine of the type that
had powered the prototype Countach and which
had spectacularly disintegrated during testing in
1971. This special V12 had a capacity of 4971cc,
internal dimensions of 85 x 73mm and developed
440bhp at 7400rpm. It was duly installed in the
first of Woolf's Countachs which was also fitted
with an innovative movable rear spoiler, squat
Pirelli P7 tyres and crudely extended wheel arches.
And therein lay the genesis of the Countach S.

Public address system

When Woolf sold the car to a Japanese enthusiast
he retained its special engine and installed it in a
second Countach that he had acquired in 1976. This
example was finished in his racing team's deep
blue and gold livery with the colours repeated in
the interior. It was also distinguished by the
provision of a public address system which
permitted the owner to hail other road users!

The 5-litre V12 engine was then again
transferred to Wolf's third Countach in which the
brakes were uprated, along with the clutch, to cope
with the demands of the enlarged unit.

He was so impressed with the results of the

changes he had made that he paid for Giampaolo Dallara, creator of the Miura, who had left Lamborghini to join De Tomaso, to return to the works to enhance the production cars in the same way. The result was the much improved Countach S.

There was also a change of road wheels. Woolf had already fitted the so-called 'telephone dial' Campagnolo alloys, and the glass-fibre flares fitted to accommodate them, together with a front spoiler, all contributed to the visual enhancements that identify the model.

Although Lamborghini eventually increased the capacity of the V12 engine to 4754cc in 1982, it was of different dimensions to the original 5-litre unit. A third stretch took place in 1985 with the enlargement of the engine to 5167cc; four-valve cylinder heads were fitted.

Such is the role played by the wealthy and enthusiastic Walter Woolf in the unfolding Lamborghini story. In fact at one stage he nearly bought the firm but, fortunately in the light of future events, wiser counsels prevailed!

Below: The model's scissor doors are one of its most distinctive features. The engine air intakes were redesigned and replaced with these wider and lower intakes. Straked air scoops at the front which appeared again just ahead of the rear wheel arches were another detail refinement.

Porsche 911 Turbo

**Top speed
153mph**
246km/h

Below: Something special: a 1980 3.3-litre Turbo with no chrome apparent, matt black being something of a Porsche speciality! The wider wheels and enhanced arches were established Turbo features by then. Less apparent is the presence of drilled brake discs arrested by Alcan four-piston calipers.

When Porsche introduced its now legendary 911 in 1962, it was capable of a respectable 130mph (209km/h) top speed. This figure progressively improved over the years but the line received a significant boost in 1974 with the arrival of 911 Turbo that was capable of 153mph (246km/h). It was able to hit 100mph (161km/h) in a mere 14 seconds.

Although Porsche's gargantuan Le Mans-winning 917 sports racer of 1970/1 had been further enhanced by a turbocharged engine, the concept had not been immediately extended to road cars. It fell to BMW to introduce, in 1973, the 2002 Turbo, which was Europe's first such street-ready model. Driven by the need to homologate its projected 935 racer in Group 4 competition, Porsche proceeded with a turbocharged version of the 911 that appeared at the 1974 Paris Motor Show.

Tea-tray spoiler

Developed under the 930 designation, the 911 Turbo was instantly identifiable by its wider wheels and accompanying flared arches while there was a large 'tea-tray' spoiler at the rear which helped to keep the back wheels firmly on the road.

Beneath was a mildly tamed race-bred, 3-litre, RSR Carrera, KKK turbocharged, six-cylinder, horizontally opposed, air-cooled engine. In this form it developed 260bhp, a good 60bhp more than the unblown 3-litre Carrera.

Fast but surprisingly flexible, the 911 Turbo was a comfortable, well-appointed car with air conditioning and electric windows fitted as standard. It was produced in this form until 1978 when the engine's capacity was increased to 3.3 litres and a competition-proven intercooler was also introduced which boosted the efficiency of the

turbocharger. Top speed was increased to 160mph (257km/h) while 100mph (161km/h) could be spirited up in a mere 12 seconds, which made this Turbo the fastest-accelerating road car of its day. Originally fitted with a four-speed gearbox, it was not until 1988 that an extra top cog arrived. This second generation Turbo was built until mid-1989, only to reappear in the spring of 1990 in revised Carrera 2 form.

The third generation Carrera Turbo arrived for 1994 with a 3.6-litre engine, twin KKK turbochargers and four-wheel drive. Accordingly sure-footed, identifiable by a distinctive howl and exceptionally rapid, it was capable of an impressive 178mph (286km/h).

The current 911 Turbo, introduced for the 2001 season, is similarly driven, has a water-cooled engine and is also available with Tiptronic semi-automatic transmission. And its top speed nudges the 190mph (306km/h) mark...

Left: The 911 Turbo's air-conditioned interior was particularly well appointed. The revolution counter dominated the instrument display and was mounted right in front of the driver with the turbocharger boost gauge set into the bottom of the dial.

Below left: This 3.3-litre Turbo was easily distinguished by the new squared-off rear spoiler with its upturned rubber surround. In addition to generating downforce, it also housed the air-conditioning radiator and served the newly introduced intercooler which reduced the temperature of the turbocharged air and so improved engine efficiency.

Specification	Porsche 911 Turbo (3 litres)
Engine location	Rear, in-line
Configuration	Turbocharged horizontally opposed six-cylinder
Bore and stroke	95 x 70mm
Capacity	2993cc
Valve operation	Single overhead camshaft
Horsepower	260bhp @ 5500rpm
Transmission	Manual four-speed
Drive	Rear
Chassis	Unitary
Suspension – front	Wishbones and torsion bar
Suspension – rear	Semi trailing arm and torsion bar
Brakes	Ventilated disc
Top speed	153mph (246km/h)
Acceleration	0-60mph (0-96km/h): 6.4 seconds

Aston Martin Lagonda

**Top speed
145mph**
233km/h

*Below: The Lagonda
prototype of 1976. Only 4ft
3in (1295mm) high, it had
plenty of boot space, but
rear passengers complained
of a lack of leg room.*

Aston Martin's luxurious and
futuristically-styled 145mph (233km/h)
Lagonda saloon was a successful initiative
which created a second product line to complement
the company's hitherto exclusively sports car range.

Aston Martin owned the Lagonda marque,
David Brown having acquired both businesses in
1947, and Lagondas remained in limited production
until the demise in 1964 of the DB4-based Rapide.
The name Lagonda was revived in 1974 for a low
production run, but as a model, rather than a
marque, designation. This was a four-door saloon
based on an extended Aston Martin V8 chassis.

Only seven were built, and production ceased in
1976. However, it did provide the company with a
platform on which to base its new car.

The firm had been placed in receivership in
1974 and a new management took over in the
following year. It commissioned a body design
from William Towns, who had styled the V8 coupé,
and the result was a low and angular four-door
saloon with concealed headlamps and a spacious
boot. The new Aston Martin was a daringly
elongated car and, at 17ft 4in (5283mm), it was one
of Europe's longest production models. It looked
like nothing else on the road.

It was powered by a detuned version of the
corporate 5.3-litre V8 engine with milder camshafts
and larger valves. Three-speed automatic
transmission was retained.

Sumptuous interior

The interior was sumptuously upholstered with
buttoned leather squabs. But the truly revolutionary
aspect of the design was a state of the art electronic
dashboard. Perfecting this feature, and coping with
the problems associated with it, nearly put paid to
the entire project.

It was mostly for this reason that there was an
two-and-a-half year hiatus before the first definitive
Lagonda left Aston Martin's Newport Pagnell

*Right: The same car as
above. The headlamps sit
under electrically activated
pop-up flaps. When the
bonnet was raised, they
remained in situ. The
supplementary halogen fog
and spot lights occupy the
recess in the slot above the
front bumper.*

*Opposite below: A 1987
Series 4 Lagonda. Towns'
original sharp lines were
somewhat softened. The
original waistline rubbing
strips were dispensed with
and the pop-up headlamps
were relocated in the nose.*

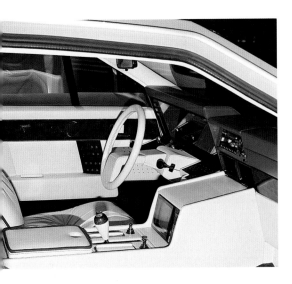

Specification	**Aston Martin** Lagonda
Engine location	Front, in-line
Configuration	V8
Bore and stroke	85 x 100mm
Capacity	5340cc
Valve operation	Twin overhead camshafts per cylinder bank
Horsepower	280bhp @ 5000rpm
Transmission	Automatic three-speed
Drive	Rear
Chassis	Platform
Suspension – front	Wishbones and coil spring
Suspension – rear	De Dion axle and coil springs
Brakes	Disc
Top speed	145mph (233km/h)
Acceleration	0-60mph (0-96km/h): 8.9 seconds

factory early in 1979. By this time the price had risen in the inflationary 1970s from £24,570 to £49,933. This was a fast car, able, on a good day, to touch 148mph (238km/h) with 100mph (161km/h) arriving in a shade over 20 seconds.

There were few production changes during its life, with the exception of fuel injection which arrived in 1986. In the following year the body was refined with the angular lines replaced by gentler curves. The pop-up headlamps were dropped to be replaced by no less than six lights positioned within the nose, a spoiler was added, along with side skirts. Alloy wheels took over from the original steel discs.

Production ceased in January 1990 after a respectable 610 examples of this unconventional saloon had been completed. The Lagonda name, for the time being at least, remains in abeyance.

Above left: In October 1983 in-house Tickford launched the much enhanced Tickford Lagonda which was fitted with no less than two colour televisions! But at £85,000 apiece there were few takers and only five examples were sold.

Porsche 928

**Top speed
135mph**
217km/h

*Right: Interior of a 1987
Series 2 928. The steering
wheel could be adjusted
vertically and, unusually,
the instrument binnacle
moved with it.*

*Below: As it was in the
beginning, a 928 of 1979
with its distinctive
'telephone dial' alloy
wheels and exposed pop-up
headlamps intended to
generate customer interest.*

Today the Porsche name is synonymous
with the enduring and enticing 911. But in
the 1970s its star was in decline as the
company pressed ahead with a range of
conventionally engined grand tourers, the flagship
of which was the 135mph (217km/h) 928.

This was a wholly new car with no legacy
passed on from previous models, although there
were family resemblances with its 924 and 944
contemporaries. All these new models were the
brainchild of Dr Ernst Fuhrmann, who had been
appointed Porsche's new chief executive in 1971.

The 928 was launched at the 1977 Geneva
Motor Show and promptly became Car of the Year
in 1978. A wide, smoothly contoured coupé with
opening tailgate, styled in-house by Anatole
Lapine, its lines appeared uncluttered by bumpers,
although they were in fact concealed beneath
deformable panels. Quite deliberately, exposed,
rather than concealed, pop-up headlamps were
specified and became a distinctive feature.

Powered by Porsche's first V8 engine, this 4.4-
litre aluminium unit, with single camshafts per
cylinder bank, drove the five-speed differential-
mounted gearbox via a flexible driveshaft contained
inside the model's tubular backbone. There was
also the option of an automatic gearbox.

Left: A 928 Series 4 of 1988. It is identifiable by its reprofiled nose, which featured a combined unit housing spot, fog and indicator lights, and hinged rear spoiler. Both changes were intended to improve the coupé's aerodynamics.

Below: The Series 4 928 was replaced by the GTS for the 1992 season. Outward changes were few but included wider air intakes and new wheels which were shared with its 968 stablemate.

Yet for all the 928's ingenious specification and good performance – 60mph (96km/h) arrived in eight seconds – and despite near perfect road manners, commentators began to wonder whether that elusive and sometimes indefinable quality of character, so apparent in the 911, somehow eluded the 928.

Porsche, believing that more performance would remedy this problem, increased the V8's capacity in 1979 to 4.6 litres. Up went acceleration and top speed rose to 145mph (233km/h) yet that all-important Porsche ingredient still remained elusive.

Improving the 928

Dr Furhmann departed in 1980 and the 911 once again moved centre stage. But this did not prevent the company from improving the 928 and in 1986 the 928-S4 appeared with sharper body lines, a new nose and the V8 stretched again, this time to 4.9 litres. More radically twin cam heads were introduced; all these ministrations produced 320bhp compared with the original's 234bhp. American customers had already had a preview of this engine, it having been fitted to US-sold 928Ss since 1985.

Now capable of 160mph (257km/h), Porsche succeeded in raising this to 170mph (274km/h) with the 928 GT of 1989. This had 330bhp on tap which made it Porsche's fastest road car.

The third and final increase in engine capacity, to 5.4 litres, came in 1991 with the arrival of the GTS. The model was discontinued in 1995, and its passing seemingly went unmourned, least of all by its manufacturer.

Specification	Porsche 928
Engine location	Front, in-line
Configuration	V8
Bore and stroke	95 x 78mm
Capacity	4474cc
Valve operation	Single overhead camshaft per cylinder bank
Horsepower	240bhp @ 5500rpm
Transmission	Manual five-speed
Drive	Rear
Chassis	Unitary
Suspension – front	Wishbones and coil spring
Suspension – rear	Semi trailing arm and coil spring
Brakes	Disc
Top speed	135mph (217km/h)
Acceleration	0-60mph (0-96km/h): 8 seconds

BMW M1

**Top speed
162mph**
261km/h

*Below: A cocktail of
influences with a body
styled by Giugiaro,
incomplete Lamborghini
engineering and finish by
Baur in Stuttgart. This road
car, which was created so
the necessary 400 units
could be built for
homologation, dates from
1980. The elongated rear
deck indicates that the 3.4
twin-cam six is mounted
longitudinally ahead of the
ZF transaxle.*

 It looked like no other BMW and was capable of over 160mph (257km/h). However, only 456 lucky owners were able to sample the delights of this race-ready mid-engined coupé.

Initiated by Jochen Neerpasch, head of BMW Motorsport, work began on the project, designated E-26, in 1976. The intention was to produce a 850bhp Group 5 car to wrest the championship from Porsche. To obtain homologation there would have to be a roadgoing version, of which 400 were required to be built over a 12-month period. There was also a 470bhp variant with appropriately tailored bodywork eligible for Group 4 GT racing.

BMW lacked the in-house facilities to undertake the (albeit limited) production of such a car, so the work was assigned to Lamborghini which was also to be responsible for the manufacture of the chassis. Styling was allocated to Ital Design and it would also undertake the construction of the glass-fibre shell.

The longitudinally-positioned engine was BMW's 3.5-litre six-cylinder unit used in the 635 CSi coupé, but here enhanced with a twin overhead camshaft/four valves per cylinder head. Output for the road car was 277bhp, a not insignificant 65 more than the norm.

Unfortunately, the programme encountered unacceptable delays, which proved to be fatal, while costs were rising alarmingly. In April 1978 BMW therefore cancelled its contract with Lamborghini and later that year Baur in Stuttgart began the assembly of the Ital-built bodies with their tubular chassis. The work was finally completed by BMW Motorsport which ensured a quality of finish in keeping with the company's other products.

Impressive road car

Formally launched at the 1978 Paris Motor Show, the M1, which sold for 100,000DM, the equivalent of £15,600, proved to be an impressive road car

able to sprint to 62mph (100km/h) in just 5.6 seconds. Although many Formula 1 drivers competed in the ProCar series of races for M1s, which were held prior to European grand prix events, the model's best placing in a sports racing event came in 1980 when Hans Stuck took third in that year's Nürburgring 1000km competition.

But the M1 never proved its worth against the real opposition because by the time it was homologated in 1981, it was beginning to date. It turned the scales at some 1985lb (900kg), which was about 440lb (200kg) more than its Porsche 936 rival. And in the competitive world of motor sport timing is all.

Left: Although only produced in left-hand-drive form, this is a British registered car. The engine produced 'only' 277bhp, thanks to 47mm inlet valves, 32mm exhausts and a 9:1 compression ratio. This compared with 48.6mm and 32.5mm for the racing units and a CR figure of 11.5:1. All M1s were fitted with essentially the same gearbox, regardless of the type of engine employed.

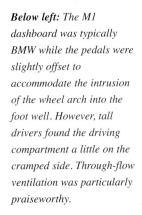

Below left: The M1 dashboard was typically BMW while the pedals were slightly offset to accommodate the intrusion of the wheel arch into the foot well. However, tall drivers found the driving compartment a little on the cramped side. Through-flow ventilation was particularly praiseworthy.

Specification	BMW M1
Engine location	Mid, in-line
Configuration	Six-cylinder
Bore and stroke	93 x 84mm
Capacity	3453cc
Valve operation	Twin overhead camshafts
Horsepower	277bhp @ 6500rpm
Transmission	Manual five-speed
Drive	Rear
Chassis	Tubular
Suspension – front	Wishbones and coil spring
Suspension – rear	Wishbones and coil spring
Brakes	Disc
Top speed	162mph (261km/h)
Acceleration	0-62mph (0-100km/h): 5.6 seconds

Audi quattro

**Top speed
137mph**
220km/h

*Right: The instrument panel
of a left-hand drive 1985
quattro included a display
to indicate whether the
centre or rear differentials
were locked or not and a
turbocharger boost gauge.*

*Below: The lines of the
1985 quattro shown to
advantage. It incorporated
aerodynamic appendages
front and rear. The badge
on the lower door panel
represented the four car
companies that constituted
the pre-war Auto Union
concern, of which Audi is
the sole surviving member.*

The 1980 quattro (the lower case 'q' is
Audi's preferred spelling) was not only a
crisply styled 137mph (220km/h)
turbocharged coupé, it was technically innovative
because all four of its wheels were permanently
driven. This was thanks to Audi's light and
ingenious system which instantly made the 4wd
concept a practical proposition in a road car. And
the motoring community was soon following in the
quattro's four-wheel drive tracks.

The seeds of the idea had been sown three years
earlier when the company's engineers were
evaluating its front-wheel drive saloons in Northern
Scandinavia. They were in company with another
Audi-designed machine – a pre-production
Volkswagen Iltis military vehicle that was due to be
launched in the following year. This easily
outpaced the Audi saloons on the snow, thanks to
its four-wheel drive system.

This revelation was not wasted on Audi's chief
chassis engineer, Jörg Bensinger, and with the
encouragement of Walter Treser, Audi's Manager of
Advanced Development and a former rally driver,
in May 1978 work officially began on what was to
emerge as the quattro.

Formidable rally contender

It was not only conceived to reinforce Audi's
already high technological profile; from 1979 four-
wheel drive cars became eligible for the World
Rally Championship, and the company recognized
that the new model could be a formidable contender
for the crown. The intention was to build 10
quattros every working day, some 2000 a year, so
the 400 cars necessary for the new Audi to qualify
for homologation could be produced quickly. (It
was not, of course, the first four-wheel drive car.

The concept was almost as old as the industry and had most recently been employed on the costly, heavy and complicated Jensen FF.)

The model was the undisputed star of the 50th Geneva Motor Show of 1980. In 1977 Audi had introduced the world's first five-cylinder petrol engine and at the beginning of 1980 this had been used in 170bhp turbocharged form in the flagship 200 model. The quattro was powered by this 2.1-litre unit. It featured a single overhead camshaft with two valves per cylinder and its output was boosted to 200bhp.

Using the Iltis system as a starting point, the Audi design team came up with an ingenious four-wheel drive concept which dispensed with the heavy transfer box and drive shaft usually associated with the system. Like all front-wheel drive Audis, the five-cylinder engine was mounted in-line rather than adopting the more usual transverse layout. The gearbox was therefore attached to the back of the power unit in the manner of rear-drive cars.

On the quattro, power was transmitted through the gearbox in the usual way to a grapefruit-sized differential located directly behind the gearbox. From there it was conveyed to a conventional rear axle. But it was also transmitted forward, via a hollow gearbox output shaft, to the differential that drove the front wheels. This was the essence of the quattro system, which was further enhanced by the latest low profile radial tyres.

Specification	Audi quattro
Engine location	Front, in-line
Configuration	Turbocharged five-cylinder
Bore and stroke	79 x 86mm
Capacity	2144cc
Valve operation	Single overhead camshaft
Horsepower	200bhp @ 5500rpm
Transmission	Manual five-speed
Drive	Four-wheel
Chassis	Unitary
Suspension – front	MacPherson strut and coil spring
Suspension – rear	MacPherson strut and coil spring
Brakes	Disc, ventilated at front
Top speed	137mph (220km/h)
Acceleration	0-62mph (0-100km/h): 7.1 seconds

Above: Produced for the 1984 season, this short wheelbase Sport quattro of 1985 with a 396bhp engine was able to reach 60mph (96km/h) in a mere 4.5 seconds.

Left: The Sport's engine with large KKK-K27 turbocharger and Bosch LH-Jetronic fuel injection. Despite its high state of tune, it was remarkably docile in traffic.

Lotus Esprit Turbo

**Top speed
175mph**
282km/h

Lotus's Esprit dates from 1975. It has stylistically and mechanically evolved over the past quarter century, and it can still show a clean pair of heels to most of the opposition with a top speed of 175mph (282km/h).

The result of a fruitful dialogue in 1972 between Lotus's founder, Colin Chapman, and Giorgetto Giugiaro of the Turin-based Ital Design, the Esprit was launched at the 1975 London Motor Show as a mid-engined, crisply styled, glass-fibre bodied coupé with Lotus's familiar backbone chassis and all-independent suspension. The engine was the corporate 2-litre, twin-cam four which developed 156bhp. Top speed was 124mph (200km/h), although Lotus claimed 138mph (222km/h).

The engine was enlarged to 2.2 litres in 1980, and the same year Lotus introduced the Esprit Turbo. With 210bhp on tap it was capable of 150mph (241km/h). The chassis had been redesigned to accept a new V8 engine which was then under development, but it would be a long time before a V8 would appear in the Esprit.

The 1988 season saw the sharp Giugiaro lines softened by Lotus designer Peter Stevens. Further styling revisions came in 1993, together with power steering, suspension changes and a new Sport 300 model with a larger turbocharger and wider wheels. This was followed in 1994 by the S4S with the Sport's mechanicals and a more luxurious interior.

High performance league

Eventually, in 1996, the Esprit received a new 3.5-litre V8 engine, twin turbocharged and developing 349bhp. At a stroke the Esprit entered a new performance league, its top speed soaring to over 175mph (282km/h) and the sprint to 62mph (100km/h) from rest taking just 4.5 seconds. But the four-cylinder car remained in production in entry-level 2.0-litre GT3 form – a model which survived, against all the odds, until 1999.

In its place Lotus offered the bargain-basement V8 GT, lacking the standard V8's rear wing and air

Above: The Esprit Turbo in its original guise (in Essex Racing colours) sporting the Giugiaro-styled body dating from the model's 1975 introduction. Both wheels and brakes were uprated for the blown version.

Right: The Turbo received its long-awaited V8 engine in 1996, the model having had a visual facelift in 1988. Outwardly similar to its four-cylinder predecessor, this mid-engined Lotus offers praiseworthy performance and handling, although with specifications rooted in the 1970s.

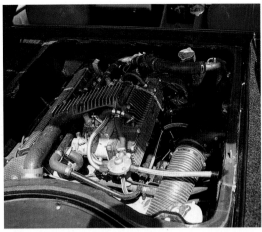

Far left: The badge is the giveaway, particularly as the four continued in production.

Left: What treasure lurks under the rear deck – the longitudinally mounted turbocharged four.

Below: The Turbo acquired this new highly distinctive dashboard for the 1998 season.

conditioning but sharing with it a roomier interior and – well overdue – a new facia.

The most extreme Esprit ever, the Sport 350, was built in 1999. Production was limited to just 50 cars, each one 176lb (80kg) lighter than the standard V8. Easily identifiable by its carbon-fibre rear wing, the Sport 350 also featured lightweight wheels and uprated running gear and an interior full of carbon fibre and aluminium alloy.

Production of the Esprit finally came to an end in February 2004. It had been on sale for nearly 30 years, in its various guises, but fewer than 11,000 had been built. Since then Lotus has concentrated on derivatives of its successful Elise – but a mid-engined supercar, a 'new Esprit', is due to appear for 2007.

Specification	**Lotus** Esprit Turbo (3.5 litres)
Engine location	Mid, in-line
Configuration	Twin turbocharged V8
Bore and stroke	81 x 83mm
Capacity	3506cc
Valve operation	Twin overhead camshafts per bank
Horsepower	349bhp @ 6500rpm
Transmission	Manual five-speed
Drive	Rear
Chassis	Backbone
Suspension – front	Wishbones and coil spring
Suspension – rear	Upper and lower link and coil spring
Brakes	Disc
Top speed	175mph (282km/h)
Acceleration	0-62mph (100km/h): 4.5 seconds

1981–1990
The Revs Begin to Rise

This was a decade again dominated by an economic recession but this situation did not prevent Porsche from embarking, in 1983, on its costly, complex and very rapid 959 coupé. And by the time that Ferrari offered its stark but sensational and even faster F40 in 1988, the industrialized world was once again basking in an era of apparent prosperity.

Further developments took place on the technical front with the revival, after an absence of some 50 years, of the supercharger. Its use in 1988 by such mainstream motor manufacturers as Ford and Volkswagen indicated that it could not be long before 'the blower' made a return to the higher echelons of the performance motor sector.

Bristol Beaufighter

**Top speed
150mph**
241km/h

*Right: Bristols have been
powered by Chrysler V8
engines since 1961 and the
Beaufighter Turbocharged
Convertible was fitted with
a 5.9-litre unit, its
performance enhanced by a
Rotomaster blower.*

*Below: The Beaufighter's
multi-purpose body was the
work of Zagato. Note the
four ventilation slots
located beneath the bumper
to aid engine cooling. The
substantial roll-over bar,
together with a steel gusset
beneath the floor, prevented
scuttle shake.*

 Take brutal and angular Zagato styling
cloaking a substantial BMW-derived
chassis rooted in the 1930s, add a
turbocharged Chrysler 5.9-litre V8 engine, and you
have the essence of the impressively engineered
Bristol Beaufighter.

Rare, expensive and appealing to a small but
discriminating clientele, Bristol is one of a handful
of Britain's post-war marques that has survived into
the 21st century. Originally it was an offshoot of
the Bristol Aeroplane Company. The 400, the first
of the line which appeared in 1947, used a potent
2-litre BMW-based six-cylinder engine.
Progressively enhanced, it remained in production
until the demise of the 406 model in 1961.

Its 407 replacement of 1962 was the first
Bristol to be powered by a Chrysler V8 engine, a
make and configuration that has been used in every
Bristol from then until the present day.

Remarkable speed

The Beaufighter of 1980 traces its origins back to
the Zagato-bodied 412 of 1975 which essentially
retained the mechanicals of its 6.5-litre 411
predecessor. The two-door four-seater with its slab-
like bonnet was remarkably fast, being effortlessly
able to attain 150mph (241km/m). Unusually, it
was a convertible and came complete with a
substantial double roll-over bar. This subsequently
evolved, in 1976, into a 'convertible/saloon'.

It featured a fixed rear window although the
company helpfully informed its customers that 'the
entire roof section may be removed in about an
hour, with an ordinary tool kit…' It was then
replaced with a canvas hood. There was an
alternative targa-style detachable roof panel.

Wartime tribute

The 1978 season saw the 6.5-litre V8 replaced by a smaller capacity 5.9-litre unit; this Series 2 model was succeeded in 1980 by the Beaufighter, named as a tribute to the wartime torpedo-carrying strike aircraft produced by Bristol Aeroplane. Although outwardly similar to the 412, the 5.9-litre V8 was retained and its power was boosted some 30 per cent by the introduction of a Rotomaster turbocharger. Like Rolls-Royce, Bristol did not disclose the output of its engine.

These ministrations were sufficient to transform its performance, and while the 150mph (241km/h) top speed remained about the same, acceleration was much improved with 60mph (96km/h) arriving in under six seconds.

The targa style was discontinued and replaced by a solid top complete with sun roof. The occupants' comfort was assured by the electrically adjustable front seats, a noteworthy refinement for the day.

The Beaufighter was joined in 1987 by the Beaufort convertible which lacked the roll-over bar which characterized its 412 predecessor. Both models enjoyed long production runs, surviving for no less than 13 years before being discontinued in 1993. Happily, Bristol is still in business.

Above: The angular rear of the Beaufighter, complete with Bristol Cars' memorable, but unduly pessimistic, number plate!

Left: The car's badge is, appropriately, a representation of the coat of arms of the city of Bristol.

Specification	Bristol Beaufighter
Engine location	Front, in-line
Configuration	V8
Bore and stroke	101 x 90mm
Capacity	5900cc
Valve operation	Pushrod
Horsepower	N/A
Transmission	Automatic three-speed
Drive	Rear
Chassis	Box section
Suspension – front	Wishbones and coil spring
Suspension – rear	Live axle, torsion bars and Watts linkage
Brakes	Disc
Top speed	150mph (241km/h)
Acceleration	0-60mph (96km/h): 5.9 seconds

Renault 5 Turbo

**Top speed
124mph**
200km/h

Right: The 5 Turbo's mid-located 1.3-litre Garrett-turbocharged engine. This is the car which won the 1981 Monte Carlo Rally.

Below: The 1981 Monte Carlo Rally winner, driven by Ragnotti and Andrie, was a specially built rally car and its balance and traction proved their worth in the Alpine snows.

It superficially resembled Renault's ubiquitous 5 but closer inspection revealed that the Turbo's engine had been transferred from the front of the car to a mid-location. The result was a raucous turbocharged 124mph (200km/h) two-seater hailed by pundits as a 'Five on steroids'.

One of Renault's big sellers of the post-war years, the 5 supermini was launched in 1972. This front-wheel-drive hatchback, with its distinctive and seemingly ageless styling, was produced until 1984. By this time some 5.4 million had been completed. It was available with a variety of engines, from 782 to 1397cc.

France's largest car maker wasted little time in producing more potent versions, the most radical of which was the 5 Turbo of 1980. This, daringly, saw a union of the hatchback's body shell with a mid-located, in-line, 137bhp, turbocharged fuel-injected version of the model's 1370cc unit.

Different suspension

Suspension also differed from the original – instead of the usual rear trailing arms, it used a wishbone and coil springs layout courtesy of the Alpine A310/V6. Inside the interior featured space age colour co-ordinated livery. There was no room for rear passengers but a little luggage could be stored under the bonnet and at the rear.

Roadholding was generally impressive, although not in the wet. The external giveaways were distinctive air intakes behind the doors and flared wheel arches. There was an altered front apron-cum-spoiler and the body was weight-saving as the roof, doors and rear hatch were made of aluminium while the bonnet, bumpers, air dam, wings and roof spoiler were plastic mouldings.

Success in the Monte Carlo Rally

There were some competition successes – an example won the 1981 Monte Carlo Rally at the first attempt. The model was replaced by the outwardly similar but more powerful Turbo 2 in 1983, by which time 1362 had been completed. Like its predecessor, this was also successful in the rally field. It could sprint to 60mph (96km/h) in a mere seven seconds and possessed excellent handling albeit with some rear end bias like its predecessor. Traction was good but ride quality was another matter – this was guaranteed to loosen the driver's deepest tooth fillings!

Only produced in left-hand-drive form, the Turbo 2 was built until 1986, two years after the mainstream 5 had ceased production. A mere 3576 examples were completed.

Above: The turbocharged Renault displaying its distinctive rear profile and hot air outlets.

Left: The enhanced cockpit of the Monte-winning Renault. Ragnotti had an eleventh hour tussle with Therier's Porsche.

Specification	Renault 5 Turbo
Engine location	Mid-located, in-line
Configuration	Turbocharged four-cylinder
Bore and stroke	76 x 77mm
Capacity	1370cc
Valve operation	Pushrod
Horsepower	160bhp @ 6000rpm
Transmission	Manual, five-speed
Drive	Rear
Chassis	Unitary
Suspension – front	Wishbones and torsion bar
Suspension – rear	Wishbones, anti-roll bar/telescopic dampers
Brakes	Disc
Top speed	124mph (200km/h)
Acceleration	0-60mph (0-96km/h): 7 seconds

Porsche 959

**Top speed
197mph**
317km/h

Right: Only produced in left-hand-drive form, the 959's interior shows some similarity to the 911 Turbo's. Despite its sophistication, this Porsche also has the virtue of being remarkably easy to drive.

Below: A 959 doing what it does best: travelling at speed. The relationship with the 911 is readily apparent. The air intakes are to help keep the massive discs cool.

It is the ultimate 911. Beneath those familiar body lines are a mind-blowing array of electro/mechanical gizmos which made the 959, for a time, the world's fastest production road car with a top speed of 197mph (317km/h).

Above all, the 959 was a reaffirmation by its makers of the spirit of the 911, with its unorthodox rear-mounted, air-cooled, flat-six engine. The 911 had taken a back seat between 1972-80, when Dr Ernst Fuhrmann was Porsche's chief executive and he decreed a switch to conventional front-engined cars such as the 928. But with the arrival of his successor, Peter Schultz, the 911 once again moved centre stage and it has remained there ever since.

Porsche unveiled its four-wheel-drive *Gruppe B* car at the 1983 Frankfurt Motor Show. Aimed at Group B competition, this required that a minimum of 200 be produced for homologation purposes. Power came from a special 2.8-litre twin-turbocharged version of the 911's air-cooled flat-six engine which had competition-proven water-cooled cylinder heads.

This element of what was to be designated the 959 was resolved relatively quickly. Unfortunately the complex four-wheel-drive system took longer to develop than expected and the first example did not reach its patient customer until April 1987, three and a half years after the model was announced.

In the meantime an early version of the car had proved its worth on the demanding Paris to Dakar rally which it won in 1984. A further success followed in 1986. However, in that year, Group B, for which the 959 had been so carefully tailored, was banned in the wake of a series of fatal crashes.

Well worth waiting for

When the definitive 959 appeared, it proved well worth the wait. Deceptively easy to drive, at the heart of the four-wheel-drive system was the computer-controlled Porsche Control Clutch which distributed the correct amount of torque between the front and rear wheels.

For fast motoring, Porsche claimed a top speed of 193mph (311km/h); in fact 197mph (317km/h) was attainable when on-board computer control lowered the body to within 4.9in (124mm) of the ground. But uneven road surfaces could be accommodated with a 5.9in (150mm) setting and the car could be electrically jacked up to 7in (178mm) if the need arose.

Only produced in left-hand-drive form, demand was such that Porsche eventually produced 250 cars, 50 more than it had intended, the last example being delivered in 1988.

Specification	Porsche 959
Engine location	Rear, in-line
Configuration	Twin turbocharged horizontally opposed six-cylinder
Bore and stroke	95 x 67mm
Capacity	2849cc
Valve operation	Twin overhead camshafts per bank
Horsepower	450bhp @ 6500rpm
Transmission	Manual six-speed
Drive	Four wheel
Chassis	Unitary
Suspension – front	Wishbones and coil spring
Suspension – rear	Wishbones and coil spring
Brakes	Ventilated disc
Top speed	197mph (317km/h)
Acceleration	0-60mph (96km/h): 3.6 seconds

Left: Much of the 959's 2.8-litre, flat-six turbocharged engine cannot be seen when the lid is raised.

Below: The fixed rear spoiler helps to keep the engine's 450 horsepower on the road.

Ferrari Testarossa

**Top speed
181mph**
291km/h

*Right: A left-hand-drive
Testarossa. Most of the
bodywork, apart from the
roof and door pressings,
was made of aluminium.
Aerodynamics were aided
by electrically activated
pop-up headlamps.*

*Below: The Testrossa's
outwardly similar 512R
successor of 1992. Its flat
12 engine was boosted from
390 to an impressive
422bhp. However, the
chassis was new and wider
rear tyres than previously
were fitted.*

The impact of Lamborghini's visually astounding Countach was not wasted on Ferrari and in 1984 it responded with the stylistically stunning Testarossa, a supercar that was capable of over 180mph (290km/h).

Named in honour of Ferrari's celebrated 1957 sports racer, the Testa Rossa (Italian for red head), it was the successor to the 4.9-litre 512BB Berlinetta Boxer of 1973 which was the second Ferrari road car to benefit from the presence of a competition-bred horizontally opposed 12-cylinder engine. The first had been its 365 predecessor.

Mounted on a tubular steel chassis, the Testarossa was similarly powered by a mid-located 'flat' 12 that was positioned in the usual Ferrari manner, in line and ahead of the rear suspension. But although its 4942cc capacity was the same as its predecessor's, and despite their outward resemblance, the two alloy units had few parts in common; this engine produced 390bhp, some 50bhp more than the Boxer's. As usual twin overhead camshafts with four valves per cylinder and mechanical fuel injection were fitted, although a revised system appeared for the 1987 season.

If there was a superficial resemblance between the two engines, the Pininfarina-designed and built body differed radically from the Boxer. This was because the radiator was moved from the front of the car and replaced by twin units located on either side of the mid-located engine to improve its cooling efficiency. Nevertheless, a frontal cooling grille was retained which allowed air to reach the front brakes and which also serviced a condenser

for the air conditioning which was a standard and welcome fitment.

Most tellingly, the relocated radiators also allowed Pininfarina to extend the stunning cooling fins to the front doors and these became the model's most readily remembered feature – one that was often copied by other manufacturers, although never as successfully. As a result the Testarossa was the widest car of its day, measuring no less than 78in (1981mm) in width.

Outstanding handling

As ever only offering accommodation for two, there was additional luggage space behind the comfortable seats. Yet despite its size the Testarossa was a far more usable car that the Boxer, its controls being light which belied the presence of a more powerful engine. Handling, in the finest Ferrari traditions, was outstanding.

Announced at the 1984 Paris Motor Show, production began in 1985 when 568 cars were built. Next year 819 examples were built, mass production by Ferrari standards, but even so there was a year's worldwide waiting list for the car that was only gradually satisfied.

Destined to remain in production until 1992, the Testarossa reasserted Ferrari's pole position as the manufacturer of the world's finest supercar.

Specification	Ferrari Testarossa
Engine location	Mid, in-line
Configuration	Horizontally opposed 12-cylinder
Bore and stroke	82 x 78mm
Capacity	4942cc
Valve operation	Twin overhead camshafts per cylinder bank
Horsepower	390bhp @ 6300rpm
Transmission	Manual five-speed
Drive	Rear
Chassis	Tubular
Suspension – front	Wishbones and coil spring
Suspension – rear	Wishbones and coil spring
Brakes	Ventilated disc
Top speed	181mph (291km/h)
Acceleration	0-60mph (0-96km/h): 5.6 seconds

Left: A 1987 Testarossa engine looking remarkably like its 512BBi predecessor, although it shared very few parts with it.

Below: A 512M of 1995 – a second reincarnation of the Testarossa – with its distinctive exposed headlamps. The 4.9-litre flat 12 engine was re-

MG Metro 6R4

**Top speed
110mph**
177km/h

*Below: The 6R4's fittings
were the result of extensive
wind tunnel testing by
aerodynamicist Bernie
Marcus. Underneath, the
familiar lines of the Metro
were clearly discernible.
Alas, this four-wheel-drive
car never lived up to its
ambitious specifications.*

 Created for the short-lived Group B
racing category, the four-wheel-drive mid-
engined MG 6R4 Metro of 1984 was a
world away from the best-selling Austin supermini
on which it was based. The 6R4 only bore a
superficial resemblance to the production Metro
because it employed four-wheel drive, the
development of this fearsome two-seater having
been entrusted to Formula 1 constructors Williams
Grand Prix Engineering.

The resulting car was unveiled in May 1985.
Powered by a purpose-designed 3-litre V6 engine
with twin overhead camshafts and four valves per
cylinder, the unit was unusual for not being
turbocharged in a field of competition which
favoured blown power units.

It was mounted back to front in the Metro, with
the forward end of the engine facing the hatchback
and with the gearbox attached conventionally
behind it and therefore in the middle of the car.
From there the permanently engaged four-wheel
drive, which employed Ferguson technology, drove
separate propeller shafts to the front and rear wheels.
All the external body panels were made of plastic,
with the exception of the doors which were steel
although these were concealed by plastic airboxes.

Two versions produced

The 6R4, the name stood for six cylinder, rally car,
four-wheel drive, was produced in two forms.
There was the so-called Clubman model which
developed some 250bhp – about 200 were made –

and a further 20 were built to International specifications which required a 380bhp engine.

At its launch in 1985 Rover announced that it would complete the necessary number of cars for homologation by November. This was undertaken at a special facility located within the Group's rambling Longbridge factory. So the car was ready in time to participate in the Lombard RAC rally of November 1985 and an example was placed a creditable third behind two Lancia Deltas. It was a good start.

In theory the prospects looked good for 1986. However, although the 6R4 was entered in the Monte Carlo, Sweden, Portugal and Corsica events, none of the Metros completed the courses. Most of the problems were related to the V6 engine which suffered from more than its fair share of teething troubles which smacked of underdevelopment.

Then, halfway through the 1986 season, Group B competition was banned because of a calamitous series of crashes. And that, in truth, was the end of this mighty Metro's front-line competition career, although the cars were run with limited successes for the remainder of the year.

At this point Austin Rover withdrew from the rallying scene. But in 1987 all the parts and engines were sold to Tom Walkinshaw Racing whereupon the V6 engine reappeared under the bonnet of the Jaguar XJ220!

Above: The 6R4's wheels grew from 13in (330mm) to 16in (406mm), partly at the request of Michelin which supplied the tyres.

Left: A standard Metro fascia was fitted although the steering wheel and attendant stalks came courtesy of the larger Maestro EFi. Note the fly-off handbrake lever.

Specification	**MG** Metro 6R4
Engine location	Mid, in-line
Configuration	V6
Bore and stroke	92 x 75mm
Capacity	2991cc
Valve operation	Twin overhead camshafts per cylinder bank
Horsepower	250bhp @ 7000rpm
Transmission	Manual five-speed
Drive	Four-wheel
Chassis	Unitary
Suspension – front	MacPherson strut reverse bottom wishbone
Suspension – rear	Strut and reverse bottom wishbone
Brakes	Ventilated disc
Top speed	110mph (177km/h) limited
Acceleration	0-60mph (0-96km/h): 4.8 seconds

Toyota MR2

**Top speed
125mph**
201km/h

*Right: A 1985 MR2
revealing the efficiency of
its pop-up headlamps. This
Toyota did everything
expected of it, the only
apparent shortcoming
according to some drivers
being a lack of cockpit
space, a not uncommon
complaint of Japanese cars.*

*Below: The 1985 car in
profile. The air intake and
low nose indicate the
presence of the mid-located
engine with the front
airdam and rear wing
providing important
aerodynamic influence. The
MR-2 was only produced in
coupé form at this stage.*

An acclaimed mid-engined coupé, the
MR2 of 1984 represented a surprising
excursion for Toyota, which had hitherto
been best known for its popular saloons. But
Japan's largest car maker made a significant
contribution to the sports sector with this wedge-
shaped coupé that was able to attain 125mph
(201km/h). A supercharged version was capable of
135mph (217km/h).

With Toyota dependent on the American market
for much of its sales, in the early 1980s it began to
manufacture a new generation of engines to
conform to the strict US emissions regulations.
This meant twin-overhead-camshaft/four-valve
cylinder heads and Toyota was soon to become a
world leader in the manufacture of such multi-valve
power units.

These engines also lent themselves to the
performance sector. In 1981 Toyota had established
links with Lotus and so it was able to draw on
Lotus' engineering expertise in the development of
its projected sports car. This was accorded the MR
prefix which stood for Midship Runabout.

It was produced in two forms. The mainstream
export version was powered by a 121bhp, 1.6-litre,
fuel-injected, twin-overhead-camshaft engine
courtesy of Toyota's Corolla GTi. There was also a
1.5-litre single-cam unit for the home market. In

both instances they were transversely mounted
behind the driver in a chunky aerodynamically
refined two-seater body with only a pair of air
intakes behind the doors to indicate the presence of
a mid-located power unit.

Supercharged for the USA

Sceptical pundits were confounded to find that the
MR2 possessed safe, predictable handling, together
with an excellent, flexible engine. And acceleration
– the 0-60mph (96km/h) time was 7.7 seconds –
was respectable for a car of this size. However, the

American market required some extra oomph and the result in 1986 was a 143bhp supercharged MR2 which increased the top speed by 10mph (16km/h) and shaved 0.7 seconds off the acceleration figure.

For the 1987 season a variation on the body style appeared in the form of the T-bar model with detachable transparent roof panels. The MR2 was destined to survive in this form until 1989, when it was replaced by a 2-litre car, instantly identifiable

by softer body lines, but which retained the same mechanical layout and name. And the enlarged engine meant a 137mph (220km/h) top speed.

It was replaced for the 2000 season by the third generation MR2, an open two-seater with, for Toyota, wacky styling, a pop-up rear spoiler and projecting head rests for the occupants. A Turbo version is capable of speeds approaching the 150mph (241km/h) mark.

Above: The third generation MR2 appeared in 2000 – a convertible, but here with optional factory hardtop.

Below left: The 1985 MR2. Power-assisted steering was fitted as standard, along with electric windows.

Specification	Toyota MR2
Engine location	Mid, transverse
Configuration	Four-cylinder
Bore and stroke	81 x 77mm
Capacity	1587cc
Valve operation	Twin overhead camshafts
Horsepower	121bhp @ 6600rpm
Transmission	Manual, five-speed
Drive	Rear
Chassis	Unitary
Suspension – front	MacPherson strut, lower arm
Suspension – rear	MacPherson strut, parallel transverse links
Brakes	Disc
Top speed	125mph (201km/h)
Acceleration	0-60mph (96km/h): 7.7 seconds

Bentley Turbo R

**Top speed
145mph**
233km/h

*Right: Bentley's winged B
badge was designed by
Frederick Gordon Crosby,
The Autocar's accomplished
artist who also designed the
original radiator. This,
however, was considerably
reduced in depth from
1965 onwards.*

*Below: A Bentley Turbo of
1984 with the radiator shell
painted in the body colour
which indicated the
presence of a turbocharged
engine. At this stage no
changes had been made to
the suspension.*

A significant milestone along the road of
the Bentley revival, the Turbo R of 1985
represented a desirable refinement of a
high-performance image that had first been crafted
three years previously with the Mulsanne Turbo.

Although owned by Rolls-Royce, the Bentley
marque had been in decline since the early 1960s.
When the Rolls-Royce Spirit, which appeared in
1980, was being planned, incredibly there were
serious thoughts about discontinuing the Bentley
version. Fortunately, wiser counsels prevailed and
the resulting model was given the Mulsanne name,
after the straight on the Le Mans circuit; it evoked
memories of Bentley's string of victories there
during the inter-war years.

Powered by the corporate 6.7-litre V8 engine,
this comfortable and luxuriously appointed four-
door saloon was capable of 120mph (193km/h).
However, perhaps inevitably the overwhelming
majority of cars built bore the Rolls-Royce badge.

Then, against a background of the recession of
the early 1980s, Rolls-Royce's marketing director,
Peter Ward, sought to re-awaken memories of
Bentley's racing heritage by turbocharging its

robust V8 engine. The resulting model, named the
Mulsanne Turbo, appeared at the 1982 Geneva
Motor Show. Outwardly distinguished by a radiator
shell painted in the body colour, rather than
manufactured in the usual chrome, it was otherwise
outwardly identical to the mainstream model, apart
from discreet *Turbo* badges on the boot lid and
front wings. Performance was transformed,
however, with top speed increased by some 15mph
(24km/h) to 135mph (217km/h).

All this was achieved with the minimum of
modification. While the transmission was
strengthened to cope with the increased power, the
twin constraints of time and available funding

meant that almost no obligatory changes were made to the suspension.

Appealing concept

The Mulsanne Turbo proved to be a great success because it appealed to a younger, more affluent generation of buyers and Rolls-Royce was sufficiently encouraged to take the concept one step further. The result, in 1985, was the Turbo R which addressed the suspension shortcomings of the original. Announced at that year's Geneva show, the Turbo R, the Mulsanne name was dropped, was the first Rolls-Royce product to be fitted with alloy wheels, in this instance wider, specially commissioned Ronal units.

The original model suffered from soft suspension which produced excessive body roll, but this problem was now redressed. The modifications principally involved increasing the stiffness of the front anti-roll bar by 100 per cent and the rear by 60 per cent. Greater resistance was also introduced to the power steering.

The output of the turbocharged engine was boosted and the Turbo R was some 10mph (16km/h) faster than its predecessor, being capable of 145mph (233km/h). It survived, in essence, for the next 12 years, the final example being completed in 1997.

Specification	Bentley Turbo R
Engine location	Front, in-line
Configuration	Turbocharged V8
Bore and stroke	104 x 99mm
Capacity	6750cc
Valve operation	Pushrod
Horsepower	298bhp @ 3800rpm
Transmission	Automatic three-speed
Drive	Rear
Chassis	Unitary
Suspension – front	Wishbones and coil spring
Suspension – rear	Semi trailing arms and coil spring, automatic self levelling
Brakes	Disc
Top speed	145mph (233km/h)
Acceleration	0-60mph (0-96km/h): 7.1 seconds

Left: The Turbo's fascia was essentially that of the standard Mulsanne, apart from the presence of the word Turbo. No rev counter was fitted.

Below: An unturbocharged 1994 Brooklands. By this time the Turbo's painted radiator had been extended to all Bentleys.

Mazda RX-7 and RX8

**Top speed
148mph**
238km/h

The Japanese Mazda company was for many years the only significant motor manufacturer to persevere with the Wankel rotary engine. In 1986 it launched a revised version of its successful RX-7 sports car and two years later came the Turbo version that was capable of speeds nudging the 150mph (241km/h) mark.

Its first Wankel-engined model, the two-seater 110S coupé of 1967, only sold 1176 examples in six years, although it was capable of 110mph (177km/h). By contrast, its RX-2 successor of 1970-78 found some quarter of a million buyers and the same engine was used in the simultaneously introduced RX-3 which shared its body with Mazda's

conventionally powered 818. Like its RX-4 contemporary, it also ceased production in 1978.

Even more successful was the RX-7 coupé, a car capable of 125mph (201km/h) which was destined to remain in production until 1985. With over 570,000 produced, it proved to be a considerable success in America.

Turbine-like power

Its 1985 replacement retained the famous RX-7 name, and it was also a two-plus-two coupé with a 2254cc two-rotor Wankel engine. Able to attain 128mph (205km/h), its engine developed 150bhp. There was also a top-of-the-range 185bhp RX-7 Turbo which could hit 148mph (238km/h). This united the Wankel's smooth turbine-like power with the accelerative qualities of a turbocharger. The 60mph (96km/h) mark arrived in less than seven seconds, but on the debit side was an average petrol consumption of some 17 miles per gallon (16.6lit/100 km).

Originally produced, like the mainstream model, in coupé form, a convertible version aimed foursquare at Californian buyers was launched in 1987. A new version arrived for 1992 but European sales suffered because of the twin bugbears of high fuel costs and unfashionable emissions problems, and it was withdrawn from Europe in 1995 while a reworked version was sold in America and Japan –

Above: A cabriolet version of the RX-7. Dating from 1985, this body variant arrived two years later. Hard and soft tops followed in 1987, the latter being electrically activated.

Right: The revised RX-7 for the 1992 season was shorter, lighter and narrower than its predecessor. More accelerative than the earlier version, thanks to its increased power (251bhp no less), there was a new injection system to ensure a near instantaneous response.

Left: The 1992 version, which, claimed Mazda, possessed better handling than the earlier car because of a lower centre of gravity and passive rear-wheel steering built into the suspension. This helped to keep the car's handling neutral during fast cornering. The twin rear aerofoils were a distinctive feature. The interior styling reflected the curved lines of the exterior.

power increased to 280bhp and a four-wheel drive RS version was offered.

At the Tokyo show in 1995 Mazda unveiled a new rotary-engined coupé concept, the RX-01. An important innovation was a new type of rotary engine with the exhaust ports relocated to the side of the combustion chamber, which allowed larger ports and improved fuel economy and emissions. By 1999 the new engine was powering another concept, the RX-Evolv, and it had acquired a name – Renesis, from 'Rotary Engine Genesis'.

The production version of the Renesis engine arrived in 2002 in a spectacular new sports car, the 250bhp RX-8, which proves that the rotary engine concept still has plenty of life left in it.

Specification	Mazda RX-7 Turbo
Engine location	Front, in-line
Configuration	Turbocharged twin-rotor Wankel
Bore and stroke	Not applicable
Capacity	2254cc
Valve operation	Not applicable
Horsepower	185bhp @ 6500rpm
Transmission	Manual five-speed
Drive	Rear
Chassis	Unitary
Suspension – front	MacPherson strut, lower wishbone
Suspension – rear	Semi trailing arms and coil springs
Brakes	Disc
Top speed	148mph (238km/h)
Acceleration	0-60mph (0-96km/h): 6.7 seconds

Left: Mazda RX-8, unveiled as a concept car at the 2001 Detroit Motor Show, is the RX-7's spiritual successor. Also powered by a twin-rotor Wankel engine, although unturbocharged, the unit develops 250bhp. Production begain in 2002. Mazda claims a top speed of 150mph (241km/h).

Ford Sierra RS Cosworth

**Top speed
145mph**
233km/h

*Right: The Sapphire-bodied
RS Cosworth of 1988
boasted an excellent driving
position, thanks to Recaro
bucket seats that were
adjustable for height, reach
and rake.*

*Below: The two-door RS
Cosworth was followed in
1988 by the four-door
Sapphire version. It was
based on the Sierra of the
same name, even if this did
not appear on the car!*

The public was stunned when in 1982 Ford unveiled the aerodynamically refined Sierra hatchback to replace its ultra-conventional best-selling Cortina. And just three years after its appearance the exclusive, potent RS Cosworth version hit the scene – this was able to attain no less than 145mph (233km/h).

From the outside it was clear that the RS Cosworth was no ordinary Sierra. At the front there was a deep air dam and a new grille panel with a larger air intake. Twin bonnet vents were provided, there were wheel arch extensions covering wider, spoked alloy wheels and a huge wing sat above the tailgate of this three-door car. But the most radical change was under the bonnet.

Northampton-based racing engine manufacturer Cosworth had been working on a twin-cam conversion kit for the popular single-cam Ford Pinto engine, and in turbocharged form it was this engine (dubbed 'YB' by Cosworth) which would power the new super Sierra. The basic YB engine produced 204bhp, and there was plenty more to come – rally-spec versions developed 300bhp, and Group A racing engines were over 340bhp.

All 5500 RS Cosworths were built in the second half of 1986 at Ford's Ghenk factory in Belgium. In 1987, 500 of them were turned into even faster RS500 cars which featured larger aerodynamic devices, a bigger turbocharger and revisions to the engine aimed at improving tuning potential. Road cars developed 224bhp, while racing machines produced in excess of 500bhp.

They were highly successful, winning a host of national and international touring car racing championships in the late 1980s.

Superb handling

For 1988 a subtler, four-door Sapphire Cosworth was introduced, and in 1990 this was given four-wheel drive and became Ford's top-line rally contender. But the heavy Sierra bodyshell always put it at a disadvantage compared to some of the lighter, more nimble opposition.

The answer was to graft Sierra Cosworth 4x4

running gear and floorpan under the lighter three-door bodyshell of the new CE14 Escort, creating the Escort RS Cosworth (which had a huge rear wing recalling the original three-door Sierra RS). With a Garrett T35 hybrid turbo the Escort Cosworth developed 227bhp, making it a swift road car and a competitive rally machine.

The final version was produced from 1994 to 1996. These final Escort Cosworths were given a smaller hybrid turbo to improve drivability, and were available without the big rear wing – for those who preferred their pace to be less conspicuous.

Above: The RS500 (left) with wide intakes below the bumper to cool the front discs. The huge rear spoiler was not retained on the Sapphire version next to it.

Below: The Sapphire Cosworth's turbocharged 2-litre twin-overhead-camshaft engine. Top speed was 145mph (233km/h).

Specification	**Ford** Sierra RS Cosworth
Engine location	Front, in-line
Configuration	Turbocharged four-cylinder
Bore and stroke	90 x 76mm
Capacity	1993cc
Valve operation	Twin overhead camshafts
Horsepower	204bhp @ 6000rpm
Transmission	Manual five-speed
Drive	Rear
Chassis	Unitary
Suspension – front	MacPherson strut
Suspension – rear	Wishbone, semi trailing arm and coil spring
Brakes	Disc, ventilated front
Top speed	145mph (233km/h)
Acceleration	0-60mph (96km/h): 6 seconds

Lancia Integrale

**Top speed
134mph**
216km/h

*Right: Only available in
left-hand-drive form, the
16-valve Integrale sported
an illuminated check panel
and a new revolution
counter. The steering wheel
was leather-rimmed.*

*Below: A 1990 Integrale
showing the distinctive
bonnet bulge demanded by
the 16-valve engine. A four-
wheel-drive model, there
was a 53/47 allocation to
rear and front wheels
respectively.*

A four-wheel-drive car that gave Lancia
the World Rally Championship for an
unprecedented six years between 1987
and 1992, the Integrale was an outwardly orthodox
four-door hatchback but with sophisticated
mechanicals. It could reach nearly 135mph
(217km/h). Paradoxically it attained its pre-eminent
position by accident rather than design.

In 1980 Fiat-owned Lancia had introduced the
front-wheel-drive Delta four-door hatchback styled
by Ital Design. It was available with a choice of 1.3
and 1.5-litre single overhead engines while the GT
version was powered by a 1.6-litre twin-cam unit.
Later, in 1984, came the HF Turbo with an
enhanced 130bhp engine which gained a further
10hp with the arrival, in 1986, of fuel injection.

Lancia had, in the meantime, produced the four-
wheel-drive S4 Delta rally car in 1984. Geared to
Group B competition, it was outwardly similar to
the roadgoing version but with a new mid-located,
1.7-litre, Abarth-designed, twin-cam four which
was both turbo- *and* supercharged.

Group A racer

The demise, in mid-1986, of Group B racing – the
result of one fatal accident too many (the final one
involved an S4) – saw Lancia rapidly respond by
replacing the S4 with the Delta HF 4WD, which
had been unveiled in prototype form at the 1982
Turin Motor Show. Tailored to Group A rules, it was
accordingly closely related to the Delta road car.

To qualify Lancia had to manufacture a minimum of 5000 examples in 1987. Such was its success that a further 500 examples of the HF Integrale, as it was known by late 1987, were also produced.

Usable road car

Unlike many homologation specials, this was a perfectly usable road car. It featured a transversely mounted, 185bhp, 2-litre, turbocharged twin-overhead-camshaft engine and a sophisticated four-wheel-drive system based, in part, on that used in the Delta S4. An epicyclic central differential produced a torque split of 56/44 from front to rear with a viscous coupling that locked when one pair of wheels began to spin. A Torsen rear differential apportioned torque at the rear end. Both suspension and brakes were uprated and wider wheels resulted in distinctive side pods being let into the wheel arches to accommodate them.

The rally cars, of course, were much more powerful. They won first time out at the 1987 Portugal event and went on to dominate the rally field for the next five years. The only significant change in specification was the arrival, in 1989, of a 16-valve cylinder head which duly appeared on the road cars.

The final Integrale of 1993 saw power upped to 215bhp and a smaller turbocharger was employed. When production ceased in 1994, Lancia ran down the curtains on its most successful rally car ever.

Above: This was the ultimate 'hot hatchback', the hatch being what most other rally drivers saw. A light in Lancia's otherwise gloomy history. This is a 1992 Evolution model, no.0015.

Specification	**Lancia** HF Integrale
Engine location	Front, transverse
Configuration	Turbocharged four-cylinder
Bore and stroke	87 x 90mm
Capacity	1995cc
Valve operation	Twin overhead camshaft
Horsepower	185bhp @ 5300rpm
Transmission	Manual, five-speed
Drive	Four-wheel
Chassis	Unitary
Suspension – front	MacPherson strut and lower wishbone
Suspension – rear	MacPherson strut and transverse link
Brakes	Disc, ventilated at front
Top speed	134mph (216km/h)
Acceleration	0-62mph (0-100km/h): 6.6 seconds

Jaguar XJR-S

**Top speed
155mph**
249km/h

Below: A 1988 XJR-S Le Mans Celebration model, launched in August and named to commemorate Jaguar's victory in the 24 hour classic just two months earlier. The first 100 examples were all sold, it was claimed, within four days of the model's announcement. In addition to the external changes, modifications were also made to the suspension but not the engine.

Jaguar's long awaited E-Type replacement, the XJS coupé, arrived in 1975. It was a more refined and luxurious product than its famous forebear, but it was to be no less than 13 years before a sporting version arrived in the shape of the XJR-S.

Introduced amidst the gloom of the post-1973 oil crisis, the XJS was powered by the company's 5.3-litre V12 engine, first seen in the Series III E-Type of 1971. Able to accelerate to 60mph (96km/h) in a respectable 7.8 seconds, the XJS's Achilles' heel was its fuel consumption of some 13mpg (21.7lit/100km). Jaguar recognized the need to address the problem and the result, in mid-1981, was the more economical HE version.

In 1982 the corporate racing programme was placed in the hands of Tom Walkinshaw's TWR group and this led to Jaguar winning Le Mans, after a 31-year absence, in 1988. TWR had been marketing Jaguar-approved performance accessories for the XJS since the mid-1980s and as

a result JaguarSport was launched in May 1988, jointly owned by the company and Walkinshaw's highly successful business.

The idea was to produce up to 500 cars a year at TWR's premises at Kidlington, Oxfordshire. The first of these, the XJR-S, was launched in August 1988, 'as a tribute to the Le Mans-winning XJR-9' and it was based on the TWR XJS V12 that Walkinshaw had been marketing, with factory approval, since 1984. At this stage no changes were made to 290bhp V12 engine but the model was instantly identifiable by its body-coloured bumpers, glass-fibre air dam, sill extensions and rear spoiler.

Improved handling

Mechanical alterations were confined to stiffening the suspension, power steering and new and wider alloy wheels. Handling therefore improved but performance remained essentially unchanged.

It was to be another year before the engine was uprated – the revised XJR-S of 1989 was the first

recipient of a JaguarSport-enlarged 318bhp 6-litre engine that was extended to the production XJS in 1993. Further work was done to stiffen the suspension. While the new engine made little difference to the 155mph (249km/h) top speed, acceleration was improved with 1.2 seconds being shaved off the original 0-60mph (96km/h) figure of 7.5 seconds.

Yet a further version arrived for the 1992 season which incorporated structural changes made to the XJS in the spring of 1991. The engine now developed 338bhp and the model survived until 1993 when it was effectively replaced by the factory-built 6-litre XJS. During this six-year period some 500 examples were completed.

Specification	Jaguar XJR-S (6 litres)
Engine location	Front, in-line
Configuration	V12
Bore and stroke	90 x 78mm
Capacity	5343cc
Valve operation	Single overhead camshaft per cylinder bank
Horsepower	318bhp @ 5250rpm
Transmission	Automatic three-speed
Drive	Rear
Chassis	Unitary
Suspension – front	Wishbones and coil spring
Suspension – rear	Trailing arms and coil spring
Brakes	Disc
Top speed	155mph (249km/h)
Acceleration	0-60mph (0-96km/h): 6.3 seconds

Above and left: The distinguishing rear spoiler was mounted on the boot lid. Inside there were JaguarSport logos, leather-bound steering wheel and gear knob and piping trim on the leather seats. The first 100 cars were enhanced with special trim and paint and victory laurels engraved on the tread plates.

Ferrari F40

**Top speed
201mph**
323km/h

*Right: Function rather than
creature comfort is the
keynote of the cockpit of a
1991 F40. Weight-saving
was a consideration – note
the drilled pedals.*

*Below: This is a pre-
production Ferrari F40 of
1988. The sliding perspex
windows are wholly in
keeping with the model's
racing pedigree although
they were subsequently
replaced by glass.*

Enzo Ferrari produced his first cars in
1947. In 1987 the F40 supercar was
unveiled, so named in celebration of his
40 years as a car maker. This was no luxurious,
refined model but a purposeful, no-frills coupé
complete with a large rear wing and a top speed of
201mph (323km/h) making it, for a time, the
world's fastest production car. It therefore
decisively eclipsed the Porsche 959's speed of
197mph (317km/h).

Based on the floorpan of the 288 GTO of 1984,
the F40 was powered by a related twin
turbocharged V8 engine of a mere 3 litres capacity,
although it developed a stupendous 478bhp. It was
rear-mounted in a longitudinal position.

Weight-saving was an overriding consideration,
and although a tubular space-frame chassis, which
provided the outline of the cabin and tail sections,
was retained, extensive use was made of Kevlar
and carbon fibre. Both materials came courtesy of
Ferrari's Formula 1 activities.

Kevlar and glass-fibre body panels also
featured, and further kilograms were saved in the
cockpit which was bereft of such niceties as
carpeting and door trim. In consequence the F40
turned the scales at just 2425lb (1100kg). While
Pininfarina had ultimate responsibility for the
styling, the F40's body was produced at Maranello
by Ferrari.

Three suspension settings

The all-independent suspension used the customary
Ferrari wishbones and coil springs and there were
no less than three settings – normal, high speed
which involved lowering it by 0.75in (19 mm), and
parking when it was raised by the same amount.

Although outwardly resembling a road car, the
acceleration was phenomenal – this most exclusive
of Ferraris was able to reach 200km/h (124mph) in
a mere 12 seconds.

If for some reason you were not satisfied with
this level of performance, for several million lire
Ferrari would extract a further 200bhp from the
trusty V8. Needless to say noise levels within the
sparsely furnished cockpit made speech between
driver and passenger virtually impossible. But then
no one ever bought an F40 to hold conversations in!

Production began early in 1988. The F40 was
priced in Britain at £193,299, some £80,000 more
that its Testarossa stablemate. It remained in
production until 1992; although it had been
intended to restrict production to just 450 cars,
worldwide demand for the model remained strong

Specification	Ferrari F40
Engine location	Rear, in-line
Configuration	Twin turbocharged V8
Bore and stroke	82 x 69mm
Capacity	2936cc
Valve operation	Twin overhead camshafts per bank
Horsepower	478bhp @ 7000rpm
Transmission	Manual five-speed
Drive	Four wheel
Chassis	Tubular steel, Kevlar and carbon fibre
Suspension – front	Wishbones and coil spring
Suspension – rear	Wishbones and coil spring
Brakes	Ventilated discs
Top speed	201mph (323km/h)
Acceleration	0-60mph (0-96 km/h): 4.7 seconds

and eventually nearly three times that number, 1311
F40s no less, had been completed before production
ceased in 1992.

It had been an extraordinarily impressive car,
daring and distinctive. Perversely, the even faster
F50 appeared in 1995, two years *before* the marque
celebrated its half century!

*Above: The F40's
unmistakable rear view; its
body was made of race-
proven fibreglass, Kevlar
and carbon fibre. This is a
1990 car with conventional
side windows.*

Above: The F40 in all its glory, utterly distinctive and sounding like a Formula 1 car when on the move.

Right: The engine of a 1991 F40, an all-alloy unit with twin water-cooled IHI turbochargers. Larger turbochargers were on offer for those owners who wished to race their F40s.

Opposite: The F40 was made from immensely strong Kevlar. Bonded to the chassis by adhesives, it was considerably lighter than steel and torsional rigidity was increased threefold.

It was wholly appropriate that the F40's launch at Maranello in July 1987 was attended by Enzo Ferrari himself, then a frail 89-year-old. The assembled multitude was treated to an insight from *Il Commendatore* regarding the thinking behind the F40's creation. 'It started in June last year when I suggested to the board a car which would be a reminder of the great days at Le Mans when you could drive a car on the streets or race it,' he revealed. There was consideration of naming the model after the 24 hour classic event which Ferrari had dominated for so many years, but the designation F40 was ultimately deemed more appropriate. And so it has proved to be.

The car can trace its ancestry back to the fabled GTO of 1962 described elsewhere in this book. Appropriately an example was on display at the unveiling to underline the association between the two. And while this celebrated sports racer reflected the model's spiritual origins, one element of its mechanical pedigree can be traced to the mid-

engined GTO road car that appeared at 1984 Geneva Motor Show.

The second branch of its family tree was provided by an one-off *Evoluzione* Ferrari of 1986, created for Group B competition which was killed off that year by the sport's organizing body. The aborted Group B was thus responsible for two of the world's fastest road cars of the 1980s, the Porsche 959 and the F40 which was some 4mph (6.4km/h) quicker.

Low drag coefficient

Pininfarina was responsible for the seductive bodywork, its brief being to produce a Ferrari that looked both backward to the marque's past glories as well as forward to the future. Great attention was paid to achieving as low an aerodynamic drag coefficient as possible and the result was a creditable Cd figure of 0.34. This was after experiments had been undertaken without the rear wing, which was eventually standardized, and the fitting of rear wheel spats, which were subsequently discarded.

A car capable of exceeding 200mph (322km/h) also required a wind-cheating underside. Pininfarina accordingly undertook pioneering experiments to ensure that the F40's wake, the spent air that was exhausted from behind the car, conformed to the most efficient 'shape' and also contributed to its stability.

The twin turbocharged V8 engine was essentially an enlarged version of the GTO unit and was created by a team headed by engineer Materazzi, who summed up the company's attitude to the F40. It represented, reported *Autocar*, 'the ideal tie between past and present'.

Enzo Ferrari died in August 1988 at the age of 90 in the first year of the F40's production. He could not have wished for a finer epitaph.

Lotus Elan

**Top speed
136mph**
219km/h

Right: The IHI turbocharged engine of a 1990 Elan SE, courtesy of Isuzu and enhanced by Lotus. Delco distributorless ignition and a Rochester fuel-injection system were fitted.

Below: An SE of 1990. Its body, created by Lotus's Vacuum Assisted Resin Injection process, was constructed of 54 pieces.

Lotus's original Elan of 1962 remained in production for no less than 12 years. However, its 136mph (219km/h) latter-day namesake of 1989 was destined for an all too short two-and-a-half year production run. Its manufacturing life was abruptly curtailed through a combination of the recession of the early 1990s and teething troubles that were then, alas, characteristic of the marque.

Lotus's founder, Colin Chapman, had taken the company upmarket in the mid-1970s with the Esprit/Eclat/Excel coupés, so a new open two-seater represented a return to the its sports car roots. But Lotus's ownership was thrown into doubt in 1982 following Chapman's sudden death from a heart attack. Four years later General Motors acquired the business.

Work on the project had begun in 1986 and the Elan retained, in essence, the backbone chassis of the original model. But there the resemblance ended. The first-generation Elan had employed a conventional front in-line engine and rear drive, but its successor was a front-wheel-drive car with the engine mounted in the transverse position.

Appropriately uprated by Lotus, it came courtesy of the GM-owned Japanese Isuzu concern and was a 1.6-litre, twin-cam, four-cylinder, 130bhp unit. However, the overwhelming majority of Elans were produced in 165bhp turbocharged SE form.

Left: The rear of the car opposite. The hood, which Lotus claimed could be lowered in less than 30 seconds, was neatly contained under the flush-fitting cover. Both the SE and basic Elan were fitted with electric windows and central door locking.

Below: Lotus racing driver and motoring journalist John Miles at the wheel of a 'Series 2' Elan, one of 800 SE examples built from spare parts in 1994. Identifiable by new wheels and a revised dashboard, purple and green metallic colours were added to the options list.

Distinctive body styling

Typically for a Lotus, suspension was all-independent with ingenious interactive wishbones at the front and wishbones and lower links at the rear. Roadholding was, as ever, outstanding. The mechanicals were cloaked in a distinctive open two-seater composite body styled by Peter Stevens, who is best remembered for having the lines of the superlative McLaren F1 to his credit.

However, when evaluated by the motoring press, doubts began to be expressed about the Elan's qualities. For while its performance more than came up to scratch, the whole experience did not perhaps match the pleasures of driving the no-frills front engine/rear drive Mazda MX-5 that cost some £7000 less. And, paradoxically, this Japanese open two-seater had been inspired, in part, by the original Elan of the 1960s.

Despite carrying the clout of General Motors ownership, only 250 Elans were sold in America in 1991 and in June 1992 Lotus announced that it was to cease production. A total of 3857 had been completed and a further 800 'Series 2' cars were built from spare parts in 1994, by which time Lotus had changed hands, again.

But this was not quite the end of the story. The tooling had been acquired, in 1993, by the South Korean Kia concern which produced Elans re-engined with a 1.8-litre Mazda-based unit until 1998.

Specification	Lotus Elan SE
Engine location	Transverse
Configuration	Turbocharged four-cylinder
Bore and stroke	80 x 79mm
Capacity	1588cc
Valve operation	Twin overhead camshaft
Horsepower	165bhp @ 6600rpm
Transmission	Manual five-speed
Drive	Front
Chassis	Backbone
Suspension – front	Wishbones and coil spring
Suspension – rear	Wishbone, lower link and coil spring
Brakes	Disc, ventilated at front
Top speed	136mph (219km/h)
Acceleration	0-60mph (0-96km/h): 6.5 seconds

Mazda MX-5

**Top speed
128mph**
206km/h

Right: Although the MX-5 was designed for fine weather, the hood of this 1993 cars offers excellent rear visibility thanks to the large back window.

Below: The front of the same car with, characteristically, the hood down. The body was steel but the bonnet was made of aluminium.

Although there were faster cars around at the same time as the Mazda MX-5, few were more influential than this crisply styled open two-seater inspired by British sports cars of the 1960s. Although nominally a Japanese car, it was created by Mazda's product planning research facility located at Irvine, California. This was because it was specifically tailored for the large and lucrative American sports car market.

At this time practically all mainstream motor manufacturers had turned their collective backs on the low-cost open two-seater sports car. The emphasis was on more expensive, better equipped closed GTs. But for their inspiration the MX-5's creators looked carefully at the sports models which had been on sale in America in 1960s, most significantly the Lotus Elan and Triumph Spitfire. Both featured in-line engines, a twin cam in the case of the Lotus, which drove the rear wheels. Suspension in both cases was independent all-round.

Introduced early in 1989, the Mazda's full name was the MX-5 Miata, and it cost a little less than $13,000, the equivalent of £7390. Under the bonnet was a 1.6-litre twin-overhead camshaft four-cylinder engine, which developed 116bhp, borrowed from Mazda's saloon range where it had

been transversely mounted. It drove the rear wheels through a five-speed gearbox and torque tube.

Well-balanced sports car

Suspension was all independent and rack and pinion steering was employed, all of which combined to produce an assured, well-balanced sports car. The body, evidently influenced by the Lotus Elan, similarly featured pop-up headlamps. Top speed was 115mph (185km/h). Later, for 1994, an alternative 1.8-litre engine was introduced.

The MX-5 was updated for the 1998 season and while the new version superficially resembled the original, the pop-up headlamps were replaced by more conventional exposed units. Once again, there were 1.6- and 1.8-litre engine options and the latter's top speed was nudging the 130mph (209km/h) mark.

For 2001 a revised front end was introduced but, more significantly, the 1.8-litre engine now benefited from Mazda's S-VT sequential valve timing system, which boosted the unit's power by 16bhp, to 156bhp. Although top speed remained about the same, acceleration was improved.

In 2005 a brand new MX-5 was introduced, based on the platform of the successful RX-8. With cleaner and more modern styling, better accommodation for taller drivers and all the driving appeal of its predecessor, it looks set to keep the MX-5 story rolling for years to come.

Specification	**Mazda** MX-5 (1.8 litres)
Engine location	Front, in-line
Configuration	Four-cylinder
Bore and stroke	83 x 85mm
Capacity	1839cc
Valve operation	Twin overhead camshafts
Horsepower	140bhp @ 6500rpm
Transmission	Manual five-speed
Drive	Rear
Chassis	Unitary
Suspension – front	Wishbones and coil spring
Suspension – rear	Wishbones and coil spring
Brakes	Discs, ventilated at front
Top speed	128mph (206km/h)
Acceleration	0-60mph (0-96km/h): 7.9 seconds

Above: The 10th Anniversary Special Edition version of the MX-5 arrived in 1999 and boasted a unique dark blue finish, tweaked suspension and, significantly, a six-speed gearbox. A total of 7500 were produced, 600 of which were sold in Britain.

Left: The MX-5 was updated for 2000 with a new nose which featured enlarged air intakes and slimmer light clusters with clear lenses, along with projector lamps. The shell was also stiffer than its predecessor, engine output was boosted and suspension tautened.

Lamborghini Diablo

**Top speed
202mph**
325km/h

*Right: In 1993 Lamborghini
announced the 30SE, built
to commemorate the
company's 30th anniversary
in 1994. Power was upped
to 525bhp but rear visibility
was not its strongest point!*

*Below: The Diablo, this
example dates from 1990, is
clearly derived from its
Countach predecessor,
although perhaps it lacks
the visual impact. It has
endured for 11 years and
has progressively improved
during this production span.*

With a top speed in excess of just over
202mph (325km/h), Lamborghini's Diablo
just pipped the Ferrari F40 as the world's
fastest car, that is until the Jaguar XJ220 came
along in 1991.

The Miura and Countach had established
Lamborghini's reputation for creating stunning
flagship supercars and while the Diablo effectively
inherited the latter's mechanicals, the durable V12
was further enlarged, this time to 5.7 litres, with
485bhp on tap.

With a wheelbase 7.9in (200mm) longer than
the Countach's, the coupé body was clearly derived
from it. It was the work of Marcello Gandini, no
longer with Bertone but now freelance, who was
responsible for the styling of both the Diablo's
illustrious predecessors. It did, however, lack some
of the impact of his earlier work.

After some input from Chrysler, Lamborghini's
owner in the years 1987 to 1994, the car was
launched at Monte Carlo in January 1990. But in
typical Lamborghini style, production did not begin
until a year later, at the height of a world recession.

The world's fastest car

The company's claim of a top speed of 202mph
(325km/h) and a 0 to 100km/h (62mph) figure of
4.9 seconds was subsequently confirmed by the
American *Road & Track* magazine which attained
202.33mph (325.60mph), just 1.33mph (2.1km/h)
quicker than Ferrari's F40. But its accolade as the
world's fastest car proved to be short-lived with the
launch, in October 1991, of the Jaguar XJ220
which could exceed 213mph (343km/h).

Left: A 1999 Diablo with its aluminium bodywork replaced by lighter, stronger carbon fibre. Arguably the best built model to date and a reflection of Volkswagen's ownership of Lamborghini.

Below left: The Diablo's instrument panel has much to commend it for functional appeal. The gear lever sits, Ferrari-like, in an open visible gate.

Improved aerodynamics

While the Diablo handled as you might expect a mid-engined car to do, its lack of power steering and anti-lock brakes were clear deficiencies. Four-wheel-drive was another but all these shortcomings were remedied in 1993 with the arrival of the Diablo VT, standing for Viscous Traction FWD. Then, for 1994, came the Diablo SE, for Special Edition, with a wildly optimistic claimed top speed of 220mph (354km/h), improved aerodynamics and engine power boosted to 525bhp.

In 1996 came the lightweight SV, which stood for Sport Veloce, with 'only' 508bhp on tap. The same year saw the arrival of the long-awaited convertible version also with four-wheel drive. Much of the styling was reworked and the detachable Targa-style roof stored externally behind the driver.

Although Lamborghini has been owned by Volkswagen since 1998, the Diablo's replacement has enjoyed a typically lengthy gestation. In the meantime the fastest-ever Lamborghini, the Diablo

GT, was unveiled in 2000 with a claimed top speed of 210mph (338km/h). The aluminium bodywork was replaced by carbon fibre which helped to reduce weight by 198lb (90kg). A 585bhp 6-litre engine arrived for 2001, which, after 11 years, was destined to be the final year of Diablo production.

Above: The long-heralded Diablo roadster appeared in 1996. Much of the bodywork was reworked, and the roof is carried outboard above the engine.

Specification	**Lamborghini** Diablo VT
Engine location	Mid, in-line
Configuration	V12
Bore and stroke	87 x 80mm
Capacity	5707cc
Valve operation	Twin overhead camshafts per bank
Horsepower	485bhp @ 7000rpm
Transmission	Manual five-speed
Drive	Four-wheel
Chassis	Tubular steel
Suspension – front	Wishbones and coil spring
Suspension – rear	Wishbones and coil spring
Brakes	Ventilated disc
Top speed	202mph (325km/h)
Acceleration	0-62mph (0-100km/h): 4.1 seconds

TVR Griffith

**Top speed
155mph**
249km/h

*Right: A driver's eye view
of a left-hand drive export
Griffith. The cabin was
acclaimed by commentators
for sympathetically echoing
the attractive external lines.*

*Below: One of the Griffith's
many virtues is that it looks
like nothing else on the
road, combining traditional
lines with assured
individuality. TVR's
subsequent models did not
disappoint either.*

 Today TVR is renowned for combining distinctive, eye-catching styling with earth-shattering performance. The Griffith can be regarded as the starting point for this renaissance; it was unveiled at the 1990 British Motor Show.

TVR dates from 1954 when Blackpool-based Trevor (hence the TVR marque name) Wilkinson began the production of glass-fibre-bodied specials powered by a variety of Ford, Coventry Climax or BMC engines. However, the business experienced many changes of ownership before it was acquired, in 1982, by Peter Wheeler, a former oil industry executive, who also possessed a formidable flair for styling. A new era for TVR had dawned.

Unusually, Wheeler carves his shapes from massive blocks of expanded polystyrene and the open two-seater Griffith represented the first outward expression of his talents. Its mechanical origins are to be found in the model S of 1986 vintage, an open two-seater with a backbone space-frame chassis and powered by a 2.8-litre Ford V6

engine. An S3 version was produced for the 1991 season. The other model in the TVR range was the angular Rover V8-powered 420 convertible.

The Griffith represented a union of these two concepts, being based on the S3 chassis and the 420's 3.9-litre V8 engine. However, its sleek open two-seater body was unique to the car. It proved to be as fast as it looked – TVR claimed a top speed of 148mph (238km/h) with 60mph (96km/h) arriving in a shattering 4.9 seconds.

Improved specification

The new model generated considerable interest on its announcement but there was to be an 18-month hiatus before the Griffith entered production early in 1992. TVR had spent this interval in improving its specification – the original S3-derived chassis was replaced by a stronger frame with all-round independent suspension, courtesy of the company's Tuscan racing car. And the Rover V8 under the bonnet was now available in two capacities, a 4.0-litre 240bhp engine and a 4.3-litre, 280bhp unit.

The body shape, which had received many plaudits on its launch in 1990, remained essentially the same but the finish of the car was carefully refined. Concealed door catches were introduced, a backlit rear number plate was fitted and the rear lights were made flush-fitting.

In 1993 an even quicker Griffith arrived. TVR's new AJP V8 engine had been planned to power this revised car, but delays developing the engine prompted TVR to return to the reliable old Rover V8, now in 5.0-litre form. This Griffith 500 model offered 340bhp and a top speed in excess of 160mph (257km/h).

The Griffith continued in production until 2002, the run ending with 100 special edition cars with slightly different styling. By then the Griffith had done its job, launching a whole new era for the Blackpool sports car maker.

Above: A Griffith with its solid detachable roof panel in place. When not in use, it filled the otherwise reasonably sized boot.

Below left: The 4.3-litre alloy V8 was a Rover-based unit which provided stunning performance and a magnificent exhaust note.

Specification	TVR Griffith 500
Engine location	Front, in-line
Configuration	V8
Bore and stroke	94 x 90mm
Capacity	4988cc
Valve operation	Pushrod
Horsepower	325bhp @ 5500rpm
Transmission	Manual five-speed
Drive	Rear
Chassis	Tubular
Suspension – front	Wishbones and coil spring
Suspension – rear	Wishbones and coil spring
Brakes	Disc
Top speed	155mph (249km/h)
Acceleration	0-60mph (0-96km/h): 4.1 seconds

Mitsubishi 3000GT

**Top speed
155mph**
249km/h

*Below: This hi-tech
Mitsubishi with its Chrysler-
designed body changed
little outwardly between its
1990 launch and 1993 when
this example was built. Less
apparent is the four-wheel
steering and computer-
controlled suspension.*

At the time of its announcement in 1990, the four-wheel drive 155mph (249km/h) Mitsubishi 3000GT was a state-of-the-art model, crammed with electronic gizmos and an abundance of mechanical refinements. It is still in production and survives as a reminder of Japanese prowess in the fields of automobile technology and increasingly integrated electronics.

The 3000GT coupé is the product of a mixed parentage, its sophisticated mechanicals having appeared in Mitsubishi's experimental HSX sports coupé displayed at the 1989 Tokyo Motor Show. It featured both four-wheel drive and also four-wheel steering which operating in conjunction with computer-controlled suspension and brakes.

These were then transferred to what was originally named the Mitsubishi Starion GTO, but the body, complete with aerodynamically refined pop-up headlamps, was courtesy of Chrysler with whom the Japanese car company had, in 1971, formed an association. It was sold on the American market as the Dodge Stealth.

Twin turbochargers

The complex mechanicals and electronics were optional fitments on Mitsubishi's luxurious Sigma saloon. Power came from the same source but the transversely mounted 281bhp V6 engine with twin overhead camshafts per bank was twin turbocharged in the 3000GT.

The suspension was designed to tailor its responses automatically to the type of terrain the car was covering. There were two settings: 'tour' was the norm while 'sport' resulted in a stiffer setting.

Inside, the driver was presented with a battery of electronically displayed information, although whether he or she really required a TV screen which indicated whether the air from the air conditioning system had reached the farthest extent of the interior is open to question!

At 3792lb (1720kg), the 3000GT was a heavy car and, despite its advanced specifications, the consensus among commentators was that the engine was outstanding, but that the model behaved better in a straight line than when it was going around corners…

Visual and mechanical updates arrived for the 1994 season. The rather dated pop-up headlamps were replaced by integrated units and engine power was boosted to 320bhp. A six-speed close-ratio gearbox replaced the original five-cog unit.

Though the turbo coupé is by far the most common, there were two other variants – the convertible Spyder, for the American market, and the 224bhp non-turbo sold in Japan.

Sales of the 3000GT ended in 2000, and so far Mitsubishi have yet to produce another big coupé. Instead its performance flagship is the rally-bred Lancer Evolution, which packs turbo power and all-wheel drive technology into a compact saloon body.

Specification	Mitsubishi 3000GT
Engine location	Transverse
Configuration	Twin-turbocharged V6
Bore and stroke	91 x 76mm
Capacity	2972cc
Valve operation	Twin overhead camshafts per cylinder bank
Horsepower	281bhp @ 6000rpm
Transmission	Manual five-speed
Drive	Four-wheel
Chassis	Unitary
Suspension – front	MacPherson strut
Suspension – rear	Wishbones, trailing arms and coil spring
Brakes	Ventilated disc
Top speed	155mph (249km/h)
Acceleration	0-60mph (96km/h): 5.8 seconds

Left: Interior of a 1995 car with six-speed gearbox that arrived for 1994 along with a passenger airbag.

Below: A 3000GT of 1995. The design had been revised in the previous year with flush headlamps replacing the pop-up variety. Mitsubishi also tidied up the strakes along the car's flanks.

Vauxhall Lotus Carlton

**Top speed
176mph**
283km/h

*Right: The Lotus Carlton's
rear spoiler was far from
just decorative – it helped
to keep the rear wheels
firmly on the road.*

*Below: The front spoiler
with its substantial air
intakes, widened wheel
arches and Ronal alloy
wheels distinguished this
model. The drag coefficient
was a creditable 0.31.*

Apart from a rear spoiler and a couple of
air intakes let into the bonnet, there was
little outwardly to signal the difference
between a Lotus Carlton and the mainstream five-
seater family model on which it was based. But
with a claimed top speed of 176mph (283km/h) it
was, in 1990, the world's fastest saloon car.

Introduced in 1986, the Carlton was the
Vauxhall version of the German-built and designed
Opel Rekord, both makes having been owned since
the 1920s by the American General Motors
Corporation. More recently, in 1986, GM had
acquired British sports car manufacturer and
engineering consultant Lotus, and this concern was
responsible not only for effecting the important
modifications but also for completing the model's
assembly. Announced at the 1989 Geneva Motor
Show, this BMW-beater did not enter production
until late in 1990 and it was also badged as the
Opel Lotus Omega in Europe.

Developing no less than 377bhp, the engine
was based on the 3-litre unit used in Vauxhall's
flagship Carlton GSi. Possessing unique 95 x
85mm internal dimensions, which gave 3615cc, it
was fitted with an aluminium twin-overhead-
camshaft four-valve cylinder head. The
turbochargers were twin Garrett T25 units, each
with its own water-cooled intercooler. There was a
phenomenal 419lb/ft of torque.

Left: The interior was another departure from the norm with leather upholstered seats supplying plenty of side support, although the rears were bucket-style. The steering wheel was adjustable for rake and the speedometer read to 180mph (290km/h).

Below: A bonnetful of engine! The great virtue of this twin turbocharged 3.6-litre V6 was its flexibility with a broad power band and no less than 377bhp on tap. Lotus had done its work well.

Drive was taken via a six-speed ZF gearbox, similar to that used on the in-house Chevrolet Corvette, to a strengthened differential. Further departures from standard were modestly uprated suspension, substantial 12.5in (317mm) ventilated all-round disc brakes with racing calipers and massive Ronal alloy wheels.

Connolly leather interior

The interior was also peculiar to the model, being trimmed throughout in Connolly leather hide with fully supportive sports front seats, each of which contained an electronic 'memory'. Electric windows and sunroof also featured.

In total nine pre-production cars were built and testing was undertaken at the Nardo high-speed circuit in southern Italy where speeds of 176mph (283km/h) were achieved. Vauxhall optimistically spoke of 180mph (290km/h) being possible. However, this prompted controversy and corporate advertisements made no mention of its potential top speed, only its impressive 0-60mph (0-96km/h) figure of 5.2 seconds.

GM envisaged making 1100 cars over three years. While it sold for a competitive £48,000, the model, alas, ran into the recession of the early 1990s. While Lotus completed them at an initial rate of 13 a week, production was curtailed a year early in December 1992. In all 950 were completed, 150 short of the original figure, with the Carlton accounting for 320 and the balance of 630 given over to the Opel version.

Specification	**Vauxhall** Lotus Carlton
Engine location	Front, in-line
Configuration	Twin turbocharged six-cylinder
Bore and stroke	95 x 85mm
Capacity	3615cc
Valve operation	Twin overhead camshafts
Horsepower	377bhp @ 5200rpm
Transmission	Manual six-speed
Drive	Rear
Chassis	Unitary
Suspension – front	MacPherson strut and coil spring
Suspension – rear	Multi link, semi trailing arm and coil spring
Brakes	Ventilated disc
Top speed	176mph (283km/h)
Acceleration	0-60mph (0-96km/h: 5.2 seconds

1991–2000
McLaren to the Fore

Britain returned to the fast car fray with a vengeance in the 1990s with McLaren's spectacular F1 supercar. It remained, for many years, the world's fastest roadgoing model, being capable of 240mph (386km/h). Like its Bugatti EB110 and Ferrari F50 contemporaries, the race-bred coupé from Woking, Surrey made extensive use of light and immensely strong carbon fibre in its construction.

It is no accident that the car's creator, Gordon Murray, pioneered the use of this aircraft industry material when working, in 1978, for racing car constructor Brabham. First extended to road models in the 1980s, it seems destined to relegate the tubular space-frame chassis to oblivion.

Honda NSX

**Top speed
161mph**
259km/h

*Right: Interior of a 3.2-litre
NSX. Like the exterior, this
has been criticized for a
lack of flair. Roadholding
is, however, outstanding.*

*Below: Honda's flagship
has remained essentially
unchanged over the years
although the 3.2-litre
version of 1997 had a
revised front spoiler.*

The NSX was designed to take on the best of Europe's supercars, and beat them. Work began on the car in 1984, but it would be another six years before the NSX would finally go on sale.

The car that emerged was a mid-engined design, Honda's first, with a transverse 3.0-litre V6 engine developing 270bhp. The brand new all alloy engine featured twin overhead camshafts on each cylinder bank, and Honda's VTEC variable valve timing system which brought a more aggressive, high-lift cam profile into action at high engine speeds to improve top-end power. A variable-length intake system was also fitted, to improve breathing at high revs and liberate more power.

Drive was taken to the rear wheels through either a five-speed manual gearbox, or an automatic transmission – the latter an unusual option for a mid-engined supercar. Anti-lock braking and a traction control system, which reduced power to the rear wheels when wheelspin was detected, were both included in the specification.

The body was aluminium and, though it was a good deal more practical than most supercars – easy to get into and out of, and with good visibility in all directions – it was an attractive shape despite perhaps lacking the design flair of some

competition. But any doubts about the NSX were dispelled when drivers got behind the wheel. It was fast – the Honda's top speed exceeded 160mph (257km/h) – and the chassis was outstanding, with safe, predictable handling. The chassis tuning had received input from none other than Ayrton Senna, F1 World Champion driving for McLaren-Honda in 1988, 1990 and 1991. Moreover, the NSX was as easy to drive as any other Honda.Unfortunately for Honda the appearance of the NSX coincided with the world recession of the early 1990s.

Lighter and faster

To expand the appeal of the car a lighter, faster NSX-R was created for the Japanese market in 1992, with a more powerful engine and less weight thanks to carbon-fibre panels. The engine was enlarged to 3.2 litres and tuned by Mugen, the tuning company owned by Soichiro Honda's son Hirotoshi. All these ministrations increased the top speed to 170mph (273km/h) and reduced the 0-60mph (96km/h) time by 0.8 seconds to 5.1 seconds.

Over time equipment levels improved, including the adoption of a passenger-side airbag and larger wheels. In 1995 a targa-top NSX-T was added to the range, proving particularly popular in the sunnier states of the USA. In 1997 the manual-transmission NSX was uprated with a 3.2-litre

engine and six-speed gearbox, though the automatic car retained the 3.0-litre engine.

The NSX's pop-up headlamps were replaced by more conventional exposed units in a restyle for 2002, and that same year a new NSX-R was introduced with a lighter and more aerodynamically efficient body. It proved to be the last major change in the NSX's production life, and the model was finally discontinued in 2005.

A 'new NSX' based on Honda's HSC show car is already under development. It has to be good – because the outgoing NSX has set Honda an extremely high standard to follow.

Above: The NSX was enhanced with a Targa-style roof in 1995 which proved particularly popular in America, although this is a UK-registered right-hand drive version. A six-speed semi-automatic gearbox arrived at the same time. Otherwise the mixture was as before with Honda's formidable engineering displayed to excellent effect.

Specification	Honda NSX
Engine location	Mid, transverse
Configuration	V6
Bore and stroke	90 x 78mm
Capacity	2977cc
Valve operation	Twin overhead camshafts per cylinder bank
Horsepower	270bhp @ 7100rpm
Transmission	Manual five-speed
Drive	Rear
Chassis	Unitary
Suspension – front	Wishbones and coil spring
Suspension – rear	Wishbones and coil spring
Brakes	Ventilated disc
Top speed	161mph (259km/h)
Acceleration	0-60mph (96km/h): 5.9 seconds

Above: The 1997 updates are not apparent from the rear. The suspension was essentially unchanged but Honda revised the steering, which was a sophisticated electric power-assisted rack-and-pinion system. Changes were also made to the brakes – Honda claimed that, in addition to their increased effectiveness, their balance was also improved.

Right: The bigger bored 3.2-litre V6 engine which developed 276bhp was actually 5.2lb (2.4kg) lighter than its predecessor because of its carbon and alloy cylinder liners. A driver-friendly dual mass flywheel had been fitted from the outset to keep clutch pressure as light as possible.

Aluminium body

The coupé body was also to have been made of steel but by the time of the Chicago launch it had also been changed to aluminium. While its lines were competently executed, the roof being finished in a contrasting black, the car perhaps lacked the design flair associated with its European competition.

However, any doubts regarding the quality of Honda's flagship were immediately dispelled once drivers got behind the black-finished wheel. The NSX's chassis was outstanding and the model exhibited predictable, safe handling, even on the tightest corners. It was fast as well – on the open road the Honda's top speed just exceeded the 160mph (257km/h) mark.

The depressed economic climate at the time the NSX was launched suggested that a different model was required. Honda responded by beginning work on a faster, lighter version which only appeared on the home market for the 1993 season. This featured carbon-fibre body panels with a reworked front end, revised suspension and wider, larger tyres. The V6 engine was enlarged to 3.2 litres and it was tuned by Mugen, a company which specialized in enhancing Formula 1 power units. It was owned by the son of the company's founder, Soichiro Honda. All these ministrations increased top speed to 170mph (273km/h) with the 0-60mph (96km/h) figure reduced by 0.8 second to 5.1 seconds.

The challenge thrown down by Toyota's newly introduced Supra of 1993 resulted in Honda uprating the model for 1994 with larger 17in wheels. Power-assisted steering, which had previously only been a feature of the automatic NSX, was also made standard. The manual gearbox was also refined to reduce the already muted transmission noise.

Targa top

A revised NSX with detachable Targa-type top was launched in the 1995 season in response to the success of Ferarri's F335. Slightly heavier than the coupé, on account of the extra reinforcement, there were further unseen improvements including a new drive-by-wire throttle and changes to the traction-control system. In consequence Honda claimed a 62mph (100km/h) figure of 5.9 seconds and a top speed of 167mph (269km/h).

An engine enlargement to 3.2 litres, foreshadowed in 1993, followed in 1997; power

was up to 290bhp. Honda also took the opportunity of lightening the car, which by this time had acquired a six-speed manual transmission. However, the automatic version, a favourite with Americans, retained the 3-litre unit.

With time running out for the NSX, a replacement must be in the offing. Honda has set itself an extremely high standard to follow.

Above: A sporting concept, the NSX-R was displayed at the 2001 Tokyo Motor Show with conventional faired-in, rather than pop-up, headlights that prefaced their appearance on the latest version of this mid-engined Honda. Carbon fibre is used for the bonnet, engine cover and the rear spoiler, hence the contrasting colour.

Left: The NSX-R's enhanced interior. Its competition heritage is underlined by the Recaro carbon-fibre Aramid bucket seats. The steering wheel is a leather-bound Momo component. Honda's publicity enthuses that the interior wraps 'the driver in an ambience tailor-made for spirited driving'.

Dodge Viper

**Top speed
172mph**
277km/h

*Right: Simplicity is the
essential theme of the Viper
and this is no more
apparent than in the no-
frills cockpit. The seats are
supportive and boast
inflatable lumbar control.
Legroom is also good.*

*Below: Although only
produced in left-hand drive
form, the car is sold in
Europe as the Chrysler
Viper because the Dodge
name is used on a French
truck. It has the virtue of
looking good when viewed
from any angle.*

 The Viper has been a remarkable success story, a hunky no-frills two-seater which began life as a concept car at the Detroit show in 1989. Created for Dodge's Chrysler parent by Carroll Shelby of Shelby Cobra fame (hence the 'Viper' name), this unashamedly 'back to basics' concept was powered by an overhead-valve V10 engine originally intended for the next generation of Chrysler trucks and sports utilities.

Such was its reception at the show, Chrysler decided to put this unconventional Dodge into production. The body, with its steel centre section and glass-fibre nose and tail and replete with Ferrari, Jaguar and Cobra echoes, was retained essentially intact, but the power unit did require some modification.

Aluminium engine block

Revamped by in-house Lamborghini, the original cast-iron block was replaced by an aluminium one; changes to the combustion chamber and valve gear produced a unit that developed 400bhp, a 100bhp improvement on the original. The red rocker boxes were Ferrari-inspired. The exhaust outlet of drainpipe-like proportions emerged from an exposed silencer just below the passenger's door.

Starting production in 1992, Chrysler claimed a top speed of 165mph (266km/h) with 60mph (96km/h) arriving in a raucous and exceedingly rapid 4.5 seconds.

The 1993 Los Angeles Motor Show witnessed the appearance of a coupé version – the GTS, as it was titled, used a more powerful 450bhp engine.

Above left: Inside the Viper's V10 engine that began life as a truck unit and was reworked by in-house Lamborghini in aluminium. A big, low-revving 8-litre, overhead valve actuation was via hydraulic tappets and pushrods.

Above right: The way forward. Chrysler's GTS/R concept Viper of 2000 forms the basis of the next generation of cars. It is longer, wider and lower than the original.

Left: Although the Viper began life as an open two-seater, a coupé version was inevitable, the GTS being unveiled in 1993. This profile underlines the success of the conversion, which looks like a new model in its own right.

Lighter than the open car and more aerodynamically efficient, it was also noticeably faster and able to attain over 170mph (274km/h). As with the roadster, there was a gap, in this instance three years, before the first production version GTS reached its customers during 1996.

In the meantime the roadster was being up-gunned and the 550bhp Venom was followed in 1997 by the Venom 600 with no less than 635bhp on tap.

Chrysler surprised everyone again at the 2000 Detroit show, unveiling the Viper GTS/R coupé with revised styling and a slightly longer wheelbase.

The GTS/R's styling was carried across to a revised Viper SRT10 production car launched in 2002. There were more than 100 improvements under the skin, including a larger 8.3-litre (actually 505cid) V10 engine which pushed the power output up to 510bhp. From the outside the most significant change was that the Viper now had a true convertible top, with no fixed roll-over bar.

Alongside the Viper roadster was a Competition Coupé, a track-only car with a lightweight composite body, race-bred running gear and safety equipment,

Specification	**Dodge** Viper GTS
Engine location	Front, in-line
Configuration	V10
Bore and stroke	4 x 3.85in (101 x 98mm)
Capacity	487cid (7990cc)
Valve operation	Pushrod
Horsepower	378bhp @ 5100rpm
Transmission	Manual six-speed
Drive	Rear
Chassis	Tubular
Suspension – front	Wishbones and coil spring
Suspension – rear	Wishbones and coil spring
Brakes	Disc
Top speed	172mph (277km/h)
Acceleration	0-60mph (0-96km/h): 5.3 seconds

and a tuned 520bhp engine. It was designed to be an affordable, but competitive, GT-class racer.

In 2005 Dodge topped off the Viper range – literally – with a new Viper coupé for the street. This still carried the 505cid, 510bhp V10 – but how long can it be before an ultra-high-performance version is unleashed?

A concept car was the starting point for the original Viper, so it is wholly appropriate that the next generation model is also based on such a vehicle. The GTS/R, unveiled at the 2000 Detroit Motor Show, sprang in essence from the sport coupés that Chrysler had raced since 1994 at Le Mans when, for the first time, GT cars were able to compete with Group C sports prototypes. For the record its best position came in 1999 when a Viper GTS/R was placed 10th. And in the three years between 1997 and 1999 the model was also ruling champion in GT2 events.

So this concept had pedigree aplenty. Designer Osamu Shikado, who had joined Chrysler from Toyota in 1994, recognized that although the car would have to be evidently different, it should also be visually related to the first generation Viper. But it is a larger car, having a 3in (76mm) longer wheelbase and a 2in (50mm) wider track. It also sits some 3.5in (90mm) closer to the road although the wheels are larger, 19in at the front and 20in diameter at the rear which compares with the 17in of the production version.

The original Viper had large hot air outlets located just behind each front wheel arch and these were perpetuated in the GTS/R but were accentuated and sculpted into the doors. Although

the car was lower in overall terms, the tail was actually taller than the original and it was used as a platform for a large rear wing to help keep the 500bhp developed by the 8-litre V10 engine firmly on the road. In a break with tradition, the power unit was converted to dry-sump lubrication and it produced 50bhp more than the production Viper.

The chassis and all-round wishbone and coil suspension were essentially unchanged but the larger diameter wheels meant uprated brakes with 13.9in (355mm) discs.

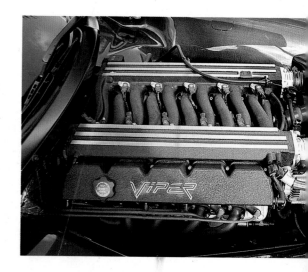

Left: The fascia is a visually pleasing combination of brushed aluminium, carbon fibre and leather. Although these juxtaposed materials will not reach the production line, the layout of the instruments will.

Below left: The GTSR legend appears behind the front wheel arches. Yet, despite the R suffix, this is a road car.

Below: The rear wing played an important visual and practical role, though it was not carried through to the production RT-10 and SRT-10 models.

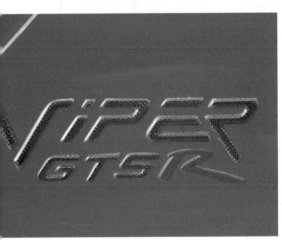

Stylish cockpit

There was a completely new interior which featured a combination of carbon-fibre, leather and brushed aluminium with the rev counter located right in the middle of the dash. The cockpit was suffused with echoes of Le Mans, even the headlining being made of carbon-fibre! However, such niceties as the beautifully crafted aluminium door hinges, front spoiler supports and substantial rear wing are, alas, being sacrificed to the realities of the production line.

Though the new RT-10 roadster would not hit the roads until 2003 the GTS/R concept car provided early pointers to the character of the new car – and paved the way for the SRT-10 coupé which was to follow in 2005.

Light Car Company Rocket

**Top speed
145mph**
233km/h

*Below: Head-on view of the
Rocket which can be
nothing else but a racer for
the road. The front double
wishbones ingeniously use
spherical bearing joints in
conjunction with anti-
vibration bushes which are
allied to high geared rack-
and-pinion steering. Double
wishbones are also
employed at the rear.*

Unconventional, light and potent, the mid-engined Rocket provides seat-of-the-pants performance and is able to hit 145mph (233km/h) although it feels like twice that figure to the lucky driver! Make no mistake, the Rocket is no whim of a garden-shed amateur. It is a deadly serious exercise, the work of respected racing car designer, Gordon Murray, better known as the creator of the McLaren F1.

Although the Rocket has been around since 1992, Murray had been mulling over the project a good 20 years before that. It was then that he and his racing driver friend, Chris Craft, using Colin Chapman's evergreen Lotus Seven as their starting point, conceived a road car which embodied some echoes of the Formula 3 motorcycle-engined 500cc racers that enjoyed popularity in Britain in the early post-war years.

The 1002cc Yamaha four chosen for the Rocket, a 143bhp engine with twin overhead camshafts and no less than five valves per cylinder, was accordingly mid-located. This was the only proprietary component to be bought in.

The gearbox was a five-speed sequential unit but the transaxle was a bespoke component, the work of Peter Weismann's US-based Traction Products, which specialized in the manufacture of transmission systems for Indianapolis cars. A feature of this unit was two alternative ratios which produced no less than 15 forward speeds and five reverse. In 1998 *Autocar's* Colin Goodwin attained a mind-boggling 101mph (162km/h) in reverse gear hurtling down the runway of a Gloucestershire airfield. A brave man!

To keep the weight as low as possible, every part was purpose-designed, from the stove-

enamelled space-frame chassis to the suspension components. This meant that the Rocket turned the scales at just 775lb (352kg). If Murray had used off-the-shelf parts, it would have added a further 325lb (147kg) to the finished product.

Pillion passenger option

Manufacture was assigned to Craft's Light Car Company with Bob Curl having the task of bringing the concept to production. He was also responsible for the design of the glass-fibre racing car-inspired body that is based on a Formula 1 Vanwall of 1957 vintage. The dashboard is made of carbon fibre, along with the cycle-type wings. While this, by its nature, is a single-seater, there is room for a second seat if the owner requires one with the passenger riding 'pillion'.

As a consequence of such a design the Rocket's weather equipment is virtually non-existent. It is devoid of such creature comforts as a hood and doors and sports only the briefest of windscreens to keep the elements at bay.

Once behind the wheel (or should that be the stick?) of the Rocket, you're never far away from the cacophony produced by the Yahama's four situated just behind the seat. The Light Car Company is currently based in Stanford in the Vale, Oxfordshire from where it continues to produce a trickle of these unusually potent roadgoing racers.

Specification	Light Car Company Rocket
Engine location	Mid, transverse
Configuration	Four-cylinder
Bore and stroke	76 x 56mm
Capacity	1002cc
Valve operation	Twin overhead camshafts
Horsepower	143bhp @ 10,500rpm
Transmission	Manual five-speed
Drive	Rear
Chassis	Space-frame
Suspension – front	Wishbones and coil spring
Suspension – rear	Wishbones and coil spring
Brakes	Ventilated disc
Top speed	145mph (233 km/h)
Acceleration	0-60mph (96km/h): 4.4 seconds

Above: The Rocket has a body made of a glass-reinforced sandwich which, happily, lacks any superfluous additions. The headrest is removable.

Left: The driver sits in a figure-hugging Tillet adjustable seat which is trimmed in leather.

Jaguar XJ220

**Top speed
213mph**
343km/h

*Right: The XJ220's lines
are stunning and it also has
the virtue of being easy to
drive at high speed. Unlike
the 1988 show car, this
model has conventional
doors rather than the
memorable upward-opening
variety. The rear wing is
barely noticeable.*

*Below: If the XJ220's
mechanical specification
was a simplified version of
that of the original show
car, the body lines were
stunning and bore no
resemblance to any other
roadgoing model. This
example is finished in
Silverstone Silver. Five
metallic finishes were
available to customers,
mostly in darker hues.*

Between the autumn of 1991 and the end
of 1993, the Jaguar XJ220, with a top
speed of 213mph (343km/h), was the
world's fastest production car. That was until the
arrival of the McLaren F1…

The starting point of what was really a very un-
Jaguar-like project came in December 1984 when
the company's director of engineering, Jim Randle,
inspired by Porsche's 959, began thinking in terms
of a 500bhp Jaguar supercar. This would be
powered by a non-standard version of the corporate
V12, a 6.2-litre unit with twin overhead camshafts
and four-valve cylinder heads, rather than the usual
5.3-litre single cam/two-valve ones.

With engineers volunteering their labour and
working on Saturday mornings, it took nearly four
years to bring the project to fruition. The completed
mid-engined silver coupé was unveiled at the 1988
Birmingham Motor Show. Clad in a stunning body
styled by Jaguar's Keith Helfet, complete with
scissor doors and with a host of refinements, it had
a theoretical top speed of over 200mph (321km/h).

Decision to proceed

Although Jaguar was acquired by Ford in 1989, the
new management decided to proceed with the
project and announced that 350 examples of a
simplified XJ220 would be built at a cost of
£361,000 each, which was about twice the price of
a Ferrari F40. The new version was unveiled in

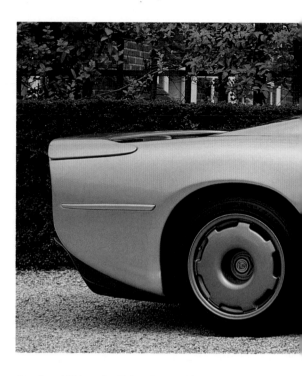

October 1991 at the Tokyo Motor Show but the
world was by then in a deepening recession.

Eight inches (203mm) shorter than the
Birmingham Show car and shorn of its V12 engine,
scissor doors, four-wheel drive, adaptive
suspension and anti-lock brakes, the coupé
nevertheless outwardly resembled the original.

Under the rear decking was a stubbier (but no
less potent) twin turbocharged 3.5-litre V6 engine
which developed an astounding 524bhp. The top
speed was a world-beating 213mph (343km/h) and
100mph (161km/h) arriving in an eye-blinking
eight seconds.

Far left: The 220's interior was not over-elaborate but was commended for its excellent driving position and body-hugging seats. The door-mounted dials were a novel feature.

Left: Around half the length of the original show car's V12, the deceptively small V6 packed a considerable punch, although critics were disappointed by its exhaust note.

12 per cent price rise

Unfortunately the 220's price had risen by some 12 per cent, to £403,000, and a number of prospective customers who had paid a £50,000 deposit found in the chill of 1991 that they were unable to complete the order.

There was also a lightened version, the XJ220-C of 1993. A trio of these cars entered that year's Le Mans 24 hour race and one example won the GT class, although it was subsequently disqualified on a technicality.

But the project continued to be overshadowed by controversy and in the event the projected production figure of 350 was cut to 275. The last car was completed in the spring of 1994.

Specification	Jaguar XJ220
Engine location	Mid, in-line
Configuration	Twin turbocharged V6
Bore and stroke	94 x 84mm
Capacity	3498cc
Valve operation	Twin overhead camshafts per bank
Horsepower	542bhp @ 7200rpm
Transmission	Manual five-speed
Drive	Rear
Chassis	Bonded aluminium honeycomb
Suspension – front	Wishbones and coil spring
Suspension – rear	Wishbones and coil spring
Brakes	Ventilated disc
Top speed	213mph (343km/h)
Acceleration	0-60mph (0-96km/h): 4 seconds

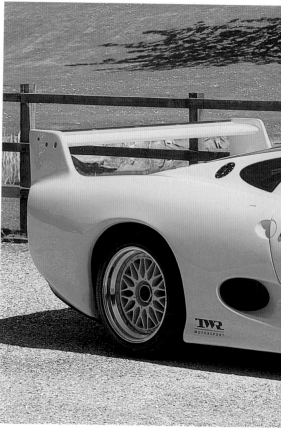

Above: The 220S was a GT racer based on the XJ220Cs that ran at Le Mans in 1993. It was not given the Jaguar name. It was a joint venture between TWR Motorsport and the Coventry-based Jaguar restorer XK Engineering. Launched in 1995, it was some 772lb (350kg) lighter than the XJ220 and 140bhp more powerful, the V6 engine being boosted to 680bhp.

Right: The 220S interior differed from the mainstream XJ220 in having leather-trimmed racing seats and a full safety harness. There was air conditioning but no CD stereo unit. While most of the body was made of composite materials, the original doors were retained.

Le Mans racers

The XJ220-C cars that TWR entered at the 1993 Le Mans event were closely related to the production versions. They differed principally in having their aluminium panels replaced with carbon-fibre sections which saved some 440lb (200kg) of weight. Changes were also made to the suspension geometry and brakes.

To conform to GT rules the cars were fitted with 1.2in (32mm) air restrictors to limit the V6's output to 500bhp, perversely some 42bhp less than it produced in the road car.

A trio of British racing green 220s entered the GT class in the 24 hour event. The fact that one car had won a GT event at Silverstone in May, the month before Le Mans, augured well for the race proper. With Porsche's 911 Turbo SLM regarded as the prime challenger, in June the 220-C's lapped Silverstone five seconds faster than the speeds they achieved on the circuit in the previous month.

Le Mans was dominated by a trio of Peugeot's 905s, and two of the TWR Racing's 220-Cs withdrew suffering from overheating, one of the cars having suffered a 'cooked' engine after the driver had switched off. However, the surviving Jaguar, driven by David Coulthard, David Brabham and John Nielson, managed to pull off the GT class victory, their task having been made easier by the Porsche crashing during the night. But they did not have an easy run and this success was achieved despite a 73-minute pit stop to replace a leaking fuel tank. In 23 hours 56 minutes the 220-C covered 306 laps which compared with the winning Peugeot's 375 circuits.

But there was to be a sting in the tail. All three cars had been declared illegal on the preparatory qualifying laps. The decision was challenged by

Left: On the 220S the original aluminium body panels were replaced, front and rear, by carbon-fibre units. It turned the scales at 2425lb (1100kg) and just 2205lb (1000kg) when the luxury refinements were removed. Note the number plate – this is TWR's Tom Walkinshaw's own car.

Below left: While the front of the 220S resembled the production XJ220, the rear of the body differed in being integral with the roof line, rather than detachable, and incorporated wing pillars to support an adjustable aerofoil. BBS wheels replaced the Speedline originals while the brake system was uprated with six-piston Brembo front calipers and AP rear ones.

TWR boss Tom Walkinshaw and they were allowed to race pending an appeal. The objection arose because the Jaguars were not fitted with catalytic converters. But the 220-C was prepared for IMSA rules to race in America and, as a road car, it was fitted with a catalyst as standard. The Le Mans authorities maintained that it should also feature on the racing version.

Unfortunately the Jaguar was stripped of its class victory on the grounds that its entrant had failed to appeal after qualifying. And that, alas, was the end of this supercar's Le Mans career.

Below: Priced at £250,000, you could have bought two for the price of just one McLaren F1. It was intended to be a drive-to-the-circuit GT racer although the 220S was seldom used in competition. Most found their ways into private collections the world over, most notably to Japan.

Toyota Supra

**Top speed
155mph**
249km/h

*Right: The Supra's low-key
interior was deliberate.
Toyota designers eschewed
the gizmos of the Mitsubishi
3000's cockpit. These seats
are finished in tan leather.*

*Below: A British-registered
1996 Supra. The car is
stable at high speeds with
handling aided by excellent
steering. The air intake
located ahead of the back
wheels helps to cool the
rear discs.*

 This is a model that progressively
improved as each generation appeared –
the best of the breed was the final version
introduced in 1993. Its top speed was limited to
155mph (249km/h), but it was capable of much,
much more.

The Supra name first appeared as a variant of
Toyota's two-plus-two Celica coupé of 1982. Then
in 1986 the Supra emerged as a model in its own
right in the form of a purpose-designed hatchback
coupé which retained its predecessor's front
engine/rear drive configuration. The engine was a
fuel-injected 210bhp 3-litre single-overhead-
camshaft unit which gave the model a top speed of
135mph (217km/h). The Turbo version of 1989 was
even quicker, able to exceed 140mph (225km/h),
but commentators deemed the handling inferior to
that of Honda's acclaimed NSX.

Like its rival, the new Supra of 1993 had
experienced a lengthy gestation period, in this
instance one of no less than eight years. But unlike
the mid-engined Honda, the new Toyota retained a
conventional mechanical layout. However,
weightsaving was an absolute prerequisite and as a
result it was 310lb (141kg) lighter than its
predecessor. This was no mean feat as model lines,
like the humans that create them, tend to get
heavier as they get older. This explained such
features as plastic petrol tanks, aluminium

suspension, a single (rather than twin) exhaust pipe and a much publicized carpet made of hollow-fibred threads!

Six-cylinder engine

Although a V8 engine was considered, a six-cylinder unit was finally employed because it was lighter and its narrower dimensions made it easier to package the turbochargers. The production version was a 320bhp twin turbocharged twin-overhead-camshaft 24-valve unit of 2997cc capacity. This was sold on the European market but there was an unblown 220bhp Supra for US customers, the engine being shared with the Lexus coupé.

Unusually for the day a manual six-speed gearbox was employed and, like its predecessor, suspension was by all-round wishbones and coil springs. Bodily the lines of the 1993 Supra's coupé had evolved from the previous generation's car, and it was again a three-door hatchback. The profile could be enhanced on the turbo model by the fitment of a rear spoiler.

Handling was an improvement and acceleration was similarly bettered, the turbocharged Supra being able to attain 60mph (96km/h) in a shade over five seconds. Top speed was limited to 155mph (249km/h), even if experimental versions had been capable of 181mph (291km/h)! Production ceased in 1997 and, for the time being at least, there were to be no more Supras.

Specification	**Toyota** Supra
Engine location	Front, in-line
Configuration	Twin turbocharged six-cylinder
Bore and stroke	86 x 86mm
Capacity	2997cc
Valve operation	Twin overhead camshafts
Horsepower	320bhp @ 5600rpm
Transmission	Manual six-speed
Drive	Rear
Chassis	Unitary
Suspension – front	Wishbones and coil spring
Suspension – rear	Wishbones and coil spring
Brakes	Ventilated disc
Top speed	155mph (249km/h)
Acceleration	0-60mph (96km/h): 5.1 seconds

Above: The rear spoiler was an optional fitting but the car looked rather tail heavy without it. However, it pushed the body's drag coefficient up a point to 0.33.

Left: What many other drivers saw as the Supra sped past. The single, rather than twin, exhaust pipes were adopted as a weight-saving measure.

Bugatti EB110

**Top speed
212mph**
344km/h

*Right: The Bugatti's
understated interior was
functional but still had
some wood trim in evidence.
The car was only available
in left-hand-drive form.*

*Below: Open wide! The
scissor doors reflect the
influence of former
Lamborghini designer
Marcello Gandini, who was
responsible for the first
version of the EB110's body.*

 During the interwar years the French
Bugatti company produced some of the
world's most famous racing and sports
cars. This mid-engined four-wheel-drive
descendant, christened the Bugatti EB110, entered
production in 1993 and its SS variant was, briefly,
the world's fastest car. Capable of 217mph
(349km/h), this was just 4mph (6.4km/h) more than
the Jaguar XJ220.

The Italian-born, French-domiciled Ettore
Bugatti was an immensely talented artist-engineer
who in 1910 began building cars under his own
name at Molsheim in Alsace. His Type 35 of 1924
is still regarded as the most beautiful racing car of
all time and it was also one of the most successful.
Bugatti died in 1947 at the age of 66 and the
company built its last car in 1952, although it
continued in business mostly undertaking sub-
contract work for the aviation industry. In 1968 it
was taken over by SNECMA, France's nationalized
aircraft company.

Revival of Bugatti

However, the first the public knew of a revival of
the marque occurred in October 1987 when
Romano Artioli, who held the Ferrari franchise for
northern Italy and southern Germany, registered
Bugatti Automobili in Luxembourg. He then
appointed Paolo Stanzani, who had been
responsible for engineering Lamborghini's

Left: The Bugatti's lines were distinctive but considered uninspiring by many. The linear intakes on the sides of the body were introduced to duct air to the rear disc brakes.

Below: The EB110's rear spoiler rose at speeds over 75mph (120km/h) and retracted when it dropped to below the 50mph (80km/h) mark. The rectangular ventilation slots were introduced to assist engine cooling.

celebrated Countach, as his technical director. Stanzani began work immediately on a purpose-designed 3.5-litre V12 engine which employed the obligatory twin overhead camshafts and no less than five valves per cylinder.

The new power unit was enhanced by the addition of no less than four tiny IHI water-cooled turbochargers and it developed a formidable 700bhp. This was some 150bhp more than what was required!

Stanzani's Lamborghini associations were reflected in the choice of Marcello Gandini, who had the lines of the Miura and Countach to his credit, to style the new Bugatti. He produced a competent, if rather dated, design which lacked the visual flair for which he was usually renowned. But then Stanzani fell out with Artioli who in July 1990 sacked him.

In the meantime work was underway on a lavishly equipped purpose-designed factory at Campogalliano on the outskirts of the town of Modena – better known as the home of Ferrari. Its designer was Giampaolo Benedeni and Artioli, dissatisfied with Gandini's styling, appointed the architect to head an in-house team which re-worked the design.

However, when the car was unveiled in Paris on 14 September 1991, the eve of what would have been Ettore Bugatti's 110th birthday (hence the EB110 name), there were collective reservations about the coupé's appearance. A few changes were effected when the model was displayed at the 1992 Geneva Motor Show although production did not begin until early in 1993.

Specification	Bugatti EB110 GT
Engine location	Mid, longitudinal
Configuration	V12
Bore and stroke	81 x 57mm
Capacity	3500cc
Valve operation	Twin overhead camshafts per cylinder bank
Horsepower	553bhp @ 8000rpm
Transmission	Manual six-speed
Drive	Four-wheel
Chassis	Unitary
Suspension – front	Wishbones and coil springs
Suspension – rear	Wishbones and coil springs
Brakes	Ventilated discs
Top speed	212mph (344km/h)
Acceleration	0-60mph (96km/h): 4.6 seconds

Right: A detail of the rear deck with a corner of the purpose-designed V12 engine revealed. In fact it was possible to view the top of the power unit through the transparent engine cover. The EB monogram on the right dates from 1910 and stands for Ettore Bugatti, creator of the legendary marque.

Below: The timidly executed radiator echoed that of the original Bugattis. The main air intake was for the mid-located engine fan-assisted radiator with the secondary one for brake cooling, essential on a high performance car. The wing mirrors were positioned to facilitate rear visibility.

Technically superb

The car was a technical *tour de force* with a light, strong but costly carbon-fibre sub-structure, appropriately the work of Aérospatiale Bugatti, so securing a bond between the marque's past and present history. With the V12 engine mounted longitudinally behind the driver, the six-speed gearbox was located within the crankcase although it was separately lubricated.

Drive to all four wheels was permanently engaged with 72 per cent of power being allocated to the rear and the 28 per cent balance conveyed to the front via a centrally located differential. Suspension was by wishbones, coil springs and pullrods at the front and double coils at the rear. The tyres were specially developed for the EB110 by Michelin.

Disappointingly the aluminium body looked visually uninspiring when set alongside its Ferrari and Lamborghini rivals, although it featured upward-opening doors in the Countach/Diablo traditions.

An uncompromising two-seater, the Bugatti was a remarkably easy car to drive with power-assisted steering, clutch and brakes. While the engine was

not particularly noisy, it emitted an agreeable and distinctive rumble at low revs. Roadholding was deemed outstanding, thanks to the permanently engaged four-wheel drive.

On the debit side was a rather cramped cockpit, a shortcoming that was compounded by a lack of boot space. On the plus side of the equation, the seats were very comfortable and the air conditioning excellent. Ride was outstanding; only left-hand-drive examples were built.

Its claimed top speed of 212mph (341km/h) was a mere 1mph (1.6km/h) slower than Jaguar's supercar, and Bugatti was keen to obtain the accolade of the world's fastest production car. To achieve this the V12 was boosted from 553bhp to 600 and a new model, the EB110 SS, for Sport Stradale or Road Racer, arrived in mid 1993. Unlike its predecessor, this was also produced in right-hand-drive form.

By stripping out many of its sophisticated accoutrements, the SS was some 440lb (200kg) lighter than the original version which was renamed the EB110 GT. The outcome was a claimed top speed of 217mph (349km/h) with 60mph (96km/h) arriving in just 3.4 seconds. However, the SS was soon overtaken by the McLaren F1 which entered production early in 1994.

Unfortunately Artioli was now overreaching himself. He had exhibited a projected EB112 four-door saloon with Ital Design-styled body at the 1993 Geneva Motor Show and later in the year acquired Lotus from General Motors. Yet in September 1995, a mere four years to the month after the EB110's launch, the Campogiallano factory closed with corporate debts of $60 million. A mere 139 cars had been built.

Just three years after that, in September 1998, the Bugatti name was acquired by Volkswagen. Its sensational Veyron prototype, which is described later in this book, possesses all the stunning individuality and sensational performance that was absent from Artioli's EB110.

McLaren F1

**Top speed
240mph**
386km/h

*Right: A unique seating
position for a special type
of road car. In the F1 the
driver sits forward of the
two passenger seats which
are located either side of
him, or her.*

*Below: A hidden refinement
was fan-assisted underfloor
aerodynamics intended to
extract the maximum
performance from the F1.
Even the electric mirrors
were wind-tunnel tested!*

Although it appeared back in 1993, the
fabulous McLaren F1 with a top speed of
240mph (386km/h) still bears the mantle
of the world's fastest production car.

McLaren is, of course, better known as the
manufacturer of Formula 1 single-seaters. It was in
the early 1990s that its chief designer, Gordon
Murray, who had long harboured the desire to
produce 'the ultimate road car', was given the
corporate green light to proceed. Murray was in the
enviable position of being able to design what
could only be named the F1 from a clean sheet of
paper. There would be no components carried over
from any other models and racing car technology
would feature prominently in its specification.

Aerodynamic styling

McLaren was also fortunate to secure the services
of stylist Peter Stevens, and his aerodynamically
efficient rakish coupé with its two distinctive
scissor doors perfectly complemented Murray's
mid-engined mechanicals.

The power unit was a longitudinally mounted
purpose-designed 6-litre BMW V12 with twin-cam
cylinder heads. Drive went to the rear wheels
(rather than all four which was the fashion) via a
six-speed gearbox. With 550bhp on tap the brakes
were four-caliper racing-type Brembo units.

The V12/gearbox unit was attached directly to a
central monocoque tub and here Formula 1 input
was immediately apparent as it was built up from

no less than 94 sections of carbon fibre, aluminium and honeycomb which were then oven-baked in McLaren's own facility.

When the F1 was unveiled on the night prior to the 1993 Monaco Grand Prix, which was appropriately won by McLaren, the company announced that just 300 F1s would be built priced at £540,000 apiece. This worked out at £180,000 per occupant because the McLaren was not a two- but a three seater. Unusually the driver sat centrally, the red upholstered seat being set forward of the others. Once so ensconced, the lucky individual would be in charge of one of the fastest, and safest, cars on the road.

With such a pedigree it was natural that the F1 would soon gravitate to the racetrack. The competition GTR version of 1994 was lighter, and with its power upped to a restricted 630bhp it won the 1995 and 1996 GT Championships. It also triumphed at Le Mans in 1995 when these extraordinary McLarens took first, third, fourth, fifth and thirteenth places. In celebration a handful of 668bhp LM F1s were built. The ultimate GT of 1997 was longer and wider than the original but only eight were produced.

Despite the mouth-watering specifications, demand for the F1 never reached the expected levels and only 100 had been completed by the time production ceased at the end of 1997.

Specification	McLaren F1
Engine location	Mid, in-line
Configuration	V12
Bore and stroke	86 x 87mm
Capacity	6064cc
Valve operation	Twin overhead camshafts per bank
Horsepower	627bhp @ 7400rpm
Transmission	Manual six-speed
Drive	Rear
Chassis	Carbon-fibre monocoque
Suspension – front	Wishbones and coil spring
Suspension – rear	Wishbones and coil spring
Brakes	Ventilated discs
Top speed	240mph (386km/h)
Acceleration	0-60mph (0-96km/h): 3.2 seconds

Left: A bespoke 6-litre BMW V12 even if the covers, that conceal twin overhead camshafts, are marked McLaren. The exhaust system incorporates four catalytic converters.

Below: Open wide! The efficiency of the brakes can be taken as read, the discs being arrested by light alloy four-piston calipers.

Above: Still bearing the dust from its triumph at the 1995 Le Mans event, the winning McLaren was displayed at that year's Goodwood Festival of Speed, which took place only days after the F1's triumph. when Yannick Dalmas, J Lehto and Masanori Sekiya averaged 104.98mph (168.99km/h) for the 24 hours.

Right: Unusually the F1 driver sits in the middle of the car so the right seat of the 1995 Le Mans-winning car was filled with electronic aids, an indication of the space age technology that now assists drivers of long-distance races.

Roadgoing racer

McLaren's 1995 Le Mans victory underlined the versatility of this extraordinary car. It was the first occasion since the 1940s that a roadgoing model had won the 24 hour event.

An increase in F1 production, coupled with pressure from customers, meant that the car could be homologated for a newly instituted GT racing series. The resulting GTR version was created for the 1995 International GT Endurance Series of races, which began in February of that year. What was effectively a lightened version of the road car was created and it dominated the season to take that year's GT championship, an achievement that the McLaren repeated in 1996.

The 668bhp developed by the BMW V12 was 41bhp more than the original power unit, but the emphasis was placed on reliability rather than flat-out performance. Modifications were confined to stripping out the interior and changes were also made to the suspension with the original compliant mountings replaced by solid anchorage, competition springs, an anti-roll bar and slick tyres.

Outwardly similar, the GTR was, however, immediately identifiable by the presence of a rear wing. Ambitiously, no less than six examples were entered in the GT class for the 1995 Le Mans event. McLaren clearly meant business.

To the collective surprise of commentators and the crowd, pundits opined that the McLarens were too slow. However, GTRs dominated the race and one car, driven by Dalmas, Lehto and Sekiya, led for all but 11 of the 298 laps. Strong opposition

came from a Porsche-engined Courage that was beaten into second place. However, one GTR succumbed to gearbox trouble.

McLaren responded to this triumph by producing the commemorative LM version that was finished in a distinctive orange hue which echoed the team's Formula 1 livery of the 1960s. It sold for £799,000, some £164,500 more than the mainstream model. Just five examples were built. Outwardly resembling the standard F1, it featured extra front-brake cooling inlets and a polished carbon-fibre rear aerofoil courtesy of the GTR. There was also an enlarged central bonnet duct to feed a rather basic cockpit ventilation system and holes in the top of each rear side window.

The LM weighed in at 2341lb (1062kg), 132lb (60kg) lighter than the GTR and 168lb (76kg) less than the standard F1 for the millionaire-in-the-street. Paradoxically, it was slightly slower than the standard F1, although designer Gordon Murray claimed that it was more fun to drive because it was quicker through the six gears…

Above: The extended tail of the longer and wider GT version of 1997.

Below: A 1996 car, chassis 068. The F1 was a costly coupé with impeccable race-bred credentials – in 1998 an example was timed at 240mph (386km/h).

Ferrari F50

**Top speed
202mph**
325km/h

*Opposite top: The F50 body
is built entirely of race-
proven carbon fibre and the
material also features in the
central monocoque tub
around which the car is
built up. Like the McLaren,
the rear wheels are wider
than the fronts.*

*Below: The view as one
overtakes you! The Ferrari
badge on the front wing
leaves you in no doubt as to
this car's pedigree. Note the
break in the rear wing line,
the rear section of the body
hinges at this point.*

Although Ferrari celebrated its 50th
anniversary in 1997, the commemorative
F50 arrived prematurely in 1995. While
outwardly resembling a 1970s sports racer, at its
heart was one of the company's successful Formula
1 racing cars re-vamped for the road.

The fastest and most powerful Ferrari of its day,
it was based on the 641 series single-seater in
which Alain Prost won six races during the 1990
season. Like so many of its contemporaries, the
F50 was built up around a central tub with a
Nomex honeycomb core skinned in epoxy resin-
bonded carbon fibre. Most of this was concealed by
the bodywork, but the material was also outwardly
apparent, being used for the body panels, seats and
even the gearlever knob.

Strong retro styling

The Pininfarina-styled body, that was produced in
coupé (with and without a detachable roof) and
open forms, displayed strong retro influences while
the big fixed rear wing was an obligatory fitment.

Both turbocharging and four-wheel drive were
eschewed. Unlike the F40 which had used a blown
V8 engine, the F50 was powered by a mid-located,
longitudinally mounted, 4.7-litre V12 that evolved
from the racer's 3.5-litre unit. Developing 513bhp,

the 109.2bhp per-litre made the F50 the most
powerful normally aspirated supercar of its day. In
consequence it was able to reach 60mph (96km/h)
in a blistering 3.7 seconds and could attain 202mph
(325km/h), just 1mph (1.6km/h) faster than its no-
frills F40 predecessor.

Drive was taken by a new six-speed gearbox, although a conventional gate, rather than the usual steering wheel-mounted push button changes, was used. The combined unit was bolted directly to the rear bulkhead.

Instrumentation consisted, in essence, of just a rev counter and speedometer. In line with Formula 1 practice, the blue-hued dials were liquid crystal displays on which the needles only appeared when the ignition was switched on.

Suspension was a compliant system which rapidly responded to road conditions via an electronic control unit. The car's construction was very weight-conscious, and the complete vehicle turned the scales at a respectable 2712lb (1230kg). But relating a road car so closely to Formula 1 technology produced its own problems because noise – the result of shackling the V12, gearbox and rear suspension directly to the cockpit – proved to be an insuperable obstacle.

Ferrari engineers therefore recognized that customers would have to live with the concept of a racer only mildly tamed for the highways of the world. Production was set at 349 cars and exactly that number was completed by the time the last example appeared on 30 July 1997, the year in which Ferrari celebrated its half centenary.

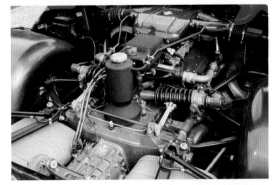

Left: This could be a shot of the engine of a Formula 1 Ferrari, and the F50's is similarly a dry-sump unit. The twin cam heads are made of aluminium although the V12 block is of cast iron. There are no less than five valves per cylinder, three inlet and two exhaust.

Specification	Ferrari F50
Engine location	Mid, in-line
Configuration	V12
Bore and stroke	85 x 69mm
Capacity	4698cc
Valve operation	Twin overhead camshafts per bank
Horsepower	513bhp @ 8000rpm
Transmission	Manual six-speed
Drive	Rear
Chassis	Carbon-fibre composite monocoque
Suspension – front	Wishbones, pushrod and coil spring
Suspension – rear	Wishbones, pushrod and coil spring
Brakes	Ventilated disc
Top speed	202mph (325km/h)
Acceleration	0-60mph (0-96km/h): 3.7 seconds

TVR Cerbera

Top speed 185mph 298km/h

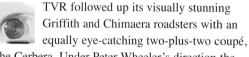

TVR followed up its visually stunning Griffith and Chimaera roadsters with an equally eye-catching two-plus-two coupé, the Cerbera. Under Peter Wheeler's direction the Blackpool company was always keen to have some new development on its stand at a major motor show, and it was the turn of the Cebera at the London Motor Show at Earls Court in 1993.

Essentially it used a longer, stronger version of the Chimaera body with the addition of a fixed coupé roof. The prototype was powered by TVR's usual tuned Rover V8 engine, which was said to give it a top speed of 158mph (254km/h) and 0-60mph (96km/h) acceleration in a little over five seconds.

Many of the concept cars TVR displayed at motor shows were never seen again, while others returned after considerable development. The Cerbera was one of the latter: it never reached production in its original Rover-powered form. But the idea of a Chimaera-based coupé lived on, and it would become the first TVR to be powered by the new family of engines. These were TVR's own in-house units, the first of them being a 4.2-litre V8, designed by engine specialist Al Melling. Called the AJP8, it belied its 'traditional' two-valves-per-cylinder layout with a hefty output of 350bhp.

TVR's stylists subtly revised the Cerbera's lines for the production cars, adding an extra 3in (76mm) to the wheelbase. The original low look was maintained but the roof line was modestly raised to permit more headroom for the rear passengers.

Above: The Cerbera is really a 'two-plus-one' coupé; there isn't much room for rear passengers. Handling is excellent and novel features abound. The electric door releases, for instance, are to be found beneath the side mirrors!

Right: This head-on view of the Cerbera emphasizes its utterly individual, yet strong and functional, shape. As a performance car this TVR could outaccelerate many of its more expensive contemporaries. The model's definitive lines were refined by TVR designers Damian McTaggert and Nick Coughlan.

Left: The view as a Cerbera accelerates away from you. Unlike the Rover V8-based power unit which emitted a disappointingly non-urgent waffle, TVR's own unit sounds rather more purposeful as a distinctive howl emanates from the twin exhaust pipes.

Below: TVR lived up to its reputation for distinctive interiors with this unusual design in which the gauges are mounted on the steering column and viewed through the lower segment of the steering wheel. The asymmetric dashboard is similarly unorthodox.

There were more radical changes inside: unusually, some of the instruments were mounted on the steering column and were viewed through the bottom half of the steering wheel.

Grand tourer Cerbera

With the new engine the Cerbera proved to be exceptionally fast, able to reach a top speed of 185mph (298km/h) and capable of sprinting from rest to 60mph (96km/h) in just four seconds. Thanks to its painstaking development process it also rode and handled better than any previous TVR, aided by the additional rigidity imparted by the fixed roof.

The original 4.2-litre V8 was joined by a 4.5-litre, 420bhp version for 1998. In 2000 the Cerbera was offered with another new TVR engine, a 4.0-litre straight six, together with chassis revisions intended to make the Cerbera Speed Six more of a 'grand tourer' than an outright sports car. Even this 'entry level' Cerbera could hit 60mph (96km/h) from rest in 4.4 seconds and go on to a top speed of 170mph (274km/h).

Revised rear lights and body-coloured A-pillars were introduced in 2000, and at the same time the fastest 4.5-litre cars were given a 'lightweight' body with a lighter bonnet and revised front wings carrying new headlamps. Production of the Cerbera continued until 2004, but by then a new era had dawned for TVR under the ownership of Nikolai Smolenski.

Specification	TVR Cerbera
Engine location	Front, in-line
Configuration	V8
Bore and stroke	88 x 86mm
Capacity	4185cc
Valve operation	Single overhead camshaft per cylinder bank
Horsepower	350bhp @ 6500rpm
Transmission	Manual five-speed
Drive	Rear
Chassis	Tubular backbone
Suspension – front	Wishbones and coil spring
Suspension – rear	Wishbones and coil spring
Brakes	Ventilated disc
Top speed	185mph (298km/h)
Acceleration	0-60mph (96km/h): 4 seconds

Bentley Continental T

**Top speed
170mph**
274km/h

*Right: The T's special
interior with engine-turned
aluminium dashboard and
centre console. Bentley's
Personal Commission
service enhances interiors
to suit an individual buyer's
own requirements.*

*Below: A Monaco Yellow
Continental T for 2000. The
model has a noticeably
shorter wheelbase than the
original. Great care is taken
with the door furniture, the
interiors of the handles
being carefully knurled.*

The Continental coupé of 1991 had the
distinction of being the first Bentley for
32 years to have its own purpose-designed
bodywork. Hitherto, the magnificently appointed
and refined saloons had been based on the products
of its Rolls-Royce parent company. When this
potent and luxurious grand tourer appeared, it
signalled the emergence of Bentley as the dominant
of the two marques after it had faced near
extinction in the 1970s.

In 1982 the Bentley Mulsanne Turbo saloon had
been unveiled. This was based on its Rolls-Royce
Silver Spirit stablemate with the 6.7-litre V8 engine
turbocharged to produce a 135mph (217km/h) car.
It was followed, in 1985, by the better-handling
Turbo R. Both models had the virtue of
immediately attracting a new, affluent and, above
all, youthful clientele which responded positively to
a revival of Bentley's long dormant performance
profile. In consequence, in 1990 Bentley
production outnumbered Rolls-Royce output for the
first time since the 1950s.

Bespoke body styling

The next step was a bespoke body which was the
work of consulting stylists, John Heffernan and
Ken Greenly. Their Project 90 concept coupé was
displayed at the 1985 Geneva Motor Show and the
public response was sufficiently encouraging for
the company to proceed with the venture. The
Continental R duly appeared six years later at the
1991 Geneva event.

Based on the Turbo R's mechanicals, the model's name was a tribute to Bentley's legendary Continental of the 1951-59 era. The blown V8's output was boosted to 328bhp and this, along with the coupé's better aerodynamics, ensured that the model was able to carry a potential four passengers in considerable comfort at speeds of up to 150mph (241km/h). Bentley had been reborn.

Subsequently, at the 1996 Geneva show, the Crewe-based company unleashed the Continental T which it billed as the fastest Bentley yet. Wider, with a 4in (100mm) shorter wheelbase and lighter than the R on which it was based, engine output was increased to 400bhp. Capable of 170mph (274km/h) and able to reach 60mph (96km/h) in a mere 5.8 seconds, the T was also enhanced by a special interior with mottled aluminium dashboard, red starter button, micro-alloy disc brakes, revised suspension and electric traction control.

An even faster-accelerating variation on the theme appeared in 2000 with the Special Commission T, identifiable by its aerodynamically refined body lines. A further 20bhp was extracted from the venerable V8 by blueprinting the engine and adjusting the management system.

The seats were upholstered in quilted Connolly leather but there were only two of them. The rear ones were removed to leave space for bespoke matching leather luggage, fittings that were very reminiscent of the sporting Bentleys of the 1920s!

Specification	Bentley Continental T
Engine location	Front, in-line
Configuration	Turbocharged V8
Bore and stroke	104 x 91mm
Capacity	6750cc
Valve operation	Pushrod
Horsepower	400bhp @ 4000rpm
Transmission	Automatic four-speed
Drive	Rear
Chassis	Unitary
Suspension – front	Wishbones and coil spring
Suspension – rear	Semi-trailing arm and coil spring
Brakes	Ventilated disc
Top speed	170mph (274km/h)
Acceleration	0-60mph (0-96km/h): 5.8 seconds

Left: The visually enhanced appearance of the Bentley Continental T's venerable aluminium V8 engine, which dates back in essence to 1959. Less apparent is the presence of the Garrett turbocharger, Bosch Jetronic fuel injection and Zytek engine management system. An electronic traction system momentarily cuts back the engine if the wheels slip or spin.

Left: When a Continental T is on the move, and during spirited acceleration and cornering, the car's viscous control differential transfers power from a spinning wheel to one with traction. This is because of the substantial amount of power and torque, to the tune of 645lb/ft at 2100rpm, developed by the big V8.

Subaru Impreza WRX STi

**Top speed
150mph**
241km/h

*Below: One of the 424
Impreza replicas that
Subaru produced in 1998 to
commemorate the fact that
it had won the World Rally
Championship for the three
successive years between
1995 and 1997. Powered by
a 2.2 'flat' four engine, it
developed some 250bhp.*

 Like Lancia's Integrale, the Impreza is a deceptive car. Introduced in 1993, outwardly it looked an unexciting model but it combined outstanding handling with formidable reliability, particularly when let loose on the rally field. In consequence Subaru won the World Rally Championship for three successive years between 1995 and 1997.

Subaru has come a long way since its first model, the diminutive rear-engined glass-fibre-bodied 360 of 1958, was described in an American consumer report as 'the most unsafe car on the market'. This one-time motor scooter manufacturer learned quickly. In 1966 it introduced an unfashionable four-cylinder horizontally opposed 'flat' engine in its FF-1 saloon. Then it offered a

four-wheel-drive version of its Leone model in 1973 and became more ambitious when it extended turbocharging to its engines in 1981.

The company moved upmarket with its Legacy saloon of 1989 and the cheaper Impreza followed in 1993. This employed four-wheel drive that could be either permanently or optionally engaged. Produced in saloon form or as a five-door hatchback, the Impreza was powered by Subaru's usual horizontally opposed four-cylinder engine that was available in 1.5, 1.6 and 1.8-litre guises. Single overhead camshafts were fitted to each cylinder bank with four valves per cylinder.

While on the debit side this meant poor accessibility, certainly compared with an in-line or transverse engine, nevertheless the 'flat' four, with

Left: Richard Burns, England's first World Rally champion, shows how it's done during his triumphant 2001 season at the wheel of his Subaru which came fourth in a series which was won by Peugeot.

Below: For 2002 the Subaru Impreza Sti will be available to British customers in two forms. There is the standard model (left), able to attain 148mph (238km/h). Its deeply spoilered Sti Prodrive neighbour is named after the company which prepares the rally cars.

its low centre of gravity, made a positive contribution to the model's superlative handling.

Commitment to competition

Subaru had rallied a Legacy RS Turbo with some success and it renewed its commitment to competition with the Impreza WRX. The turbocharged and reworked 2-litre engine with twin cam heads produced no less than 240bhp. For homologation purposes, 2500 examples of a road car were built. It was outwardly identifiable by the presence of a large bonnet scoop, wide alloy wheels, a deep front air dam and twin fog lights.

A coupé version of the Impreza arrived in 1994 and this formed the basis of the 22B rally version which was specially constructed by the corporate motorsport division, Tecnica International, and prepared by Prodrive of Banbury, Oxfordshire.

The WRX was soon proving its worth, although in 1993-94 international rallying was dominated by Toyota. However, in 1995 the Impeza gave Subaru its first ever World Rally Championship win and its star performer, Colin McRae, won the driver's title – the first Briton to attain that accolade. Subaru was to repeat the triumph in the next two years, although in 1998 it lost out to Mitsubishi.

This first generation Impreza was replaced in 2000 by a new version which retained its proven, successful and unusual mechanicals. After all, if ain't broke, don't fix it!

Specification	Subaru Impreza WRX STi
Engine location	Front, in-line
Configuration	Horizontally opposed four-cylinder
Bore and stroke	92 x 75mm
Capacity	1994cc
Valve operation	Twin overhead camshafts per cylinder bank
Horsepower	280bhp @ 6500rpm
Transmission	Manual five-speed
Drive	Four-wheel
Chassis	Unitary
Suspension – front	MacPherson strut
Suspension – rear	MacPherson strut dual link, anti-roll bar
Brakes	Ventilated disc
Top speed	150mph (241km/h)
Acceleration	0-60mph (96km/h): 4.7 seconds

Jaguar XKR

**Top speed
155mph***
249km/h
*limited

Right: Although the XK8 on which the R is based can be regarded as the E-Type's successor, it is a much more refined product and is only available with automatic transmission.

Below: The Jaguar XKR is distinguished by its meshed radiator grille that is similar to that on the XJR saloon which shares the same 4-litre supercharged engine. Note the absence of bumpers.

The XKR, which Jaguar claims is its fastest-accelerating car, can reach 60mph (96km/h) in just 5.2 seconds. It made its debut at the 1998 Geneva Motor Show. That was two years after the XK8, on which it is based, appeared at the same venue.

Available in coupé and convertible forms which revealed plenty of visual reminders of its famous E-Type forebear, the XK8 of 1996 was an all-new car powered by a 4-litre, 290bhp, V8 twin-cam engine that was making its debut in the model. However, refinement was the order of the day because it was only available with five-speed automatic transmission courtesy of Mercedes-Benz.

The engine was subsequently extended to the existing XJ6 saloon which was accordingly transformed into the XJ8 for the 1998 season. A new XJR supercharged version, in which the V8 was enhanced by the fitment of a Eaton M112 blower boosting output to 370bhp, was capable of a limited 155mph (249km/h) top speed and was able to hit 60mph (96km/h) figure in 5.3 seconds.

50th anniversary

The similarly upgunned XKR followed at the 1998 Geneva event, which was also the 50th anniversary of the introduction of Jaguar's legendary XK120 sports car. The XKR shaved a second off the blown saloon's time to 60mph (96km/h), attaining this figure in the aforesaid 5.2 seconds, while the top speed remained the same.

Left: The XKR 100 of 2001 is a limited edition model created to commemorate the centenary of the birth of Jaguar's founder, William Lyons. Enhancements include matt black finish, '100' badges and alloy wheels in the manner of the impending F-Type sports car. Some XJR saloons are similarly enhanced.

Below: The model also gets a black leather interior, sports steering wheel, Momo gearknob, DVD satellite navigation system, reverse park control and automatic windscreen wipers. Production is limited to 1000 examples of all three cars.

Although outwardly resembling the XK8, the R, which is available in both open and closed forms, was easily identifiable by its bright mesh radiator grille. This provided a visual link with the XJR saloon that sports a similar feature.

When the blown 4-litre V8 engine was transferred to the sports car, adequate cooling became a major factor, so two louvred panels were set into the bonnet to let the hot air out. A red background to the Jaguar radiator badge, alloy wheels and a discreet rear lip were the only other identifying features.

The XKR is also enhanced by the presence of CATS, which stands for Computer Active Technology Suspension. As its name suggests, this provides electronically controlled adaptive damping, but the damper settings were also altered to make the car's handling even firmer.

Limited edition

To celebrate Jaguar's entry to Formula 1 in 2000, the company produced the limited edition XKR Silverstone with uprated suspension, enhanced interior and silver, rather than the usual gold, alloy wheels. The engine was unchanged; just as in the mainstream model, you might think that you were in a standard XK8, that is until you pressed hard on the accelerator…

Specification	Jaguar XKR
Engine location	Front, in-line
Configuration	Supercharged V8
Bore and stroke	86 x 86mm
Capacity	3996cc
Valve operation	Twin overhead camshafts per bank
Horsepower	370bhp @ 6150rpm
Transmission	Automatic five-speed
Drive	Rear
Chassis	Unitary
Suspension – front	Wishbones and coil spring
Suspension – rear	Wishbones and coil spring
Brakes	Ventilated disc
Top speed	Limited to 155mph (249km/h)
Acceleration	0-60mph (96km/h): 5.2 seconds

Mercedes-Benz CLK-GTR

**Top speed
199mph**
320km/h

Below: Awesome and
purposeful, the radiator and
headlamp treatment of the
CLK-GTR was shared with
the CLK coupé; this road-
tamed racer even
incorporates Mercedes-
Benz's famous tri-star
mascot. Although often
regarded as a successor to
the 300SL coupé of the
1950s, the doors are not
of the gullwing variety
although the car does
possess a similarly high
sill line.

 With a price tag of £1.1 million, the CLK-GTR Mercedes-Benz of 1998 is the most expensive car in this book – and seven years on it is still one of the fastest cars Mercedes has built, being capable of 199mph (320km/h).

It is a spiritual successor to the fabled 300SL gullwing coupé of 1954-57, although it does not possess such memorable doors, using front-mounted scissor ones instead of gullwings. It was conceived as a roadgoing version of the company's racer which won the 1997 and 1998 GT championships. Homologation required that just one road car should be made, but Mercedes-Benz, which approved the project in March 1997, decided to build a 'small quantity' for private customers. The first of the strictly two-seater coupés was delivered in November 1998 with the last of 25 examples being finished in the summer of 1999.

Built in batches of three, each taking four to six weeks to complete, the work was undertaken by AMG at its factory at Ludwigsburg near Stuttgart. Since 1998 AMG had been Mercedes-Benz's in-house performance arm. The car only differed in detail from the track-ready GTRs. The Kevlar bodyshell was reinforced, the suspension retuned to increase the ride height, and 18in (457mm) wheels were fitted. Inside there were sports seats, three-point safety belts, twin air bags and an integrated roll cage.

There were visual reminders of the newly introduced CLK coupé although these were confined to the radiator grille, the four headlamps and instrumentation.

Racer tamed for the road

Built up around a carbon-fibre monocoque, the car's occupants could be in little doubt that this was a racer tamed for the road. Mounted longitudinally and directly attached to the rear bulkhead in the manner of the Ferrari F50, the 6.8-litre unit was based on the 5.9-litre V12 used in the S600 passenger models but developed by the UK-based Ilmor Engineering. Developing 612bhp with a massive 572lb/ft of torque, it raucously drove the

rear wheels through a six-speed manual gearbox which was operated by twin paddles located behind the steering wheel. Unlike the similar unit used by Ferrari, the CLK-GTR was fitted with a clutch. Acceleration was astounding with 62mph (100km/h) arriving in just 3.8 seconds.

Interestingly, this latter day 'silver arrow' was diametrically opposed in concept to McLaren's celebrated F1 which featured racing technology in a car that was specifically designed for road use. This awesome Mercedes-Benz coupé was, by contrast, a racer tamed for the highway. In consequence, it was fitted with power steering, power brakes and traction control, all refinements that were noticeably absent from the F1.

Specification	Mercedes-Benz CLK-GTR
Engine location	Mid, in-line
Configuration	V12
Bore and stroke	89 x 92mm
Capacity	6898cc
Valve operation	Twin overhead camshafts per bank
Horsepower	612bhp @ 6800rpm
Transmission	Manual six-speed
Drive	Rear
Chassis	Carbon-fibre monocoque
Suspension – front	Wishbones, pullrod and coil spring
Suspension – rear	Wishbones, pullrod and coil spring
Brakes	Ventilated disc
Top speed	199mph (320km/h)
Acceleration	0-62mph (0-100km/h): 3.8 seconds

Above: Although it is not a particularly practical road car, the 'Silver Arrow' could not be anything but a Mercedes-Benz. The body panels are made of Kevlar and the rear spoiler is an essential aid to produce stability and downforce.

Left: The cockpit is a little congested although safety features abound with the presence of an integrated roll-over cage, and airbags for driver and passenger.

Maserati 3200GT

**Top speed
174mph**
280km/h

*Right: The long-awaited
Spyder convertible, which
arrived for the 2002 season,
is powered by a new
Ferrari-developed 4.2-litre
V8 engine. The Ital Design-
styled open car is
distinguished by its
conventional rear lights
which differ from the
coupé's distinctive 'hockey
stick'-shaped lenses.*

*Below: Hot Maserati: the
Asetto Corsa 3200 of 2001
with a special handling
pack that includes variable
suspension settings and
tauter springs. It marks the
end of the line for Maserati's
long-running 3.2-litre
V8 engine.*

 In 1993 Maserati, after suffering decades of corporate uncertainty, was acquired by Fiat. The first visible fruits of this change of ownership was the arrival, in 1998, of the 3200GT coupé, a car capable of over 170mph (274km/h). The omens looked good.

Work on the project began following the 1993 take-over and a coupé concept was commissioned from Ital Design. The new model was to be powered by Maserati's proven 3.2-litre V8 engine but it was extensively revised to the extent that no less than 90 per cent of the component parts were new. In 1997 management of the company was assigned to in-house Ferrari, with the Maserati range being priced some 25 per cent below the products of its erstwhile rival.

Announced at the 1998 Paris Motor Show, the 3200 represented a clean break for a company that had previously been starved of investment to the extent that build quality had been compromised. Not only was the worth of the new coupé, a genuine two-plus-two, apparent for all to see, its lines were soberly executed so as not to clash with the more visually extravagant Pininfarina-styled Ferraris. The 3200 was evidently aimed at Aston Martin DB7 and Jaguar XK8 territory.

With a claimed top speed of 174mph (280km/h) and a credited 0-62mph (100km/h) figure of 5.1

seconds, in the main the 3200 lived up to expectations. It also boasted traction control and adaptive damping. Its impressive performance and high speed stability reflected the results of many hours of wind tunnel testing.

Automatic option

It was originally fitted with a manual six-speed Getrag gearbox, but some commentators found this heavy in operation until the oil warmed up, and the clutch less than smooth. A welcome automatic option arrived in 1999. Its top speed of 168mph (270km/h) and acceleration rate were, inevitably, slightly down on the manual version. But it had the virtue of being easier to drive than the original.

The Assetto Corsa (Racing Order) version marked the end of the 3200 in its original form. Just 350 were built, all boasting tauter springs, uprated anti-roll bars and new 15-spoke wheels.

For 2002 there was a revised GT with a normally aspirated 4244cc V8 engine, which shared much of its architecture with the unit Ferrari mid-mounted in its F430. The new engine also went into an open-topped version, the Spyder, which sat on a shortened platform with 8.7in (220mm) removed from the wheelbase. Both the coupé and Spyder were available with a semi-automatic gearchange Maserati called Cambiocorsa. The GT and Spyder introduced a new generation of drivers to Maserati. But with the news that Maserati has been moved from Ferrari to Alfa Romeo, both under Fiat control, the future for the Modena firm is uncertain.

Above: Nice lines – the 3200GT with the classic outline of the Ital Design-styled coupé body shown to advantage.

Left: The Spyder of 2002. The wheelbase of this open car is 8.7in (220mm) shorter than the coupé's and it boasts computer-controlled suspension.

Below left: The Spyder's well-appointed cockpit is upholstered in leather and features hi-tech navigational aids.

Specification	Maserati 3200
Engine location	Front, in-line
Configuration	V8
Bore and stroke	80 x 80mm
Capacity	3217cc
Valve operation	Twin overhead camshafts per cylinder bank
Horsepower	370bhp @ 6250rpm
Transmission	Manual six-speed
Drive	Rear
Chassis	Unitary
Suspension – front	Wishbones and coil spring
Suspension – rear	Wishbones and coil spring
Brakes	Ventilated disc
Top speed	174mph (280km/h)
Acceleration	0-62mph (100km/h): 5.1 seconds

Audi TT

**Top speed
145mph**
233km/h

*Right: Audi's stylistically
adventurous TT. This is the
more powerful 225bhp
version in which four-wheel
drive is a compulsory
fitting. Sure-footed and
rapid, this turbocharged
model has sold well.*

*Below: A TT roadster of
2000. Unlike the coupé
version, this is strictly a
two-seater with obligatory
roll-over bars for driver
and passenger protection.
The distinctive wheels echo
those of the Bugatti marque
of the 1920s.*

Outwardly unconventional, stylistically distinctive and capable in its most potent form of 145mph (233km/h), Audi's TT is a skilful combination of old and new themes. It comes courtesy of the hi-tech arm of Volkswagen's growing family of marques.

Like Porsche's Boxster and the Dodge Viper, the TT sprang from a concept car. It was conceived at Audi's California-based design centre and from the outset its stylist, Freeman Thomas, drew inspiration from German Bauhaus design themes of the 1930s.

The TT appeared at the Frankfurt Motor Show in 1995. It was based on a shortened version of the floorpan to be used in Audi's upcoming A3 hatchback, itself closely related to the next generation VW Golf, and powered by a 1.8-litre, twin-cam, four-cylinder engine from the Audi A4 saloon line.

Such was the enthusiastic reception accorded to the TT that Audi decided to put it into production, first as a coupé and then in open form, the latter concept having been revealed at the 1995 Tokyo show. Outwardly almost identical to the concept car, apart from the addition of rear quarter-lights and an enlarged air intake, the TT coupé was

launched at the 1998 Paris Motor Show.

Two engines were offered, turbocharged, 1.8-litre in-line fours with twin overhead camshafts and five valves per cylinder, the entry level version developing 180bhp and the top-line engine 225bhp. The definitive TT specification included four-wheel drive, but this was a different system to Audi's existing four-wheel drive transmission. Normally the front wheels did the driving, and the TT transmission incorporated a Haldex clutch which

delivered torque to the rear wheels if the front wheels started to spin. In entry-level 180bhp guise the TT could reach a top speed of 140mph (225km/h) with 60mph (96km/h) arriving from rest in 7.1 seconds. The 225bhp version reached 145mph (233km/h) and was about a second quicker over the standard sprint from rest.

Soon after the coupé's introduction, a series of high-speed accidents prompted Audi to revise the TT's suspension and add a small tail spoiler. In 1999 Audi also announced a new model, a two-seater Roadster.

Audi upped the ante again in 2002 with the introduction of a 3.2-litre V6 engine, shared with the Golf R32, which developed 240bhp. It was mated to the new Dynamic Shift Gearbox (DSG), which gave drivers fingertip control of the gearchange, together with lightning-fast changes. There was also a super-smooth fully automatic mode. The rest of the car received minor tweaks, most noticeably bigger wheels and tyres and a restyled grille.

The TT has been a great success for Audi. However, a new model – a little larger, but using aluminium for lightness – is expected for 2007.

Below left: The cockpit of the TT coupé is replete with echoes of Bauhaus design themes from the 1930s.

Below: A TT coupé of 2000 with a rear spoiler introduced, along with suspension modifications, to address safety scares (now resolved) that surfaced soon after its unveiling.

Specification	Audi TT
Engine location	Front, transverse
Configuration	Turbocharged four-cylinder
Bore and stroke	81 x 86mm
Capacity	1781cc
Valve operation	Twin overhead camshafts
Horsepower	225bhp @ 5900rpm
Transmission	Manual six-speed
Drive	Four wheel
Chassis	Unitary
Suspension – front	MacPherson strut and wishbone
Suspension – rear	Wishbones and coil spring
Brakes	Ventilated disc
Top speed	145mph (233km/h)
Acceleration	0-60mph (96km/h): 6.2 seconds

Aston Martin DB7 Vantage

**Top speed
185mph**
298km/h

*Below: The Vantage coupé
and Volante versions of the
DB7, a line that dates from
1993 and which was
enhanced in 1999 by the
arrival of V12 power.*

Aston Martin's expensive, hand-built V8
cars found just 46 buyers in 1991.
Economic recession hit Aston harder than
most car makers, and for years the tiny British
supercar manufacturer had wanted to add a smaller,
lighter, cheaper car to its range to help it survive
through leaner years. That opportunity finally came
thanks to the efforts of a new Aston chairman,
Walter Hayes.

It had been Hayes who had suggested to Henry
Ford II that Ford should buy Aston Martin, which
happened in September 1987. Now, as Chairman of
the company, it would be Hayes who would convince
Ford management to bankroll a new, smaller Aston.

In 1989 Ford acquired Jaguar, and set about
restructuring the company. One of the first
casualties was Jaguar's F-type sports car – pretty,
but years late and grossly over-complicated and
over-weight. An alternative plan was put forward
by TWR, who were running Jaguar's works racing
effort and were redeveloping the XJ220 for
production. TWR suggested marrying the F-type
body to the existing Jaguar XJ-S platform and
adding its own four-cam version of Jaguar's V12

Left: The Volante version of the DB7 was introduced in 1996. Its Vantage V12-engined equivalent arrived, like the coupé, in 1999. The open model is a beautifully refined car and is also produced at Aston Martin's Oxfordshire factory.

Below: The 5.9-litre V12 engine which powers the DB7 Vantage and, in essence, the Vanquish began life as two Ford Duratec V6 engines mounted end to end. It was magnificently refined by in-house Cosworth.

engine, but that idea was turned down on the grounds that it would be too costly to manufacture.

But the idea appealed to Hayes, who realised that at Aston Martin's lower volumes the cost of manufacture was less important. Soon TWR was redeveloping its idea as an Aston, swapping the V12 engine for a supercharged version of Jaguar's latest AJ6 straight-six, producing 335bhp. The car's shape was created by TWR designer Ian Callum, incorporating classic Aston design cues such as the 'shouldered' air intake and the teardrop plan form of the cabin.

By the time of its public debut at the Geneva show in March 1993 it had acquired a name – DB7, harking back to Aston's glory days under the leadership of David Brown. Production began, a little late, at the end of 1994, and a drophead Volante version followed in 1996.

In 1999 the DB7 Vantage and Vantage Volante appeared, with a new Cosworth-built V12, loosely based on two Ford Mondeo/Taurus Duratec V6s laid end to end to produce a 5.9-litre, 60-degree V12 with 420bhp. The DB7's top speed went up to 185mph (298km/h) and its 0-60mph (96km/h) time dropped to around 5.0sec.

Aston Martin and Zagato got together to produce a run of just 99 DB7 Zagatos in March 2002, followed by the Zagato-built DB American Roadster 1 for the US market. The final DB7 derivative was the GT, with a 435bhp engine and revised suspension. Production ended in 2003 after just over 7000 DB7s had been made. It was the most popular Aston yet built.

Specification	**Aston Martin** DB7 Vantage
Engine location	Front, in-line
Configuration	Supercharged V12
Bore and stroke	89 x 79mm
Capacity	5935cc
Valve operation	Twin overhead camshaft per cylinder bank
Horsepower	420bhp @ 6000rpm
Transmission	Manual six-speed
Drive	Rear
Chassis	Unitary
Suspension – front	Wishbones and coil spring
Suspension – rear	Wishbones and coil spring
Brakes	Disc, ventilated at front
Top speed	185mph (298km/h)
Acceleration	0-60mph (96km/h): 5 seconds

Panoz AIV

**Top speed
130mph**
209km/h

*Below: There isn't a lot of
room in the AIV's cockpit.
The instruments are
courtesy of Mustang Cobra
and easy to read. However,
you sit high and the tops of
the doors are low, so you're
exposed to plenty of
buffeting!*

*Below right: The body, like
the space-frame it conceals,
is made from aluminium
and defies description while
the windscreen comes
courtesy of the Volkswagen
Super Beetle. The badge on
the bonnet incorporates the
Irish shamrock, a pointer to
the origins of the Panoz
marque.*

 It's rare, raucous and rapid. For this V8-
engined open two-seater, which rather
resembles a beached whale on wheels, is
perfect transport for the enthusiast who wants
something a little different (gulp) from the norm.

Panoz Auto Developments, based in Georgia,
USA, sold its first cars in 1992 with a chassis based
on the Irish-built TMC kit car of 1983-88 vintage.
This unlikely liaison occurred because Donald
Panoz, whose father emigrated to America from
Italy in the early 1900s, established Elan
Pharmaceuticals in Ireland. In 1988 his 26-year-old
son, Daniel, applied for a job with the Thompson
Motor Company, only to find that it was in the
process of being liquidated.

He duly acquired the rights to the space-frame
that had been designed by Frank Costin, a man
whose distinguished engineering career embraced
the design of the Vanwall, Lotus Mark 8 and
Marcos chassis. In 1989 Panoz established a
factory at Hoschton, some 50 miles (80km) from
Atlanta, and in 1997 he entered a GT at Le Mans,
initiating a commitment to the event that continues
to this day.

As far as its road cars were concerned, Panoz
engineers replaced the TMC's original four-
cylinder Ford units with a 5-litre V8 engine,
courtesy of the Ford Mustang, and this evolved into
the AIV open two-seater of 1996. The services of
stylist Freeman Thomas, who had essayed the lines
of the Audi TT, were retained and he came up with
the distinctive open two-seater cycle-winged
aluminium body that, it should be said, looks like
nothing else on the road.

Aluminium intensive

The original space-frame was replaced by a modern
and considerably lighter aluminium backbone
chassis and this metallic theme was extended to the
engine which was a new Ford alloy 4.6-litre V8
with twin-cam heads and 32 valves. Now the
reason for the AIV name, it stands for Aluminium
Intensive Vehicle, becomes apparent.

If the styling is controversial, there is no
argument about this Panoz's performance,
notwithstanding the provision of a five-speed

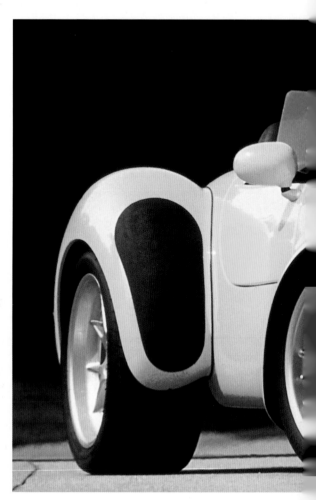

Specification	**Panoz** AIV
Engine location	Front, in-line
Configuration	V8
Bore and stroke	90.2 x 90mm
Capacity	4601cc
Valve operation	Twin overhead camshafts per cylinder bank
Horsepower	305bhp @ 5800rpm
Transmission	Automatic five-speed
Drive	Rear
Chassis	Backbone
Suspension – front	Wishbones and coil spring
Suspension – rear	Wishbones and coil spring
Brakes	Disc, ventilated at front
Top speed	130mph (209km/h)
Acceleration	0-60 mph (96 km/h): 4.5 seconds

energy-absorbing automatic gearbox. With its excellent power-to-weight ratio, the AIV can sprint to 60mph (96km/h) in 4.5 seconds, reach the ton in 13.5 and it has a top speed of 130mph (209km/h).

Behind the wheel you can feel the full effects of this performance which is accompanied by buffeting aplenty. The robust chassis, coupled with all-round wishbones suspension, means that the AIV corners like a racer. Perhaps it's not everyone's cup of tea, but how boring the motor industry would be without such imaginative excursions into unorthodoxy.

Above left: Panoz's Esperante of 2000 is, in effect, a conventionally bodied AIV, which has now ceased production. It has a Ford Mustang engine.

BMW M5

**Top speed
160mph**
257km/h

*Below: A picture is worth a
thousand words: an M5 at
speed. The understated
5-series modifications
include twin scoops in the
front bumper which feed the
engine's induction system
while the fog lights are oval
and headlights xeon. Less
discernible is the radiator
chrome surround that is
wider than usual.*

For two decades BMW's M5 models have
been refined saloon cars which cosset
their drivers and passengers in a
comfortable, air-conditioned cabin and cruise
quietly in their long-legged top gears. The M5s
have also been impressive performance cars which
will run rings round many a so-called supercar.

M stands for Motorsport, a division of the
Munich company which was established in 1972.
One of its roles was to produce specially modified
versions of BMW's already impressively
engineered sports saloons. The first of these was
the M535i of 1980, which used the largest of
BMW's six-cylinder engines in the compact 5-
series body. In 1984 Motorsport went one better,
inserting its 24-valve engine – derived from the
racing engines used in the 1970s CSLs, and then in
the BMW M1 supercar – into the latest 5-series

body to form the first M5. A second-generation
version ran from 1990 to 1996.

Significantly more power

Then there was a hiatus until the third-generation
M5 broke cover for 1999. Like its predecessors,
external modifications were kept to a minimum. Its
starting point was the already outstanding 4.3-litre
V8-powered 540i. At its heart was a 4.9-litre V8
which BMW claimed was 95 per cent new. With an
output of 400bhp, a significant 114bhp more than
that developed by the 540 unit on which it was
based, almost every component was different and
engine efficiency was enhanced by a Vanos variable
valve timing system.

A drive-by-wire throttle was fitted and flicking
a *Sport* button on the dashboard produced a more
rapid response from the car than the normal setting

Specification	BMW M5
Engine location	Front, in-line
Configuration	V8
Bore and stroke	94 x 89mm
Capacity	4941cc
Valve operation	Twin overhead camshafts per cylinder bank
Horsepower	400bhp @ 6600rpm
Transmission	Manual six-speed
Drive	Rear
Chassis	Unitary
Suspension – front	MacPherson strut
Suspension – rear	Multi link and coil spring
Brakes	Ventilated disc
Top speed	160mph (257km/h)
Acceleration	0-60mph (96km/h): 5.4 seconds

allowed. Adjustments were also made to the steering to provide the driver with easier parking and straight line precision.

Important modifications were made to the suspension which was lowered by 0.6in (15mm) at the front and 0.4in (10mm) at the rear with the springs and dampers uprated accordingly. With gunmetal alloy wheels peculiar to the model, the M5 was also distinguished by the presence of four – rather than the usual two – exhaust pipes.

The M5 is now a fixture in BMW's 5-series line, and the latest car is even more impressive than its forebears. The most powerful road car BMW has ever built, it boasts 507bhp from its 5.0-litre V10 engine and is electronically limited to no more than 155mph (250km/h). Without the limiter it could have reached 205mph (330km/h)…

Above left: The alloy 4.9-litre 400bhp V8. Note the precision twin induction pipes uppermost on the left and the outer banks of cam boxes just visible.

Above: The alloy wheels have a satin finish and the famous M5 badge is mounted low on the right of the boot lid.

Left: The M5's bespoke streamlined side mirrors fold up out of the way to improve aerodynamics.

Shelby Series 1

**Top speed
170mph***
274km/h
*Claimed by
manufacturer

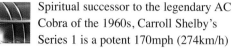

Spiritual successor to the legendary AC
Cobra of the 1960s, Carroll Shelby's
Series 1 is a potent 170mph (274km/h)
open two-seater from the American master of
performance motoring. Unlike his previous projects
which were based on other manufacturers' cars, this
car is purpose-designed, although it does employ a
proprietary engine.

Announced at the 1997 Detroit Motor Show,
the Series 1 was based on a square-section tubular
steel chassis enhanced with a carbon-fibre and
glass-fibre body replete with Ferrari and Cobra
themes. However, after some 50 years of being
associated with Ford projects, the Series 1 is
powered by a 4-litre General Motors V8, courtesy
of Oldsmobile's Aurora saloon.

In a bid to reduce weight, the original chassis
was dispensed with and replaced by an aluminium
space-frame. The all-round coil and wishbone
suspension was also aluminium-based. A
modification was also made to the gearbox which
in the 1997 show car was mounted in unit with the
engine. Production versions have a ZF transaxle
with power being delivered by a torque tube which
also has a structural role.

The Detroit event also provided Shelby with the
opportunity of gauging public reaction to the
interior which originally reflected a stark, no-frills
specification. By contrast, the production Series 1
is far better equipped and has air conditioning,
electric windows and a CD player.

Most of the interior fittings come from the GM
parts bin but the leather upholstered seats are
peculiar to the car and are the work of Shelby, a
one-time racing driver, himself.

Above: The Shelby's body,
made from carbon and
glass fibre, which is replete
with European and
American retro themes. The
bonnet bulge has a
practical function and
conceals a duct to expel hot
air away from the radiator.

Right: The distinctive
spoilered tail is readily
apparent as are the vents on
the front wings. Apart from
having a decorative
function, they permit heated
air generated by the front
disc brakes to escape. The
car is only produced in left-
hand-drive form.

Speedway tuition

The extensive use of lightweight materials means that the Shelby turns the scale at 2597lb (1178kg), and it can reach 60mph (96km/h) in well below five seconds. On the road, in addition to its accelerative qualities, the Shelby has been praised for its predictable roadholding and excellent steering. Production is based at Shelby's new factory located alongside the Las Vegas Speedway and included in the car's price is a day's tuition around the circuit.

The Shelby experienced a protracted birth and production did not begin until 2000. And the original price, the equivalent of £63,000, has risen to a more viable £81,000, because Venture Industries, an American engineering concern, has taken a 75 per cent stake in the business. This has meant increased production and an improvement in build quality.

Above: The well-equipped cockpit is in contrast to the first version of the car.

Left: The Shelby's strictly two-seater styling should stand the test of time.

Below left: The console which is faced with carbon fibre contains both a radio and a CD player.

Specification	Shelby Series 1
Engine location	Front in-line
Configuration	V8
Bore and stroke	87 x 84mm
Capacity	3995cc
Valve operation	Twin overhead camshafts per cylinder bank
Horsepower	320bhp @ 6500rpm
Transmission	Manual six-speed
Drive	Rear
Chassis	Space-frame
Suspension – front	Wishbones and coil spring
Suspension – rear	Wishbones and coil spring
Brakes	Ventilated disc
Top speed	170mph (274km/h)*
Acceleration	0-60mph (96km/h): 4.4 seconds*
	*Manufacturer's claim

Pagani Zonda C12

**Top speed
200mph***
322km/h
*Claimed by
manufacturer

*Right: The Mercedes-Benz
6-litre V12 engine has been
enhanced by AMG, the
company's in-house tuner
and engine enhancer.
Having initially powered
the discontinued S-type
saloon, it has been easily
adapted to its new
mid-location.*

*Above: Other drivers will
be in no doubt that they
have a Pagani in front of
them. The inspiration for
this cluster of quadruple
exhaust pipes is the
American space
programme. NASA has got
a lot to answer for!*

*Right: The Zonda S with its
distinctive split rear spoiler
uses a more powerful 7-litre
engine. Other outward
changes have been made to
the distinctive carbon-fibre
body which amply reflects
the car's impressive
performance.*

One of the latest recruits to the supercar
league, the Pagani is a sensationally
styled mid-engined coupé with a claimed
top speed of 200mph (322km/h). It is the brainchild
of Argentinian-born Horacio Pagani, who as a
young man became friends with his fellow
countryman, five times world motor racing
champion Juan Fangio. The letter of introduction
from Fangio to Maserati's former chief engineer,
Giulio Alfieri, then at Lamborghini, resulted in
Pagani obtaining a job there.

Concentrating on styling and recognizing the
potential of light and immensely strong carbon-
fibre structures, Pagani was responsible for the
lines of the Countach Anniversary model of 1988.
However, soon afterwards he left Lamborghini,
setting up Modena Engineering to concentrate on
design and carbon-fibre technology, and he quickly
built up an international clientele of customers.

Then he decided to produce his own car, which
he originally intended to name Fangio, after his
mentor. Although he eventually settled for Zonda,
which means wind from the Andes, the former
champion's influence is apparent in Pagani's use of
a Mercedes engine. Mechanically inspired by the
Sauber-Mercedes sports racers, he claims that the
body lines were influenced by the voluptuous
contours of his wife Cristina's figure!

Sensational debut

The Zonda made a sensational debut at the 1999
Geneva Motor Show. The chassis was a
combination of a carbon-fibre backbone and steel
space frames at either end. It was powered by a
V12 Mercedes-Benz 6-litre engine, courtesy of its
recently discontinued S series cars. Longitudinally
located, it drives the rear wheels via a five-speed
ZF gearbox. Weighing just 2756lb (1250kg), its
makers claimed, optimistically as it turned out, a
0-60mph (96km/h) figure of under four seconds.

Left: The Zonda's lines take visual inspiration from Pagani's wife Cristina and the wind tunnel. The front of the Zonda S (below) has a more clearly defined nose and repositioned headlights.

Below left: The current Zonda is fitted with a factory developed six-speed gearbox which replaces the original five-cog ZF unit. Early owners will be able to upgrade to the later gearbox.

Following the Geneva debut, Pagani announced that it would also be offering an even faster version with the engine enlarged to 7 litres and enhanced by Mercedes-Benz's in-house tuner AMG. Appearing at the 2000 Geneva event, this version was designated the Zonda S and it differed outwardly from the base model in having a more clearly defined nose with the aerofoil, which had been a feature of the 1999 car, now divided – a modification which also makes a contribution to the car's extraordinary visual impact.

The Zonda S also differed mechanically in possessing a Pagani-developed six-speed manual gearbox which replaced the five-cog ZF original. Although longer by 1.9in (50mm) than the standard C12, its makers say that weight remains the same, ensuring brutally rapid acceleration and a top speed of over 200mph (322km/h).

The announcement of a limited-edition Zonda Roadster, of which only 40 will be built, has only added to the appeal of the Pagani range.

Specification	Pagani Zonda C12
Engine location	Mid, longitudinal
Configuration	V12
Bore and stroke	89 x 80mm
Capacity	5987cc
Valve operation	Twin overhead camshafts per cylinder bank
Horsepower	394bhp @ 5200rpm
Transmission	Manual six-speed
Drive	Rear
Chassis	Monocoque
Suspension – front	Wishbones and coil spring
Suspension – rear	Wishbones and coil spring
Brakes	Ventilated disc
Top speed	200mph (322km/h)*
Acceleration	0-62mph (96km/h): 4.5 seconds*
	*Manufacturer's claim

Lotus Exige

**Top speed
124mph**
200km/h

*Below: A racer for the
road, an Exige on the move.
Note that in addition to the
mid-located engine air
intakes, a secondary roof-
mounted duct also directs
air to the power unit. The
roof line is higher than
might be expected because
it has to accommodate an
owner's helmeted head! The
wheels are shod with
specially developed
Yokohama tyres.*

The Exige coupé was another development
stemming from Lotus's successful mid-
engined roadster, the Elise. Based on the
Sport Elise racer, the closed car underlines the
versatility of a concept that first appeared in 1995.
Conceived during the era when Bugatti owned Lotus,
the model was named Elise after the granddaughter
of its chairman Romano Artioli. But his business
collapsed in 1995 and in the following year Lotus
was acquired by the Malaysian Proton concern.

The Elise, spiritual successor to the no-frills
Lotus Seven of the 1950s, was powered by a
118bhp version of Rover's 1.8-litre K-series
engine, and featured an advanced extruded-
aluminium epoxy-bonded chassis which weighed a
mere 154lb (70kg). All-round aluminium composite
brakes represented another significant first. A glass-
fibre body was also synonymous with the marque.

Able to attain 124mph (200km/h) and reach
60mph (96km/h) in 5.9 seconds, the Elise
possessed the roadholding and distinctive character
on which Lotus had built its reputation. However,
on the debit side was undue engine noise and a
fabric roof that could be difficult to erect.

Of greater significance as far as the future
Exige was concerned was the 150mph (241km/h)
200bhp Sport Elise coupé conceived for a one-
make race series run in 2000 by Lotus Motorsport.
Announced in April 2000, the Exige is effectively a
mildly detuned version of the Sport powered by a
177bhp version of the Rover four, although a more
potent 190bhp version is also available.

This performance is assisted by the lines of the
coupé body that possesses about the same drag
coefficient as the roadster although it exerts more
downforce. And, like the racer, it is fitted with a
rear wing.

Based on the Sport Elise chassis, in the interests
of practicality the Exige dispensed with the racer's
central driving position. It reverted to two-abreast
seating although only the driver's seat can be
adjusted fore and aft.

Respectable performance

While Lotus claimed a 0-100mph (161km/h) figure of a respectable 12.3 seconds and a top speed of 136mph (219km/h), in reality these claims appeared somewhat optimistic, the actual figures being 13.7 seconds and 124mph (200km/h) respectively. Nevertheless, the Exige, like its parent, possesses oodles of noisy character, to which is coupled outstanding steering and handling.

Left: An Exige on the Lotus stand, which the company claimed to be its largest ever, at the 2000 British Motor Show. The hot air outlets can be seen on either side of the twin exhaust pipes.

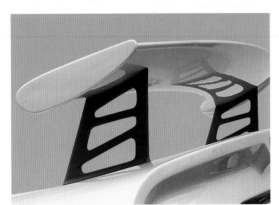

Specification	Lotus Exige
Engine location	Mid, transverse
Configuration	Four-cylinder
Bore and stroke	80 x 89mm
Capacity	1796cc
Valve operation	Twin overhead camshafts
Horsepower	190bhp @ 7800rpm
Transmission	Manual five-speed
Drive	Rear
Chassis	Extruded aluminium
Suspension – front	Wishbones and coil spring
Suspension – rear	Wishbones and coil spring
Brakes	Ventilated disc
Top speed	124mph (200km/h)
Acceleration	0-60mph (96km/h): 5.5 seconds

Above left: The rear wing of the Sport Elise was replaced by this rather smaller version which Lotus maintained produced aerodynamic characteristics that were more appropriate for the road user. It generates 99lb (45kg) of downforce at 100mph (161km/h) and it thus considerably assists the Exige's roadholding.

Left: The no-frills philosophy of the Exige is underlined by the cockpit – while the driver's seat is adjustable, the passenger's is fixed. The belts are a full four-point mounting. Perversely, it is possible to have an in-car entertainment facility, indicated by the radio aerial and speaker mounts.

Morgan Aero 8

**Top speed
160mph**
257km/h

By any standards it is a sensational car, but for an old established company like Morgan it is positively light years removed from its other products. The 160mph (257km/h) Aero 8 made its sensational debut at the 2000 Geneva Motor Show and it combines the traditional looks for which the marque is justifiably famous with state-of-the-art mechanicals.

The model, which revives a name previously associated with its formative three-wheeler line, sprang from a racing car that Charles Morgan, the company's present managing director, campaigned during the 1997 season. The work of Jaguar's former engineering director, Jim Randle, and created for that year's GT championship, its chassis was constructed from laser-cut aluminium sections. These were then glued and bonded together in much the same way in which the Lotus Elise frame is constructed.

Hitherto every Morgan since the marque's foundation in 1910 featured sliding pillar independent front suspension. But the GT2 racer used an unrelated and distinctive all-independent system which has been inherited by the Aero 8. This uses long cantilever upper arms with lower wishbones at the front with long transverse rear wishbones and coil springs as the suspension medium. While the racer's chassis came up to scratch, its Rover V8 engine, based on the unit used to power the Plus 8, was beginning to show its years and rendered the car uncompetitive.

Morgan has made no such mistakes with its new road car and it is powered by BMW's current 286bhp 4.4 V8, as used in the 5-Series saloon, but of a unique specification to Morgan. The gearbox is also German and is a six-speed Getrag unit.

Controversial bodywork

Perhaps the most controversial aspect of the new car is its bodywork with the front headlight treatment producing raised eyebrows in some quarters. But at least this new Morgan cannot be mistaken for anything else! The lines of the open

Above: The aerodynamically refined front end gives the Aero 8 a personality all of its own. Power is courtesy of BMW and, unlike previous examples of the marque, all-independent suspension is employed.

Right: Benefiting from low weight and a combination of old and new themes, the Aero's alloy wheels are individually etched with the Morgan badge. They allow plenty of air to reach the all-round discs.

two-seater evoke some of the spirit of the traditional Morgans, but the Aero 8 only uses about a dozen parts, namely the hinges, bonnet latches and doors, in common with its contemporaries. However, it does retain the time-honoured ash frame used with an aluminium monocoque.

It may come as a surprise to discover that the Aero was wind tunnel-tested. The drag coefficient figure of 0.39 is not outstanding but it is a revelation in Morgan terms, and is 40 per cent lower than that achieved by the Plus 8 whose body lines are firmly rooted in the 1930s.

With a selling price of just under £50,000, some £16,500 more than the Plus 8, the Aero 8 represents a considerable gamble by Morgan which is one of Britain's few remaining indigenous car companies.

Above: The Aero's handling and performance have been praised, this being aided by the car's light weight.

Left: The new Morgan as it appeared at the 2000 British Motor Show. Access to the car is good, thanks to the long doors.

Below left: The interior similarly echoes old and new themes. The windscreen is electrically heated and the ash frame, rather than being concealed by trim, is exposed.

Specification	**Morgan** Aero 8
Engine location	Front, in-line
Configuration	V8
Bore and stroke	82 x 92mm
Capacity	4398cc
Valve operation	Twin overhead camshafts per bank
Horsepower	286bhp @ 5500rpm
Transmission	Manual six-speed
Drive	Rear
Chassis	Aluminium monocoque
Suspension – front	Cantilever, wishbones and coil spring
Suspension – rear	Wishbones and coil spring
Brakes	Ventilated disc
Top speed	160mph (257km/h)
Acceleration	0-60mph (0-96km/h): 4.7 seconds

BMW Z8

**Top speed
155mph***
249km/h
*limited

*Right: The Z8's instrument
panel contains retro
elements. Moving the
instruments to the centre of
the dash means that the
driver has an uninterrupted
view down the bonnet.*

*Below: Inspired by BMW's
507 of the 1950s, with the
wing-mounted side vents
echoing that model, the Z8's
structure makes extensive
use of aluminium and is
essentially a hand-made
product.*

 The ancestry of the Z8 roadster is evident
to see: it clearly draws its visual
inspiration from BMW's classic 507
roadster of the 1950s. Produced between 1957 and
1959, the 507 was powered by a 3.2-litre V8 engine
and could be wound up to 135mph (217km/h). But
it was expensive for its day and only 250 were
produced. Now in demand by collectors, it fired the
imagination of BMW's chairman and old car fan
Bernd Pischetsreider and his fellow board member
and classic car enthusiast Wolfgang Rietzle.

The result, the work of Henrik Fisker, the
Danish head of BMW's California studio, was the
Z8 concept car. It was unveiled at the 1997 Tokyo
Motor Show. While some features of the concept
car were sacrificed for the production line, the Z8,
which appeared for the 2000 season, closely
resembled the show version. But this was no
pastiche of the original. It also incorporated a raft
of 1960s features, courtesy of Austin-Healey,
Jaguar and Aston Martin. However, the most
significant difference between the two cars is that

the production version has been shorn of its D-
Type-inspired rear fin. It has been replaced by more
production-friendly twin roll-over hoops.

Aluminium space frame

Aluminium featured extensively in the construction
of the Z8, most significantly the space frame that
was welded and glued together, while the
suspension components were made of the same
metal. It therefore comes as no surprise to find that

the body panels are also aluminium with the bumpers and boot lining made from strong and ultra-light carbon fibre. The Z8 weighs a very respectable 3494lb (1585kg).

It also perpetuated the spirit of the 507 in having a V8 engine, although this is a 5-litre unit developing an awesome 400bhp and comes courtesy of BMW's formidable M5 saloon. Under-bonnet warm air escapes through distinctive 507-style vents positioned on each side of the front wings.

Retro styling

There was a choice of a six-speed manual gearbox and an SMG sequential version of the same unit. Inside the retro themes were continued with a chrome-plate and leather-bound steering wheel. These went hand in hand with the latest gizmos, such as satellite navigation, a ten-speaker stereo and a hands-free mobile phone.

Although the Z8's top speed was limited to 155mph (249km/h), without this restriction it could probably attain 180mph (289km/h) and it can sprint to 62mph (100km/h) in just 4.7 seconds.

Unlike its much cheaper Z3 relative which was produced in America, the Z8 was assembled by hand in Germany. This was no mass-produced car; just ten a week were built and production ended in 2003. Its owners are the fortunate few.

Above: The rear lights are distinctive and the twin exhaust pipes indicate a V8 engine. The back tyres are wider than the front ones.

Left: The model's 4.9-litre V8 engine is inherited essentially intact from BMW's potent M5 saloon. The Z8 is fitted with electronic stability and traction control.

Specification	BMW Z8
Engine location	Front, in-line
Configuration	V8
Bore and stroke	94 x 89mm
Capacity	4941cc
Valve operation	Twin overhead camshafts per bank
Horsepower	394bhp @ 6600rpm
Transmission	Manual six-speed
Drive	Rear
Chassis	Tubular aluminium
Suspension – front	MacPherson strut and coil spring
Suspension – rear	Multi link and coil spring
Brakes	Ventilated disc
Top speed	Limited to 155mph (249km/h)
Acceleration	0-62mph (0-100km/h): 4.7 seconds

Ultima GTR

**Top speed
231mph**
372km/h

*Below: The Ultima is the
supercar you can build
yourself: the company
supplies comprehensive
self-build kits, and a variety
of engine specifications are
available.*

Look hard and you will find a few supercars which can better the Ultima GTR's top speed, maybe even one or two which can keep up with it in a sprint from a standing start. But when it comes to performance per pound, nothing can touch an Ultima. No European high-tech supercar offers so much for so little. No American muscle machine matches the Ultima's pace at the Ultima's price. This is the ultimate bang for your bucks.

The GTR was launched in 1999 after a 14-month development programme. The starting point was Ultima's existing Sports model, which contributed its proven tubular spaceframe chassis and double wishbone suspension. The glass-fibre bodyshell was completely redesigned with the emphasis on aerodynamic efficiency, the new body shape being extensively tested at the Motor Industry Research Association (MIRA). Compared to the Sports, the GTR has a lengthened tail which cleans up the airflow over the rear of the car, reducing drag and improving downforce at speed.

Though the GTR is a fixed-roof car, with forward-opening doors, lovers of open-air motoring are catered for too. The open-top Ultima Can-Am, based on the GTR, takes as its inspiration the incredibly powerful racing cars of the Can-Am series in the 1960s and 1970s.

Power for all the Ultima models comes from a tuned Chevrolet small-block V8, available in a variety of specifications from Ultima's engine supplier American Speed in Moline, Illinois. Outputs range from 300bhp to well over 700bhp, though most buyers opt for a 350 cubic inch (5.7-litre) unit with 350-400bhp. Even these provide rapid performance, but pick a motor from the top end of the scale and the Ultima is extraordinarily fast. At the Millbrook Proving Ground in April

Left: This 685bhp Ultima set a new 0-100mph-0 world record in 2005.

Below left: With the rear bodywork removed, the engine, suspension and chassis are visible.

Below: Various different engine specs are available from Ultima's supplier, American Speed.

2005 a standard Ultima with a 685bhp engine set a new 0-100mph-0 world record of just 9.8 seconds, and the company claims that the car is capable of a top speed of 231mph (372km/h).

And all this from a car which, if you want, you can build yourself. Though Ultima build several fully completed cars every year, the GTR is also available in kit form for the buyer to assemble, further reducing the cost. Buyers can choose anything from a basic chassis package to a complete kit including every last nut and bolt. Assembling the car takes most buyers about six months of part-time work. The result is a bargain performance car which can outrun many a million-dollar mega-machine.

Specification	Ultima GTR
Engine location	Mid, in-line
Configuration	V8
Bore and stroke	N/A
Capacity	6178cc
Valve operation	Pushrod
Horsepower	685bhp @ 6800rpm
Transmission	Porsche five-speed transaxle
Drive	Rear
Chassis	Tubular spaceframe
Suspension – front	Double wishbone and coil spring
Suspension – rear	Double wishbone and coil spring
Brakes	Ventilated disc
Top speed	limited to 231mph (km/h)
Acceleration	0-60mph (96km/h): 2.7 seconds

Aston Martin Le Mans Vantage

**Top speed
200mph+**
322km/h

Unashamedly purposeful and with a top speed in excess of 200mph (322km/h), this potent Aston Martin was able to hit 100mph (161km/h) in under 10 seconds. Little wonder that the supercharged V8 engine developed no less than 600bhp.

It represented the final expression of a line that began with the lacklustre Virage coupé of 1989. Since 1950 Aston Martin has applied the Vantage name to the most powerful model of its day and this Virage-based car was the flag-bearer developed for 1993.

The output of its 5.3 V8 engine was boosted from 310 to 550bhp, principally by the fitment of two Eaton superchargers. With a top speed approaching 190mph (306km/h), its brakes needed to be good and the 14in (356mm) diameter discs, courtesy of the corporate Group C racer, were the largest then fitted to a production car.

Three years on, in August 1995, a Mark II version of the model appeared that could be easily identified by a distinctive crackle-finished radiator grille. Beneath the surface no less than 700 modifications had been effected to refine handling, improve the gear change and reduce noise levels.

Then for 1998 came the top-of-the-range Vantage 600, the output of the venerable but robust V8 having been boosted to 600bhp, each blower now boasting its own intercooler. There was a new

Right: Aston Martin banished the usual wood veneer in the Le Mans for titanium, a theme that echoed the Project Vantage concept car of 1998.

Below: The front of the Le Mans is noticeably different from the Vantage on which it was based. The nose and the bonnet and wing air intakes are all peculiar to the model.

five-speed gearbox, actually a Chevrolet Corvette ZR1 unit but with the top gear blanked off. Speeds in excess of 200mph (322km/h) were attainable.

Outward changes were minimal and discreet; for instance, the shape of the radiator grille was accentuated by a thin chrome surround. There was also a small but significant badge which declared *Works Prepared* and *Newport Pagnell* which is where this Aston Martin was built.

Anniversary of Le Mans victory

The 1999 Geneva Motor Show witnessed the arrival of the ultimate version, the Le Mans Vantage, which celebrated the 40th anniversary of Aston Martin winning the 1959 24 hour classic

event and the World Sports Car Championship. Available in 550 and 600bhp guises, the Le Mans was instantly identifiable by its reworked nose with enlarged radiator ducts in a new grille panel. It also incorporated an extended spoiler to aid downforce.

The range of colour schemes included the almond green paint of a hue used by the 1959 works team. Inside, the Le Mans revealed the influence of the interior of the Project Vantage concept car of the previous year. Just 40 cars, one for each year, were produced.

The last Le Mans off the line appeared at Aston Martin's stand at the 2000 British Motor Show, so allowing the V12-engined Vanquish to take centre stage in 2001.

Below: The number plate says it all! The Le Mans is based on the Vantage 600 which appeared in 1998. The thin chrome surround was a distinctive feature.

Bottom left: The Vantage engine. The output of the two Eaton superchargers, introduced in 1993, was boosted so that the V8 developed 600bhp. Each unit has its own intercooler and water pump.

Specification	Aston Martin Le Mans Vantage
Engine location	Front, in-line
Configuration	Twin supercharged V8
Bore and stroke	85 x 100mm
Capacity	5340cc
Valve operation	Twin overhead camshafts per bank
Horsepower	600bhp @ 6750rpm
Transmission	Manual six-speed
Drive	Rear
Chassis	Unitary
Suspension – front	Wishbones and coil spring
Suspension – rear	Wishbones and coil spring
Brakes	Ventilated disc
Top speed	Over 200mph (322km/h)
Acceleration	0-60mph (96km/h): 3.9 seconds

Noble M12 GTO

**Top speed
155mph***
249km/h
*Claimed by
manufacturer

*Right: The instrumentation
is functional with analogue
dials set in a dashboard
that matches their contours.
The rest of the cockpit
echoes this basic approach.*

*Below: The Noble doing
what it does best, on the
move and offering owners a
ride that is both pliant and
controlled.*

Superlative roadholding coupled with impressive performance are the hallmarks of the mid-engined Noble M12 GTO coupé announced in 2000. Capable of 155mph (249km/h), this car firmly occupies Lotus territory and, according to rumour, it is in some respects superior to the acclaimed Elise.

Engineer Lee Noble has been a significant player in the precarious world of specialist sports car manufacture since 1985. He originally created a Group C-inspired coupé with a finely engineered space frame chassis, and this appeared in revised and more curvaceous Rover V8-powered Mark 3 form in 1987. It survived until 1990 but was revived as the Ultima sports car in 1992. Noble was also responsible for the design of the 200mph (322km/h) Ascari coupé of 1995.

In 1998 Noble produced the M10 roadster. Based on a space frame chassis, it was available with a choice of two mid-located Ford engines: a 1.8-litre four-cylinder Zetec unit or a 2.5-litre V6. But while it was a highly competent mechanical confection, commentators deemed that the glass-fibre body lacked flair.

The M12 coupé that appeared two years after the M10 in 2000 is an ingenious derivative. The glass-fibre body is distinctive, agreeably executed

and possesses a rear wing. Power comes courtesy of a Ford V6 engine. Unlike the roadster, it develops no less than 310bhp, thanks to its twin Garrett turbochargers. Combined with a remapped engine management system, this provides a flexible, responsive engine with all the bite expected from a blown power unit. Significantly the M12 is an extremely light car and turns the scales at a mere 2160lb (980kg).

Minimalist design approach

Lee Noble's particular area of expertise is chassis design and the frame is essentially the same as that of its roadster predecessor. However, there are detail differences in the design of the wishbone suspension, this being used at the rear in place of the M10's radius arms. The driving compartment contains no-frills, light, padded bucket seats reflecting a minimalist design approach adopted to keep weight down.

The M12 is, in truth, a track car that has been tamed for road use. For more serious track use there is the even more extreme M400, so-called because its power to weight ratio is 400bhp/tonne. Now Noble's range is expanding in a different direction, with the M14 announced in 2004. More upmarket, more convenient and with a higher-quality interior the M14 takes Noble into a new market where it challenges the best that Porsche and Ferrari have to offer.

Above: The Noble manages to combine a distinctive, thoroughly professionally executed body with an outstanding chassis.

Left: Bucket seats with a minimum of padding are fitted together with two racing harnesses. However, conventional seat belts are available as well.

Specification	Noble M12 GTO
Engine location	Mid, transverse
Configuration	Twin turbocharged V6
Bore and stroke	82 x 79mm
Capacity	2595cc
Valve operation	Twin overhead camshafts per cylinder bank
Horsepower	310bhp @ 6000rpm
Transmission	Manual five-speed
Drive	Rear
Chassis	Space-frame
Suspension – front	Wishbones and coil spring
Suspension – rear	Wishbones and coil spring
Brakes	Ventilated disc
Top speed	155mph (249km/h)*
Acceleration	0-60mph (96km/h): 3.9 seconds*
	* Manufacturer's claim

Chevrolet Corvette Z06

**Top speed
171mph**
275km/h

Right: The Z06 name is inspired by a special Corvette Sting Ray of the 1960s although the hp figure refers to the higher American SAE rating.

Below: Based on the Corvette Hardtop, the Z06's styling changes include new 10-spoke alloy wheels, air vents behind the front wheels and mesh-covered frontal air intakes.

One hundred miles an hour (161km/h) from standstill in less than a tyre-scorching 10 seconds is just one of the attributes of the Z06, the latest version of the legendary Corvette, which was unveiled in 2000.

It was named in memory of the 1962 racing Sting Ray coupé, of which only 199 examples were built. But this latter-day version is rather more plentiful and will account for about 20 per cent of Corvette production. With annual output running at some 33,000 cars, that's the equivalent of about 6500 examples per year.

The current Corvette shape appeared in 1997 and it is the fifth generation of a line that began back in 1953. It had a glass-fibre body, just like the original, and a full length perimeter seamless tubular chassis lurked beneath those distinctive and aerodynamically refined contours, which accounted for an impressive 0.29 drag coefficient. A notable feature was the fact that the all-independent suspension was available with an active option.

Coupé and convertible models

Power was provided by a new LS1 all-alloy 345cid (5.7-litre) V8 which developed 345bhp and drove through a six-speed manual gearbox. Produced in coupé and convertible forms, these were joined for the 1999 season by a hardtop with detachable lift-out roof panels. It is this latter version, which is lighter than the coupé, that forms the basis of the Z06. Outwardly similar to the mainstream 'Vette, it can be identified by new ten-spoked alloy wheels and discreet air intakes introduced in the front spoiler and ahead of the rear wheels.

Left: This Corvette's lines are not interrupted by bumpers. The air vents in the rear apron are another feature peculiar to the Z06. The Eagle F1 tyres are specially developed by Goodyear, the wheels being one inch (25mm) wider than the originals.

Below: The new wheels with their forged alloy rims display the all-round ventilated discs to good effect; brakes are activated by a Bosch anti-lock system. The Corvette's petrol tank can hold 15 gallons (68lit) of fuel.

However, the real changes were to be found beneath the bonnet with the revised LS6 V8 now producing 385bhp. Improvements to harness the extra horses included high compression cylinder heads, redesigned inlet manifolding for better breathing, a 'hotter' camshaft and less restrictive titanium exhaust system.

Active-handling system

The already rigid suspension was also uprated with a new tauter rear springs; transverse front and rear, they are made from a composite material. The real secret of the Z06's roadholding is General Motors' second-generation active-handling system. Subtle and ingenious, its most significant feature is that it senses possible trouble ahead and the fuel supply and Bosch anti-lock disc brakes are unobtrusively trimmed accordingly. The driver, benefiting from supportive and distinctive red and black seats, will probably be unaware of its intervention!

Sure-footed, fast – it's capable of 171mph (275km/h) – and an uncompromising sports car, the Z06 is the latest manifestation of a line which, nearly 50 years on, shows itself to be as vibrant as ever.

Specification	Chevrolet Corvette Z06
Engine location	Front, in-line
Configuration	V8
Bore and stroke	3.9 x 3.6in (99 x 92mm)
Capacity	345cid (5654cc)
Valve operation	Pushrod
Horsepower	385bhp @ 6000rpm
Transmission	Manual six-speed
Drive	Rear
Chassis	Tubular steel
Suspension – front	Wishbones and transverse leaf spring
Suspension – rear	Wishbones and transverse leaf spring
Brakes	Ventilated discs
Top speed	171mph (275km/h)
Acceleration	0-60mph (0-96km/h): 4 seconds

Renault sport Clio V6

**Top speed
145mph**
233km/h

*Right: Perhaps surprisingly,
the interior is standard Clio
although air conditioning
and a CD changer are
available at extra cost. It is,
of course, only a two-seater.*

*Below: Not only does the
deep front spoiler with its
enlarged air intakes
indicate something special,
the mid-located air intakes
reveal the presence of a
V6 engine.*

The Clio supermini of 1990 was Renault's
big seller of the decade – the sport is a
low-production second-generation
145mph (233km/h) car for the discriminating
enthusiast who craves impressive performance and
outstanding handling. In truth Renault has revived
the concept of the 5 Turbo of 1983 and, like its
predecessor, this hot Clio's V6 engine occupies the
space usually reserved for the rear passengers!

This is a project that originated as a concept car
which Renault unveiled at the 1998 Paris Motor
Show. After two years of development in
conjunction with the British specialist engineering
group TWR, the Clio V6 appeared at the start of
the 2001 season. The price was a competitive
£25,995.

The build process was protracted. In France
Renault sport (the lower-case 's' is Renault's
choice) took delivery of 3-litre V6 engines used in
the top-line version of the Laguna saloon. It then
reworked the engines with new pistons, a raised
compression ratio, improvements to the inlet ports

and a new exhaust system. The result was a 20bhp
increase in power, up to 230bhp. The engines and
standard bodies were then shipped to TWR's
Uddevalla plant in Sweden, where the necessary
modifications were made to the three-door
hatchback hulls and the cars were assembled at the
rate of 12 per day.

The V6 was mounted transversely behind the
front seats, driving the rear wheels through a bespoke
six-speed gearbox. The standard Clio's torsion

beam rear suspension was replaced with a multi-link layout, and the track was widened considerably at both ends – by 4.3in (110mm) at the front and 5.4in (138mm) at the rear. The wheelbase is also slightly longer, by 1.2in (30mm) and the Clio V6 sits 2.6in (66mm) closer to the ground. With its wide tracks, low stance and mid-mounted engine the Clio generated massive grip in corners, though it could be difficult to handle at the limit.

That problem was addressed in a second-generation Clio V6, which had revised suspension together with improvements to the brakes and a more inviting interior. More power was on tap, too, as the V6 had been reworked again to develop 255bhp. Production of the revised car began at Renault sport's Dieppe factory in 2004, but manufacturing was not to last long: the final cars were delivered in 2005.

By then a new mainstream Clio hatchback was on sale, though Renault sport said it had no plans to drop a V6 into the back. But it will not be too long before we see more fast cars from Dieppe.

Above: The Clio V6 generates massive grip, but can be tricky to handle on the limit.

Below left: The badging says it all and this is the world's only mid-engined hatchback. There's even a little luggage space.

Specification	**Renault** sport Clio V6
Engine location	Mid, transverse
Configuration	V6
Bore and stroke	87 x 82mm
Capacity	2946cc
Valve operation	Twin overhead camshaft per cylinder bank
Horsepower	230bhp @ 6000rpm
Transmission	Manual six-speed
Drive	Rear
Chassis	Unitary
Suspension – front	MacPherson strut
Suspension – rear	Multi link and coil spring
Brakes	Ventilated disc
Top speed	145mph (233km/h)
Acceleration	0-60mph (96km/h): 6.7 seconds

Ferrari 550 Barchetta Pininfarina

**Top speed
186mph**
299km/h

*Right: While the instrument
panel is related to the 550
Maranello, the Barchetta's
seats are new and are
leather-trimmed carbon
fibre. Competition-inclined
owners can have a racing
harness fitted.*

*Below: The Barchetta's
nose is also 550-based, and
the presence of an air
intake is a reminder that
this is a front-engined V12
Ferrari. The wheels are
split-rim alloys.*

Ferrari built a mere 448 examples of the
550 Barchetta Pininfarina, the open
version of its 550 flagship coupé unveiled
at the 2000 Paris Motor Show. Produced to
commemorate the 70th anniversary of the creation
of the famous Turin-based styling and
coachbuilding establishment, it was priced at
£172,000; wealthy collectors were said to be
offering £30,000 above this asking price, even for
second-hand examples.

After 23 years of producing mid-engined
supercars, in 1996 Ferrari unveiled the 550
Maranello coupé with a front-located 485bhp 5.4-
litre V12 engine. Capable of 199mph (320km/h), it
is no surprise to find that it consumed petrol at a
rate of 7.9mpg (35.5 litres/100km) for town
driving, a figure that soared to around 18mpg (15.6
litres/100km) on long runs!

Originally the 550 was fitted with a six-speed
manual gearbox which operated through the
traditional Ferrari visible gate. However, from the
1998 season it became available with a Selespeed

automatic box which dispensed with the
conventional clutch pedal. Borrowing technology
from Ferrari's Formula 1 cars, gear changes were
effected by two paddles mounted just behind the
steering wheel rim.

Cloaked in a magnificently proportioned but
understated Pininfarina body, this uncompromising
two-seater boasted Ferrari's traditional tubular steel
chassis, all-independent suspension and
sophisticated ASR traction control.

After four years production, the coupé was joined in 2000 by the celebratory open-topped version. It was named the Barchetta in memory of Ferrari's first production car, the delectable Touring-bodied 166 open two-seater of 1948. Even more significantly it celebrated Pininfarina's foundation in 1930. First associated with Ferrari in 1952, and exclusively so since 1955, it is a partnership that continues to amaze and delight the motoring world.

No-frills barchetta concept

With a windscreen reduced by 3.9in (100mm) in height, the open 550 remains true to the no-frills barchetta concept by dispensing with a hood although a rudimentary cover is provided to protect the car's occupants in the event of sudden rain.

Twin roll-over bars feature at the rear with their contours echoed in the twin humped boot lid. Inside there are new carbon-fibre leather trimmed seats, with lucky customers being able to specify their own exterior colour and interior trim.

Although weighing about the same as the coupé (the lack of roof is offset by a reinforced body substructure), the Barchetta is slightly slower flat out than its stablemate, on account of the closed car's superior aerodynamics. It is thus capable of a mere 186mph (299km/)!

Below: Classic lines: by the nature of its body, the Barchetta's windscreen is considerably shallower than that fitted to the 550M coupé.

Bottom left: Note that the retro-style twin fairings moulded into the boot cover echo the double roll-over hoops. The model comes complete with a rudimentary hood.

Specification	Ferrari 550 Barchetta Pininfarina
Engine location	Front, in-line
Configuration	V12
Bore and stroke	88 x 75mm
Capacity	5474cc
Valve operation	Twin overhead camshafts per bank
Horsepower	485bhp @ 7000rpm
Transmission	Automatic
Drive	Rear
Chassis	Tubular steel
Suspension – front	Wishbones and coil spring
Suspension – rear	Wishbones and coil spring
Brakes	Ventilated disc
Top speed	186mph (299km/h)
Acceleration	0-60mph (0-96km/h): 4.6 seconds

Spyker C8 Spyder

**Top speed
187mph**
300km/h

*Below: The Dutch Spyker
marque was revived in 2000
with the C8. The car was
built using an aluminium
space frame, and powered
by a 4.2-litre Audi V8 engine.*

Spyker was a respected Dutch marque in the 1920s, selling expensive, quality cars to a rich clientele. Sadly its customers proved to be too rare a breed and the last of those early cars was built in 1925. But the name lived on.

The Spyker marque was revived in 2000 by Dutch engineer Maarten de Bruijn and entrepreneur Victor Muller. The cars that the new company would build were to be craftsman-built sports cars which have proved to be amongst the fastest cars ever made.

The new company's first model was the C8 Spyder, unveiled at the Birmingham International Motor Show in 2000. This lightweight roadster was based on an aluminium space frame chassis which was so stiff there was no need for a full windscreen frame to add to the car's strength, and the resulting 'frameless' screen enhanced the open-air feel of the C8's cabin. Inside fine leather trim and aluminium detailing combined to create a welcoming environment. Between the seats sat an exposed, polished, gear linkage which controlled a six-speed Getrag manual transmission. Power came from a 4.2-litre all-alloy V8 engine from Audi, which propelled the Spyker to a claimed maximum of 187mph (300km/h).

Spyker's range then expanded to include the C8 Laviolette, a fixed-roof version of the C8 with a glass roof panel, and in 2002 the company unveiled the C8 Double 12 R, which had been developed for GT racing, and released a road-going version of the racer called the Double 12 S. The Double 12

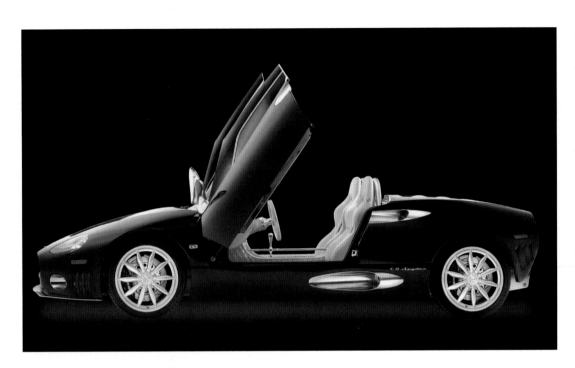

Left: The Spyker's doors open upwards and forwards. Note the exposed gearchange rod in the cabin.

Below left: An ornate interior includes retro-styled instruments and an 'engine-turned' dash panel.

Below: With nearly 400bhp available from its mid-mounted V8 engine, the Spyker C8 can exceed 180mph (290km/h). Twin-turbo V8 and W12 cars are also available.

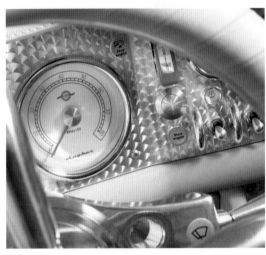

chassis was wider and longer to allow the engine to be positioned lower, and wheel arch extensions were riveted to the aluminium body panels to cater for wider racing tyres. The car was available with a racing-type dog-engagement gearbox and, on the racing R version, chassis-mounted air jacks.

The latest developments from Spyker are a pair of even faster cars. The C8 Spyder T is powered by a Cosworth Technology-developed twin-turbo version of the Audi V8 engine with 525bhp on tap, and is said to reach a top speed of 200mph (322km/h). The C12 LaTurbie is normally aspirated, but swaps the 4.2-litre Audi V8 for a 6.0-litre Audi W12 engine with 500bhp. Spyker hope to begin production of the C12 late in 2006.

Specification	Spyker C8 Spyder
Engine location	Front, in-line
Configuration	In-line six
Bore and stroke	84.5 x 93.0 mm
Capacity	4172cc
Valve operation	Twin overhead camshafts per bank
Horsepower	394bhp @ 6500rpm
Transmission	Six-speed manual
Drive	Rear
Chassis	Aluminium space frame
Suspension – front	Double wishbone with coil springs
Suspension – rear	Double wishbone with coil springs
Brakes	Ventilated disc
Top speed	187mph (300km/h)
Acceleration	0-62mph (100km/h): 4.5 seconds

2001 onwards
Bugatti Poised to Conquer

McLaren's reign as the world's fastest car is finally over. First Koenigsegg and now Bugatti have built even faster machines, the latter with a projected top speed in excess of 250mph (402km/h).
Volkswagen now owns three top marques – Bugatti, Lamborghini and Bentley – which can challenge the fastest and most exciting cars available anywhere in the world.
Add to this a resurgent Aston Martin, with its Vanquish, DB9 and V8 Vantage, Porsche's awesome Carrera GT and revitalised 911, and Mercedes-Benz's latest collaboration with its F1 partner McLaren, the SLR, and there has never been a more exciting time in the history of the fast car.

Porsche GT2

**Top speed
196mph**
315km/h

*Right: The GT2's interior
is functional and devoid of
such weighty items as air
conditioning and electric
windows. The seats are
comfortable and the driving
position is excellent.*

*Below: The spoilered rear
reveals that this is a far
from ordinary 911, with a
large air intake for the 3.6-
litre flat-six engine and rear
outlets for the heat
generated by the adjacent
ceramic discs.*

Capable of 196mph (315km/h), the twin-
turbocharged 911 GT2 was the fastest
road car Porsche had ever built when it
was launched in 2001, at the Detroit show. It was
faster flat out than even its extraordinarily rapid
four-wheel drive Turbo stablemate. The GT2
combined the lightweight, rear-wheel-drive chassis
of the Porsche's no-frills, competition-honed,
limited edition GT3 road car of 1999 with the latest
water-cooled 3.6-litre 911 Turbo engine, plus an
extra 36bhp.

At 3175lb (1440kg), the GT2 weighed a
significant 485lb (220kg) less than the current
Turbo. While the absence of four-wheel drive
accounted for some of this weight-saving, it also
reflected the rear seats, the electric activation of the
front ones and an air conditioning system all being
removed. This figure included a 35lb (16kg) saving
from an unexpected quarter because the GT2 is the
first production car to be fitted with race-bred
carbon ceramic brakes. They had the virtue of not
only improving the coupé's stopping power, but
also its steering.

Instantly identifiable

Outwardly the GT2 was modified to improve brake
cooling and engine ventilation. It is instantly
identifiable by the substantial air intakes incorporated
in the front spoiler to cool the 13.8in (350mm)
discs – the ducts mounted ahead of each rear wheel
arch perform the same function. Greater downforce
is provided by a fixed rear spoiler. It also sits 0.7in
(20mm) lower than the standard cars and uses
wider tyres on larger 18in (457mm) alloy rims.

Although designed with competition in mind,

the GT2 is a practical road car, although, as one overtakes you, any doubts about its identity will be banished by the presence of the name modestly adorning the back of the engine cover.

Power increase

Beneath the engine cover is the horizontally opposed

six-cylinder GT3-based power unit with four valves per cylinder. It develops 456bhp rather than the Turbo's 420, a power increase principally achieved by increasing the boost pressure developed by the twin KKK K64 turbochargers. In addition, titanium connecting rods were fitted to permit the engine speed to soar to an impressive 7900rpm.

For 2004 the 911 GT2 was uprated with still more power – 483bhp – thanks to higher boost pressure and more efficient intercoolers. The GT2, along with the GT3, Carrera 4 and Turbo models, remained in production even after the new two-wheel drive 997-series 911s came along for 2005, but it surely will not be long before a new generation of ultra-high performance turbocharged 911s is unleashed.

Above: The GT2 rides lower than the mainstream 911 with new wheels and tyres added to cope with the great increase in power. Further weight has been saved by not retaining the Turbo 911's four-wheel drive; only the GT2's rear wheels are driven. Created with track use in mind, just 300 examples were completed during 2001.

Specification	**Porsche** 911 GT2
Engine location	Rear, in-line
Configuration	Twin turbocharged horizontally opposed six-cylinder
Bore and stroke	100 x 76mm
Capacity	3600cc
Valve operation	Twin overhead camshafts per bank
Horsepower	456bhp @ 5700rpm
Transmission	Manual six-speed
Drive	Rear
Chassis	Unitary
Suspension – front	McPherson strut and coil spring
Suspension – rear	Multi link and coil spring
Brakes	Ceramic disc
Top speed	196mph (315km/h)
Acceleration	0-60mph (0-96km/h): 4.1 seconds

Aston Martin Vanquish

**Top speed
196mph**
315km/h

*Right: The cockpit
perpetuates many of the
themes displayed in Project
Vantage. Gear changes are
effected by using racing-
style paddles behind the
steering wheel.*

*Below: Immensely
impressive, the Vanquish
represents a formidable
British challenger to
Ferrari. Handling has won
much praise.*

When, in 1997, stylist Ian Callum began
work on the design of what was to
become the Vanquish, he took a backward
look as well as casting his eyes forward. As a result
the company's new V12-engined coupé of 2001 is
visually related to the legendary DB4 GT Zagato of
1960 vintage.

Born of a desire by Ford's DB4-owning
president, Jac Nasser, to elevate Aston Martin,
which Ford has owned since 1987, to the status
Ferrari enjoys in Italy, this important corporate
project is also intended as a showcase for the
technological advances being made by the parent
company. There is no shortage of them!

Project Vantage concept car

As a first step Nasser sanctioned the Project
Vantage concept car which was launched at the
1998 Detroit Motor Show. And for all its retro
elements, beneath the coupé's gleaming green-

painted aluminium panels was a state-of-the-art
chassis. Receiving a rapturous reception from the
public, Ford accordingly gave the project the green
light and the result, some three years later, was the
beautifully built Vanquish.

Unveiled at the 2001 Geneva Motor Show, the
£158,000 model is outwardly almost identical to

the 1998 concept car although it is narrower by a mere 5.9in (151mm). The more obvious changes have taken place inside where detail alterations have been made to the dashboard, seats and controls. And there isn't a trace of wood veneer to be seen, just burnished aluminium. Available in a choice of styles, the Vanquish comes as an uncompromising two-seater or as a rather cramped two-plus-two.

The Vanquish was built like no Aston before it. A strong carbon-fibre transmission tunnel was bonded and riveted to extruded aluminium members which formed the front and rear bulkheads. The engine, steering and front suspension were mounted on a subframe constructed from carbon fibre, steel and aluminium, and bolted to the front bulkhead. Ahead of this subframe sat a deformable composite crash structure. The outer panels were made using a new process called 'Superforming', but were still finished and fitted by Aston's skilled craftsmen.

Under the bonnet was a 5.9-litre V12 engine, with twin overhead camshafts per bank and four valves per cylinder, which was first seen as a mock-up at the Turin show in 1994, and then powered the Ford Indigo show car of 1996. In 1999 it went into the DB7 Vantage in 420bhp guise, but for the Vanquish it was revised and uprated to produce 460bhp and driven through a six-speed semi-automatic gearbox. The Vanquish could achieve a top speed of 196mph (315km/h) and sprint from rest to 60mph (96km/h) in 4.8 seconds.

An even quicker Vanquish S was announced in 2004. Further development boosted the V12 engine

to 520bhp, and pushed the top speed beyond 200mph (320km/h). The suspension, steering and aerodynamics all came in for subtle reworking on this, the fastest production Aston ever built.

Above: Vanquish hides a sophisticated aluminium and composite structure under its aluminium skin. The car is assembled by hand at Aston Martin's Newport Pagnell factory.

Left: The alloy V12 has been hailed as one of the outstanding aspects of the new Aston Martin Vanquish's specification. An underbonnet plate reveals the name of the individual who built this complex unit.

Specification	**Aston Martin** Vanquish
Engine location	Front, in-line
Configuration	V12
Bore and stroke	89 x 79mm
Capacity	5935cc
Valve operation	Twin overhead camshafts per bank
Horsepower	460bhp @ 6500rpm
Transmission	Manual six-speed
Drive	Rear
Chassis	Aluminium/carbon-fibre monocoque
Suspension – front	Wishbones and coil spring
Suspension – rear	Wishbones and coil spring
Brakes	Ventilated disc
Top speed	196mph (315km/h)
Acceleration	0-60mph (0-96km/h): 4.8 seconds

Lamborghini Murcielago

Top speed 205mph*
330km/h
*Claimed by manufacturer

Right: Evolution rather than revolution – the visual relationship between the wedged-shaped Murcielago and its Diablo predecessor is very apparent.

Below: Scissor doors, a familiar Lamborghini feature that reach back to the Countach and were continued in the Diablo.

It has been hailed as the best designed and built Lamborghini for years, even if the Murcielago name is nothing like as memorable as Miura or Countach! Capable of 205mph (330km/h), this magnificent four-wheel-drive coupé for 2002 will, thanks to the investment of its Volkswagen owner, re-establish Lamborghini as a front-line supercar manufacturer.

In truth this Diablo replacement has been a long time a-coming, work on the project, coded L147, having begun in 1995 when Lamborghini was owned by the Indonesian consortium which had acquired it from Chrysler in 1993. In 1995 the long-running V12 engine had a capacity of 5.7 litres. The intention was to increase this to 6 litres to power the Diablo GT of 2000 before the powerplant was extended to the standard car and then to its successor.

The latter was to be called the Canto and in 1996 Lamborghini commissioned styling house Zagato to body four prototypes. The Milan company addressed the important matter of engine cooling by introducing two pronounced pod-like air scoops into the rear wings.

Acquired by Volkswagen

Although corporate reservations regarding the design centred on fears that it would date too quickly, cash shortages meant that Lamborghini was stuck with it. That was until July of 1998 when the company was acquired by Volkswagen, which allocated the business to its Audi subsidiary – the performance arm of the VW empire.

Audi wasted little time in commissioning, in the early spring of 1999, a new design from Bertone which, in the person of its stylist Marcello Gandini, had been responsible for the celebrated lines of the Miura and Countach. Further initiatives were canvassed from Italian stylist IDEA and the French Heuliez concern.

With work underway on the body, Lamborghini's engineering director Massimo Ceccarani, now with greater funding available, recognized that the new model would be greatly enhanced by a more powerful engine. In mid 2000 the V12 was experimentally and reliably enlarged to 6.2 litres by lengthening the stroke from 84 to 86mm. The revised unit produced 571bhp at 7500rpm, an increase of 29bhp over the 6-litre.

But Volkswagen was still dissatisfied with the appearance of the new car. It therefore turned to one of its own in-house stylists for his ideas regarding the design of what had to be one of the most prestigious cars in the motoring world. Belgian designer Luc Donckerwolke had previously been responsible for the exterior lines of the Audi 2 saloon and had also undertaken work for sister company Skoda.

Above: The Murcielago is extraordinarily wide, measuring 80.3in (2040mm), or 0.2in (5mm) more if the retractable exterior wing mirrors are extended. The tyres are Pirelli's new P-Zero Rosso covers.

Specification	Lamborghini Murcielago
Engine location	Mid, longitudinal
Configuration	V12
Bore and stroke	87 x 86mm
Capacity	6192cc
Valve operation	Twin overhead camshafts per cylinder bank
Horsepower	571bhp @ 7500rpm
Transmission	Manual six-speed
Drive	Rear
Chassis	Steel space-frame
Suspension – front	Wishbones and coil spring
Suspension – rear	Wishbones and coil spring
Brakes	Ventilated disc
Top speed	205mph (330km/h)*
Acceleration	0-60mph (96km/h): 3.8 seconds*

* Manufacturer's claim

Porsche Carrera GT

Top speed 205mph*
330km/h
Claimed by manufacturer

Below: The mouth-watering Carrera GT, launched to the public at the 2000 Paris Motor Show. Porsche was heartened by the wholly positive worldwide response to the new car, although the announcement to proceed with the design was not finally made until more than a year later, at the 2002 Detroit show. Production began late in 2003.

Porsche's Carrera GT, announced in production form in 2003, is powered by a 605bhp V10 engine, which makes it the fastest road car the Stuttgart company has ever built. It bristles with features, acting as a showcase for Porsche's formidable competence in the fields of automobile design and technology.

The starting point for this state-of-the-art Porsche is a racer that the company withdrew from the 2000 Le Mans race and mothballed. But the engineering behind the race car would not go to waste: its carbon-fibre monocoque hull was to form the basis of the Carrera GT road car. Although the engine is located at the rear in 911 fashion, the Carrera GT bears no visual relationship to the current 911. Instead the company's California-based design studio, which created its impressive aerodynamically honed lines, drew on the body shape of Porsche's 718RS Spyder racing car of 1961 vintage for inspiration.

Targa top

While the car unveiled at the model's Paris launch was a roadster, the production Carrera GT features a more practical detachable Targa-style roof panel. And after over 50 years of producing horizontally opposed rear-mounted engines, the company is opting for a V10 to power the new car. Based on the unit developed for its aborted 2000 Le Mans sortie, this alloy 68 degree 5.5-litre engine is fitted with robust race-proven connecting rods so that it can rev to beyond 8000rpm. Attached directly to the monocoque hull, this compact engine drives the rear wheels courtesy of a racing-type three-plate clutch and six-speed gearbox.

Suspension has an impeccable pedigree, being also race-proven and is based on Porsche's GT1 that won Le Mans in 1998. It uses conventional wishbones at the front while rose-jointed wishbones are employed at the rear and they operate in conjunction with coil springs and pushrods.

Porsche claim a 0-60mph (96kmh) acceleration time of 3.8 seconds, and 0-124mph (200km/h) in 9.9 seconds. The Carrera GT has a top speed of 205mph (330km/h).

The new car's inviting interior does without some of the excesses of the original Carrera GT show car, including its digital instrumentation. Unusually in a car full of high-tech composites, the gearknob is wooden – a tribute to the Le Mans-winning 917, which was given a balsa wood gearknob as a last-minute weight-saving measure!

Production of the Carrera GT is based at Porsche's new Leipzig factory, which also builds the luxurious (and rapid) Cayenne SUV. Though several new Porsche models are expected in the next few years, for now and probably for quite some time to come, this is undoubtedly the ultimate Porsche.

Above: The mid-located V10 engine is a 68 degree unit and is a remarkably compact one, being only 22.4in (570mm) long.

Left: The Carrera GT concept car's cabin was toned down before production.

Below left: The concept car's rear deck. The production Carrera GT has a Targa-type removable roof panel.

Specification	Porsche Carrera GT
Engine location	Mid, in-line
Configuration	V10
Bore and stroke	N/A
Capacity	5.5 litres
Valve operation	Twin overhead camshafts per cylinder bank
Horsepower	605bhp @ 8000rpm
Transmission	Manual six-speed
Drive	Rear
Chassis	Monocoque
Suspension – front	Wishbones and coil spring
Suspension – rear	Wishbones, coil spring and pushrod
Brakes	Ventilated disc
Top speed	205mph (330km/h)*
Acceleration	0-60mph (96 km/h): sub-4 seconds*

* Manufacturer's claim

Mercedes-Benz SLR McLaren

Top speed 207mph*
334km/h
*Claimed by manufacturer

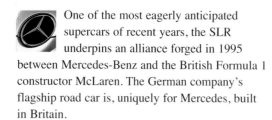

One of the most eagerly anticipated supercars of recent years, the SLR underpins an alliance forged in 1995 between Mercedes-Benz and the British Formula 1 constructor McLaren. The German company's flagship road car is, uniquely for Mercedes, built in Britain.

Its forerunner, the SLR concept car, made its memorable debut at the 1999 Detroit Motor Show. With overall design responsibility vested in Gordon Murray, creator of the McLaren F1, the appropriately named Vision SLR was an alluring two-seater silver coupé and one of the undisputed stars of the event. And, unlike many concepts, this vehicle was a runner which retained Mercedes-Benz's long-established and conventional front engine/rear drive configuration.

Based on the chassis of the impending SL convertible which appeared for the 2002 season, the Vision SLR's aluminium and carbon-fibre body was awesome, innovative but indisputably Mercedes-Benz. Stylistically it was the work of Franz Lezher, who had previously been responsible for the lines of a diametrically opposed Mercedes concept: a quirky F300 three-wheeler that appeared at the 1997 Frankfurt Motor Show.

This SLR incorporates visual elements from the McLaren-Mercedes MP4/13 Formula 1 racer along with design cues from the SL coupé of 1954. The upward-opening doors are a distinctive feature, although they are not of the gull-wing type that featured on the legendary 300SL of the 1950s.

Above: The Vision SLR's cabin featured simple instrumentation and an unusual oval steering wheel. Alcantara and aluminium dominated. The console incorporated a colour navigation screen.

Right: The Vision SLR gave a good indication of the production car's shape, though there were many detail differences including the operation of the doors.

A year after the Vision SLR study appeared, DaimlerChrysler announced that the production SLR would look a little different. The production SLR, unveiled in 2003, was broadly similar to the concept but had many detail differences, including doors which now pivoted on the windscreen pillars so they opened upwards and outwards.

Carbon construction

Under the skin the SLR was constructed using F1-style carbon structures, including the first example of a carbon-fibre crumple zone at the front of the car. It was powered by a 5.4-litre V8 engine with just a single overhead camshaft on each bank of cylinders, and three valves per cylinder. Twin superchargers helped to boost the V8's output to 626bhp, which provided a top speed of 207mph (334km/h) and a 0-62mph (100km/h) acceleration time of 3.8 seconds. The job of hauling down the speed fell to an electrohydraulic 'brake by wire' system, using carbon-ceramic brake discs. A computer-controlled air brake flap was also deployed during heavy braking from high speeds.

The McLaren-built SLR managed to evoke memories of the fabulous Gullwing Mercedes SL road and racing cars of the 1950s, but at the same time it introduced advanced new technology – some of which would filter down to other Mercedes road cars in due course. It was a truly remarkable fast car.

Specification	**Mercedes-Benz** SLR McLaren
Engine location	Front, in-line
Configuration	Twin-supercharged V8
Bore and stroke	97 x 92mm
Capacity	5439cc
Valve operation	Single overhead camshaft per cylinder bank
Horsepower	626bhp @ 6500rpm
Transmission	Five-speed automatic
Drive	Rear
Chassis	Carbon-fibre monocoque
Suspension – front	Double wishbone and coil spring
Suspension – rear	Multi-link coil spring
Brakes	Ventilated disc
Top speed	207mph (334km/h)*
Acceleration	0-62mph (100km/h): 3.8 seconds*

* Manufacturer's claim

Left: The new 5.5-litre supercharged V8 engine develops 557bhp although it uses single- rather than the usual twin-overhead camshafts.

Below: The Vision, Mercedes-Benz's flagship coupé, is awash with retro-themes, while also looking remarkably modern.

Ferrari Enzo and Fxx

**Top speed
220mph**
354km/h

The day after Ferrari secured its fourth consecutive F1 Constructor's World Championship crown, it announced its fastest ever road-going car. Mid-engined, packing a 660bhp punch and incorporating innovative new braking and electronics systems, the new machine was to be named after the founder of the company, Enzo Ferrari.

The chassis of the new car was an immensely strong and rigid structure built from carbon fibre

and aluminium honeycomb, weighing a featherweight 92kg, clothed in composite body panels. Careful shaping of the bodywork and automatic control of twin front flaps ensured that the Enzo's aerodynamic balance was retained under all circumstances. Ground effects were utilised to create downforce without the need for a large inverted wing at the back of the car.

A new V12 engine powered the Enzo, an ultra-light 6.0-litre unit boasting variable inlet and exhaust valve timing and a drive-by-wire throttle control system. The motor was coupled to a six-speed gearbox with electro-hydraulic change, operated by the driver from paddles behind the steering wheel – just like in an F1 Ferrari. The driver could choose from 'Sport', 'Race' and 'Super' gearchange modes, the latter cutting gearchange times by 50 per cent, to just 150 milliseconds. These settings also changed the point at which the traction control system intervened.

Right: The Enzo and Fxx were powered by a new V12 engine, 6.0-litres and 660bhp in the Enzo, 6.3-litres and 800bhp in the Fxx. The engines were coupled to six-speed gearboxes with paddle shift.

Below: The nose of the Enzo and Fxx was inspired by the design of modern Formula 1 cars, with a prominent central snout and horizontal air intakes which echoed the front wing of the F1 car.

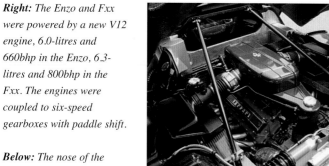

A year after the Vision SLR study appeared, DaimlerChrysler announced that the production SLR would look a little different. The production SLR, unveiled in 2003, was broadly similar to the concept but had many detail differences, including doors which now pivoted on the windscreen pillars so they opened upwards and outwards.

Carbon construction

Under the skin the SLR was constructed using F1-style carbon structures, including the first example of a carbon-fibre crumple zone at the front of the car. It was powered by a 5.4-litre V8 engine with just a single overhead camshaft on each bank of cylinders, and three valves per cylinder. Twin superchargers helped to boost the V8's output to 626bhp, which provided a top speed of 207mph (334km/h) and a 0-62mph (100km/h) acceleration time of 3.8 seconds. The job of hauling down the speed fell to an electrohydraulic 'brake by wire' system, using carbon-ceramic brake discs. A computer-controlled air brake flap was also deployed during heavy braking from high speeds.

The McLaren-built SLR managed to evoke memories of the fabulous Gullwing Mercedes SL road and racing cars of the 1950s, but at the same time it introduced advanced new technology – some of which would filter down to other Mercedes road cars in due course. It was a truly remarkable fast car.

Specification	Mercedes-Benz SLR McLaren
Engine location	Front, in-line
Configuration	Twin-supercharged V8
Bore and stroke	97 x 92mm
Capacity	5439cc
Valve operation	Single overhead camshaft per cylinder bank
Horsepower	626bhp @ 6500rpm
Transmission	Five-speed automatic
Drive	Rear
Chassis	Carbon-fibre monocoque
Suspension – front	Double wishbone and coil spring
Suspension – rear	Multi-link coil spring
Brakes	Ventilated disc
Top speed	207mph (334km/h)*
Acceleration	0-62mph (100km/h): 3.8 seconds*

* Manufacturer's claim

Left: The new 5.5-litre supercharged V8 engine develops 557bhp although it uses single- rather than the usual twin-overhead camshafts.

Below: The Vision, Mercedes-Benz's flagship coupé, is awash with retro-themes, while also looking remarkably modern.

Ferrari Enzo and Fxx

**Top speed
220mph**
354km/h

The day after Ferrari secured its fourth consecutive F1 Constructor's World Championship crown, it announced its fastest ever road-going car. Mid-engined, packing a 660bhp punch and incorporating innovative new braking and electronics systems, the new machine was to be named after the founder of the company, Enzo Ferrari.

The chassis of the new car was an immensely strong and rigid structure built from carbon fibre

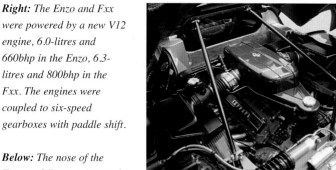

Right: The Enzo and Fxx were powered by a new V12 engine, 6.0-litres and 660bhp in the Enzo, 6.3-litres and 800bhp in the Fxx. The engines were coupled to six-speed gearboxes with paddle shift.

Below: The nose of the Enzo and Fxx was inspired by the design of modern Formula 1 cars, with a prominent central snout and horizontal air intakes which echoed the front wing of the F1 car.

and aluminium honeycomb, weighing a featherweight 92kg, clothed in composite body panels. Careful shaping of the bodywork and automatic control of twin front flaps ensured that the Enzo's aerodynamic balance was retained under all circumstances. Ground effects were utilised to create downforce without the need for a large inverted wing at the back of the car.

A new V12 engine powered the Enzo, an ultra-light 6.0-litre unit boasting variable inlet and exhaust valve timing and a drive-by-wire throttle control system. The motor was coupled to a six-speed gearbox with electro-hydraulic change, operated by the driver from paddles behind the steering wheel – just like in an F1 Ferrari. The driver could choose from 'Sport', 'Race' and 'Super' gearchange modes, the latter cutting gearchange times by 50 per cent, to just 150 milliseconds. These settings also changed the point at which the traction control system intervened.

The Enzo's electronic control systems for the engine, gearbox, suspension, anti-lock brakes, traction control and aerodynamics constantly shared information. During a gearchange, for instance, the gearbox subsystem managed the clutch, engine and suspension settings to give the fastest, smoothest gearchange while preventing the car from pitching.

Another innovation was the use of carbon-ceramic disc brakes, a first for a road car. The F1-style discs were lighter than steel discs, provided greater stopping power and were designed to last the life of the car.

Ferrari announced that 349 Enzos would be built for sale. But that wasn't quite the end of the story. The same basic design was adapted to become the Maserati MC12, and then in 2005 Ferrari announced a further run of 20 or so examples of a track-only derivative, the Fxx. Not intended for racing, the Fxx was instead designed for wealthy enthusiasts to enjoy in special non-competitive track events. It was even wilder than the Enzo, with revised high-downforce bodywork and a 6262cc V12 engine developing no less than 800bhp.

Above: Fxx was a track-only derivative of the Enzo. The bodywork was revised to improve downforce, and the engine was enlarged. Owners enjoyed them at exclusive non-competitive track events.

Left: Just as on a modern F1 car, the Enzo and Fxx carried many of its controls on the steering wheel – but even the track-orientated Fxx had space for a passenger.

Specification	Ferrari Enzo and Fxx
Engine location	Mid, in-line
Configuration	V12
Bore and stroke	92 x 75.2mm
Capacity	5999cc
Valve operation	Twin overhead camshaft per cylinder bank
Horsepower	660bhp @ 7800rpm
Transmission	Six-speed sequential semi-auto
Drive	Rear
Chassis	Carbon fibre and aluminium honeycomb monocoque
Suspension – front	Double wishbone and coil spring
Suspension – rear	Double wishbone and coil spring
Brakes	Carbon ceramic ventilated disc
Top speed	220mph (354km/h)
Acceleration	0-62mph (100km/h): 3.7 seconds

Bentley Continental GT

**Top speed
198mph**
319km/h

*Right: The Continental
GT's interior offers all the
sumptuous luxury expected
of the marque, with lashings
of traditional wood and
leather trim.*

*Below: The 6.0-litre W12-
engined Continental GT
offers the pace of a supercar
with the refinement and
comfort of an executive
saloon car.*

 Effortless, supercar-shredding pace is what the Bentley Continental GT is all about. Six turbocharged litres deliver more than 550bhp and a top speed that nudges towards 200mph (322km/h), but the Bentley is no highly-strung racing machine. While the driver and passengers recline in the sumptuous comfort of a limousine-like interior and with the engine barely turning above tickover, the Continental GT can surge into the distance in a manner few cars can match.

The source of all this impetuous is a 12 cylinder engine of 5998cc, based on Volkswagen's existing W12 engine from the Phaeton saloon. Where a conventional V12 has two banks of six in-line cylinders, the W12s cylinders are staggered – effectively each bank of cylinders is a narrow-angle V6. Staggering the cylinders in this way means that they can be mounted closer together on a shorter crankshaft, with the result that Volkswagen's W12 engine is the shortest 12-cylinder unit in production anywhere in the world.

The W12's 414bhp, though ample for an executive saloon, was less than adequate for the kind of performance the company had in mind. So the Bentley engineers turned to forced induction – a recurring theme in Bentley's history since 1928.

This latest 'Blower Bentley' was fitted with a pair of KKK turbochargers, which boosted the W12's maximum power output to 552bhp, and its peak torque, a not inconsiderable 479lb ft, was delivered at just 1600rpm. This monstrous urge was fed to a six-speed ZF automatic gearbox which could be controlled using a conventional selector lever, or gearchange paddles mounted behind the steering wheel. Drive was delivered to all four wheels.

Inside the Continental GT blended traditional trim materials with the latest technology – classic Bentley bullseye ventilation ducts with organ-stop controls, for instance, shared the wood-veneer dashboard with a multi-function LCD display. High-quality leather was swathed over the cabin, which had all the ambience and comfort to be expected from the company that built HM The Queen's State Limousine.

Bentley claimed, with some justification, that the Continental GT shared just the same core values as the cars W.O. Bentley had been building 80 years earlier. Certainly it proved that a glorious British marque founded in the early years of the 20th century was alive and kicking at the start of a new millennium.

Specification	Bentley Continental GT
Engine location	Front, in-line
Configuration	W12
Bore and stroke	84 x 90.2mm
Capacity	5998cc
Valve operation	Twin overhead camshaft per cylinder bank
Horsepower	552bhp @ 6100rpm
Transmission	Six-speed ZF automatic
Drive	Four-wheel drive
Chassis	Steel monocoque
Suspension – front	Double wishbone with air springs
Suspension – rear	Multi-link with air springs
Brakes	Ventilated disc
Top speed	198mph (319km/h)
Acceleration	0-62mph (100km/h): 4.8 seconds

Left: Bentleys of the 21st century reflect similar core values to those of the founder, W.O. Bentley, back in the 1920s. Effortless performance and quality manufacture are uppermost.

Left: Four-wheel drive and a sophisticated air suspension system gives the Continental GT road manners to match its awesome straight-line pace.

Ford GT

**Top speed
205mph**
330km/h

*Right: The GT is powered
by a supercharged V8 engine
developing 550bhp. Note
the extruded aluminium
members forming part of
the car's space frame.*

*Below: Back to the future –
the Ford GT evokes strong
memories of its racing
forebear, though the shapes
of the old car and the new
are subtly different – and
the new car is much bigger.*

Bill Ford unveiled the Ford GT concept at the North American International Motor Show in 2002, and just 45 days later Ford stunned the pundits by announcing that a production version was on the way. Forty years on from the original Ford GT40, a new car with the same stunning styling and electrifying performance was to go on sale.

Though the new GT looks much the same as the old, the two cars have surprisingly little in common. The 2004 GT is four inches (100mm) taller than the 1960s racer, and no less than 18in (457mm) longer, and it is constructed using an aluminium space frame which uses 35 extrusions, seven complex castings, two semi-solid formed castings and various stamped aluminium panels. Unlike the glass-fibre body panels of the original car the new GT's are superplastic-formed aluminium, and the underbody is shaped to cut the high-speed

rear-end lift which always bedevilled the 1960s GTs.

Suspension is by unequal-length double wishbones and coil-over damper units at all four corners, while huge braking forces are available

Left: The new GT is taller and longer than the original GT40, and constructed in a different way. In the 1960s the GT40's steel and glass fibre construction was state-of-the-art – the new GT uses a modern aluminium space frame, with aluminium external panels. The rear underbody is shaped to cut lift, a problem on the old car.

thanks to four-piston aluminium monoblock calipers from Brembo, acting on cross-drilled and vented brake discs which sit inside vast BBS alloy wheels with Goodyear Eagle F1 tyres.

V8 power

The GT is powered by a development of Ford's biggest modular V8, an all-aluminium 5.4-litre unit with a mouth-watering specification. Central to it is a massively strong forged steel crankshaft, acted on by forged aluminium alloy pistons and H-beam alloy conrods. Twin overhead camshafts on each cylinder bank operate four valves per cylinder, the intake valves controlling high-pressure air from an Eaton screw-type supercharger. The end result is a maximum of 550bhp at 6500rpm, making the GT one of the few road cars to exceed 100bhp per litre. Power is delivered to the rear wheels through a six-speed Ricardo transaxle which incorporates a helical limited-slip differential. Top speed is said to be 205mph (330km/h).

But the GT's performance is secondary to its looks. This is a supercar which draws a direct line to the world-beating race cars of the 1960s, and to emphasise that a Tungsten Grey limited edition model was released for 2006 to commemorate the 40th anniversary of Ford's famous 1-2-3 victory at Le Mans in 1966.

Left: The GT dashboard recalls the facia of the GT40, but the instruments and switchgear are all modern items. As on the original, the doors are cut into the roof to improve access.

Specification	Ford GT
Engine location	Mid, in-line
Configuration	V8
Bore and stroke	90.2 x 105.8mm
Capacity	5409cc
Valve operation	Twin overhead camshafts per bank
Horsepower	550bhp @ 6500rpm
Transmission	Six-speed manual transaxle
Drive	Rear
Chassis	Extruded aluminium spaceframe
Suspension – front	Double wishbone and coil spring
Suspension – rear	Double wishbone and coil spring
Brakes	Ventilated disc
Top speed	205mph (330km/h)
Acceleration	0-60mph (96km/h): 3.6 seconds

Aston Martin DB9

**Top speed
186mph**
300km/h

*Right: The DB9 is powered
by the latest development of
Aston Martin's 5.9-litre V12
engine, delivering up to
450bhp, coupled to a six-
speed manual or automatic
transmission.*

*Below: Elegant with the
roof up or down, the DB9
Volante provides wind-in-the-
hair motoring or the snug
comfort of a saloon car.*

With the launch of the DB9 late in 2003, Aston Martin marked a number of 'firsts'. This was the first Aston to be built entirely at the company's new purpose-built headquarters and factory complex at Gaydon in Warwickshire, and it was the first production Aston to utilise a new aluminium structure known as the 'VH' (for 'vertical/horizontal') platform, which would underpin all future Aston Martins.

The DB9's bold new shape was sharper and crisper than that of the DB7 it was replacing, in part reflecting the industry-wide trend away from the organic curves of the 1990s towards shapes with more structure and definition. The body incorporated what Aston called 'swan wing' doors, which rose at an angle as they were opened to avoid high kerbs. But the classic Aston styling cues such as the 'shouldered' grille shape and the vents in the wings were still very much in evidence. The DB9 was true to its heritage, but still looked sophisticated and modern.

The aluminium VH structure was built up from die-cast, extruded and stamped aluminium components, some of them fixed together using self-piercing rivets and others bonded with adhesive, which was applied by a robot – the only one at Aston Martin. The new structure made the DB9 body 25 per cent lighter than that of the outgoing DB7, while at the same time being twice as stiff.

Impressive torque

Powering the DB9 was a new development of the V12 engine seen in the DB7 Vantage and the Vanquish. New inlet and exhaust manifolds, camshafts, crankshaft and engine management boosted power to 450bhp, and ensured that 80 per cent of the impressive maximum torque of 420lb ft was available at just 1500rpm. The new version of the V12 was also 11.8kg (26lb) lighter than before. Two transmission choices were offered, a six-speed Graziano manual or a six-speed ZF automatic.

Inevitably the DB9 coupé was swiftly followed by a drophead Volante version, which was unveiled at the Detroit show early in 2004. Later that year Aston Martin revealed plans to enter international GT racing with a team run by Prodrive, using the DB9-based DBR9. In its first year the car won its class at Sebring and Silverstone, and finished third in its class at Le Mans. The DBR9 was joined in 2005 by the DBRS9, a club and national GT racing version.

The DB9 shows how Aston Martin has reinvented itself in the last decade. It is confident and forward-looking – and it makes some of the fastest and most exciting cars on the planet.

Above: Classic Aston Martin styling cues such as the distinctive grille shape are blended with a sharp modern style in the DB9. This is the Volante, revealed in 2004.

Left: The DB9's lines are clearly related to those of its big brother the Vanquish, and the V8 Vantage which was unveiled in 2005.

Specification	Aston Martin DB9
Engine location	Front, in-line
Configuration	V12
Bore and stroke	89 x 79mm
Capacity	5925cc
Valve operation	Twin overhead camshafts per bank
Horsepower	450bhp @ 6000rpm
Transmission	Six-speed manual or automatic
Drive	Rear
Chassis	Bonded aluminium monocoque
Suspension – front	Double wishbones and coil springs
Suspension – rear	Double wishbones and coil springs
Brakes	Ventilated disc
Top speed	186mph (300km/h)
Acceleration	0-60mph (96km/h): 4.7 seconds

Bristol Fighter

**Top speed
210mph**
338km/h

*Below: From the very
beginning Bristol's cars
have been shaped to
maximise aerodynamic
efficiency – hence the
Fighter's cabin narrows
towards the rear to
minimise drag. The 'gull-
wing' doors are a new
departure for Bristol.*

Never a company to slavishly follow automotive fashions, Bristol has travelled its own, individual road for more than five decades. While most of its expensive, hand-made cars have been elegant four-seater saloons, it has on occasion built fast two-seaters, and the Fighter is the latest in that line. This is Bristol's very individual interpretation of a supercar for the 21st century – a car which blends massive power and aerodynamic refinement to achieve a top speed well in excess of 200mph (322km/h).

Underpinned by a strong steel chassis structure with aluminium floors and bulkheads, the Fighter is skinned in hand-formed aluminium panels, with carbon-fibre doors and tailgate. The combination delivers strength, light weight and, importantly, the low centre of gravity essential for a high-performance car. The shape of the car has been designed with optimum aerodynamic efficiency in mind, with a compact frontal area and careful control of the air flow both over and under the car resulting in a low drag coefficient of 0.28.

Viper power

The 8-litre V10 engine powering the Fighter, developed from the unit fitted to the Dodge Viper, is positioned in front of the passenger cabin but behind the front wheels to improve weight distribution and handling. The all-aluminium engine produces 525bhp in standard form and 628bhp in 'S' specification – and Bristol are quick to point out that careful design of the intake system results in a supercharging effect at 200mph, increasing the engine's power output still further.

A six-speed close-ratio manual gearbox is fitted as standard, with sixth gear high enough to allow 100mph cruising with the big V10 spinning at just 2450rpm. At the other end of the scale, a tall first

Above: Unlike most Bristols down the years, the Fighter is a two-seater.

Far left: The Bristol's small frontal area improves aerodynamic efficiency.

Left: Power comes from a Chrysler V10 engine, which is reworked by Bristol.

gear allows the Fighter to reach 60mph from rest without a gearchange, in just four seconds.

Gull-wing doors provide access to an interior which offers no concessions to the car's extraordinary performance. In contrast to the cramped cabins of many supercars, the Bristol provides ample space for tall drivers, and the same high levels of trim and equipment which are found in Bristol's saloon cars.

Bristol's individual approach does not endear it to everyone, but there can be no denying the quality of the cars it produces. And there seems to be no shortage of wealthy enthusiasts prepared to spend £230,000 or more to own one of these magnificent machines.

Specification	**Bristol** Fighter
Engine location	Front, in-line
Configuration	V10
Bore and stroke	101.6 x 98.6mm
Capacity	7996cc
Valve operation	Twin overhead camshafts per bank
Horsepower	525bhp @ 5600rpm
Transmission	Six-speed manual or automatic
Drive	Rear
Chassis	Steel box section
Suspension – front	Double wishbones and coil springs
Suspension – rear	Double wishbones and coil springs
Brakes	Ventilated disc
Top speed	210mph (km/h)
Acceleration	0-60mph (96km/h): approximately 4.0 seconds

Ferrari 612 Scaglietti

**Top speed
199mph**
320km/h

*Below: The 612 Scaglietti
was the first V12 Ferrari
to use an aluminium space
frame construction. More
than 3500 hours of wind
tunnel work went
into refinining the
aerodynamics.*

Look back at the classic Ferraris and you
will find that many were styled by
Pininfarina, and many of those had their
bodies crafted by Sergio Scaglietti. Eventually
Scaglietti sold his business to Ferrari, and today the
sophisticated all-alloy structures of Ferrari's latest
models are built at the Scaglietti Light Alloy
Technologies facility in Modena, a few miles from
Ferrari's Maranello base. It is there that Ferrari
builds the chassis and body of the 612 Scaglietti.

The 612's structure builds on the lessons Ferrari
learned with the all-aluminium 360 Modena. It is
the first V12 Ferrari to drop the traditional steel
tubular space frame in favour of an aluminium
space frame developed in conjunction with the

American company Alcoa. The alloys used in the
construction of the chassis are ductile – easily
shaped – during the pressing and extrusion
processes, but are then heat-treated to improve their
toughness. Ferrari claim the 612 to be 40 per cent
lighter than a conventional car of similar size, and
the new car is 60 per cent stiffer in torsion than the
outgoing 456 model.

More than 3500 hours of work went into
refining the aerodynamics of the bodyshell, first
using computer programs created by the University
of Pisa and later in the wind tunnel, using scale
models. The underside of the 612 came in for
particular attention to ensure optimal air flow. At
the rear, a diffuser helps remove heat from the

exhaust system and the gearbox oil cooler.

Power for the 612 comes from a 5748cc development of the 65-degree V12 already seen in the 575M, developing 540bhp at 7250rpm – nearly 100bhp more than the V12 in its predecessor, the 456M. Power is fed to a six-speed transaxle, either with a traditional manual gearchange or Ferrari's F1A electro-hydraulic system, operated by paddles behind the steering wheel. The result is near-200mph (322km/h) performance and a 0-62mph sprint time of just 4.2 seconds.

And this is no stripped-out racer: the 612 Scaglietti offers comfortable and luxurious accommodation for four people, with more headroom for rear passengers and easier entry and exit than the old 456M. Most supercars are centred around the driver and just one passenger – with the 612 Scaglietti, you can share the experience of your Ferrari with your friends.

Left: Like most Ferraris, the 612 Scaglietti was styled by Pininfarina. It was a controversial shape, particularly the nose with its large air intake and small headlamps. Many preferred the outgoing 456.

Below: Despite space for four people, the 612 provided all the performance expected of a Ferrari. Under the bonnet was a 5.7-litre V12 engine developing 540bhp.

Specification	Ferrari 612 Scaglietti
Engine location	Front, in-line
Configuration	V12
Bore and stroke	89 x 77mm
Capacity	5748cc
Valve operation	Twin overhead camshaft per cylinder bank
Horsepower	540bhp @ 7250rpm
Transmission	Six-speed manual or sequential semi-auto
Drive	Rear
Chassis	Aluminium space frame
Suspension – front	Double wishbone and coil spring
Suspension – rear	Double wishbone and coil spring
Brakes	Ventilated disc
Top speed	199mph (320km/h)
Acceleration	0-62mph (100km/h): 4.2 seconds

Koenigsegg CCR

**Top speed
245mph***
395km/h

*claimed by
manufacturer

*Below: The menacing front
end of the CCR, with its
extraordinary doors
open. This is officially the
fastest production car in
the world, though it may
not hold the title for very
much longer.*

 Koenigsegg may be one of the newest
supercar manufacturers around, but what
counts is not how long they have been in
business but whether their machinery is up to the
job – and they have proved in no uncertain terms
that it is. In February 2005 a Koenigsegg CCR
driven by renowned test driver Loris Bicocchi
recorded a top speed of 241mph (387.87km/h) at
the Nardo test track in southern Italy, making the
CCR officially the world's fastest production car.

The impetus for this extraordinary speed comes
from a 4.7-litre, all-alloy V8 engine which belies its
relatively humble Ford roots with an output of no
less than 806bhp (making the CCR also, for the
moment, the world's most powerful production
car). Koenigsegg's major rework of the engine
includes the addition of twin Rotrex superchargers
supplying up to 1.4bar (21psi) boost through an
intercooler, and carbon-fibre valve, timing and front
covers which cut engine weight by 12kg (26lb).

The engine's air intake system is also moulded
entirely from carbon fibre. The engine is a stressed
chassis member, bolted to the back of a carbon-
fibre/aluminium honeycomb tub which forms the
main part of the car and which weighs, remarkably,

just 62kg (136lb). Power is taken through a six-
speed transaxle supplied by Italian manufacturer
Cima, driving the enormous rear wheels through a
limited-slip differential.

All of which produces a supercar with
remarkable ability, and not just the ability to hit
very high speeds in a straight line. On the steering
pad Koenigsegg claim a rousing 1.3g cornering
acceleration. From rest the CCR will hit 60mph
(96km/h) in a fraction over 3.0 seconds, aided by
its dry weight of just 1180kg (2596lb), which
makes it the featherweight of its class.

But it is the Koenigsegg CCR's top speed
potential which grabs the headlines, and this is so
great that even that record run in 2005 did not
extract the last ounce of performance. The Nardo
track is a circle with a 7.8-mile (12.5km)
circumference, which means that during the run the
Koenigsegg was always subject to the extra tyre
drag of cornering. According to company boss
Christian von Koenigsegg, a long straight, such as
the one at Volkswagen's Ehra-Leissen proving
ground where the McLaren F1 set its record
maximum speed, should see the CCR achieve
245mph (395km/h). Or maybe more…

Left: Koenigsegg's CC8S, from which the CCR was developed. With a 655bhp V8 engine, the CC8S was the most powerful production car in the world until the CCR came along.

Specification	Koenigsegg CCR
Engine location	Mid, in-line
Configuration	V8
Bore and stroke	N/A
Capacity	4700cc
Valve operation	Twin overhead camshafts per bank
Horsepower	806bhp @ 6900rpm
Transmission	Cima six-speed manual
Drive	Rear
Chassis	Carbon fibre semi-monocoque
Suspension – front	Double wishbone and coil spring
Suspension – rear	Double wishbone and coil spring
Brakes	Ventilated disc
Top speed	limited to 245mph (395km/h)
Acceleration	0-62mph (100km/h): 3.2 seconds

Above left: The view other drivers see, and then not for long. The rear end of the CCR incorporates twin venturi tunnels to generate downforce at speed.

Left: The Koenigsegg CCR is built around a carbon-fibre tub, reinforced with aluminium honeycomb, which weighs just 62kg (136lb). The roof panel can be removed and stowed under the front boot lid.

Lamborghini Gallardo

**Top speed
192mph**
309km/h

 Lamborghini's bullfighting connections continue with its newest model, the Gallardo – the name is a breed of fighting bull. Work began on this compact mid-engined Lamborghini in 2000, starting with an Italdesign-Giugiaro styling concept which was refined by Lamborghini's in-house styling team. Like the Murcielago and Diablo before it, the Gallardo continues the dramatic 'monovolume' wedge shape introduced by the Countach but with a modern cab-forward stance.

Audi's Aluminium Space Frame system provided the body structure. Extruded aluminium members welded to cast aluminium joints provided the structural strength and the mounting points for the external aluminium and thermoplastic panels. The result was a high degree of torsional stiffness – essential for precise handling – and a body weight of 1430kg. Careful aerodynamic work led to the use of a flat underside to minimise parasitic drag and an electronically controlled rear spoiler which popped up at high speed.

And high speeds were the Gallardo's forte. Mounted in the back was an all-alloy 5.0-litre V10 engine, with a 90-degree included angle between the cylinder banks rather than the more common 72 degrees. The V10 inherited the wider angle from Audi's V8 engine, from which it was descended, though the choice also helped to reduce the height of the engine and lower its centre of gravity. The unit had dry-sump lubrication like a race car engine, a variable geometry intake and continuously variable valve timing for both the intake and exhaust. Maximum power from the four-valve V10 was 500bhp, delivered to all four wheels through a sophisticated transmission system which

Below: Lamborghini's parent company Audi provided the technology underpinning the Gallardo: it is based on the Aluminium Space Frame system used in the Audi A2 and A8.

pushed most of the torque to the rear unless grip was in doubt. Drivers could choose from a six-speed manual gearbox and a semi-automatic which Lamborghini called eGear.

Originally the Gallardo had a top speed of 192mph (309km/h) and could sprint from rest to 62mph (100km/h) in 4.2 seconds, but in 2005 even quicker variations arrived. Revisions to the engine brought the V10 up to 520bhp for the Gallardo SE, a limited edition run of 250 cars which were recognisable by their two-tone paintwork. That cut the 0-62mph (100km/h) time to 4.0 seconds, and boosted the top speed to 196mph (315km/h).

The Gallardo Spyder was also launched in 2005, and featured the same 520bhp engine as the SE, together with shorter gear ratios, recalibrated suspension and, most important of all, an electric folding roof. Lamborghini claimed a top speed of 195mph (314km/h) with the roof up and, for the ultimate wind in the hair experience, 191mph (307km/h) with the roof down!

Specification	**Lamborghini** Gallardo
Engine location	Mid, in-line
Configuration	V10
Bore and stroke	82.5 x 92.8
Capacity	4961cc
Valve operation	Twin overhead camshaft per cylinder bank
Horsepower	500bhp @ 7800rpm
Transmission	Six-speed manual, optional sequential semi-auto
Drive	Four-wheel drive
Chassis	Aluminium space frame
Suspension – front	Double wishbone and coil spring
Suspension – rear	Double wishbone and coil spring
Brakes	Ventilated disc
Top speed	192mph (309km/h)
Acceleration	0-62mph (100km/h): 4.2 seconds

Left: The Gallardo's clever four-wheel drive system biases torque to the rear of the car unless traction is lost, providing keen drivers with optimum handling characteristics.

Left: Chunky styling of the Gallardo echoes its modern Lamborghini stablemate, the Murcielago. An open-top Gallardo Spyder was added to the range in 2005, along with a limited-edition Gallardo SE.

Left: The Gallardo's 90-degree V10 was related to Audi's V8 engine. The 5.0-litre, 500bhp unit was mated to either a six-speed manual gearbox or Lamborghini's semi-automatic eGear transmission.

Ferrari F430

**Top speed
196mph**
315km/h

*Below: Ferrari's F430 is
the latest of a line of mid-
engined V8 cars dating back
to the Dino 308GT4 and
308GTB in the 1970s. But
the F430 is a very modern
machine, with F1-influenced
engineering and an up-to-
date shape drawn by
Pininfarina, in conjunction
with Ferrari Head of
Design Frank Stephenson.*

Ferrari replaced its 360 Modena with this, the F430, in 2004. Though this is an 'entry level' model – if such a description can be applied to any Ferrari – the F430 embodies the best of the Ferrari tradition, with race car technology applied to a road-going car to deliver the greatest possible driving experience.

Like most Ferraris the F430's shape was created by Pininfarina, this time working in conjunction with Ferrari's design chief Frank Stephenson. At the front the aggressive new nose featured distinctive twin air intakes which drew their inspiration from the 1960s 'shark nose' Ferrari F1 car. Large vents ahead of the front wheels exhausted cooling air from the front-mounted radiators, and another set of intakes over the rear wheels sucked in intake air for the mid-mounted engine.

The engine itself was a normally aspirated 90-degree V8 with a race-style flat-plane crankshaft and dry-sump lubrication. The engine had a capacity of 4308cc, revved to 8500rpm and produced 483bhp. Both the inlet and exhaust camshafts featured continuously variable valve timing and were driven by a gear system rather than the previous gear/toothed belt combination.

Power was sent to either a six-speed manual gearbox operated through a classic Ferrari open-gated lever or a semi-automatic six-speed F1 transmission operated by paddles behind the steering wheel. The semi-auto transmission was given a new control strategy which improved the speed and smoothness of gearshifts, which could be accomplished in just 150 milliseconds.

The F430 was the first road Ferrari to be fitted with an electronic differential called E-Diff, which transferred torque between the rear wheels to maximise traction and roadholding. E-Diff played its part in making the F430 three seconds faster than the outgoing 360 Modena around Ferrari's Fiorano test track.

Left: The twin air intakes at the front of the F430 were inspired by those of the 'shark nose' Ferrari F1 cars of the early 1960s.

Below: Air from the front-mounted radiators exits through ducts ahead of the front wheels, while intake air for the engine enters through scoops above the rear wheels.

Bottom left: The F430's 4308cc V8 engine is visible through the car's rear window. The engine delivers 483bhp at a screaming 8500rpm, propelling the F430 to 196mph (315km/h).

Responses from both the electronic differential and the F1 transmission, if fitted, could be tailored to the conditions using a rotary switch or 'manettino' fitted to the steering wheel. The switch had five positions – ice, low grip, sport, race and CST, the latter activating or deactivating the F430's stability and traction control systems.

Like the 360 Modena before it, the F430 was built entirely from aluminium at the Scaglietti facility in Modena. But the F430 offered significant improvements in stiffness and crash performance, despite a minimal increase in overall weight.

The F430 is as close to a 'mass market' product as Ferrari ever gets – but even this latest mid-engined Maranello masterpiece can be appreciated only by the fortunate few.

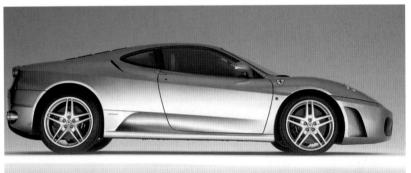

Specification	Ferrari F430
Engine location	Mid, in-line
Configuration	V8
Bore and stroke	92 x 81mm
Capacity	4308cc
Valve operation	Twin overhead camshaft per cylinder bank
Horsepower	483bhp @ 8500rpm
Transmission	Six-speed manual or F1 semi-automatic
Drive	Rear-wheel drive
Chassis	Aluminium space frame
Suspension – front	Double wishbone with coil springs
Suspension – rear	Double wishbone with coil springs
Brakes	Ventilated disc
Top speed	196mph (315km/h)
Acceleration	0-62mph (100km/h): 4.0 seconds

Porsche 911

**Top speed
182mph**
293km/h

*Below: Porsche's latest
iteration of the 911
phenomenon is this, the
997 series.*

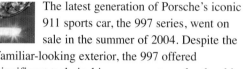

The latest generation of Porsche's iconic
911 sports car, the 997 series, went on
sale in the summer of 2004. Despite the
familiar-looking exterior, the 997 offered
significant technical improvements under the skin
aimed at making the new car more efficient, safer
and more fun to drive.

The new 911 was distinctively different. Over
recent years successive generations of 911 had
looked bigger and fatter, but the 997 sought to turn
back the clock and bring a new leanness to the 911.
Oval headlamps made a welcome return, and wider
tracks front and rear with matching arches gave the

997 a more pronounced waistline. The revisions
also improved the body's aerodynamic efficiency,
improving the drag coefficient from an already
impressive 0.30 to an excellent 0.28.

Two models were launched simultaneously –
the 3.6-litre, 325bhp 911 Carrera and the 3.8-litre,
355bhp Carrera S. Both were fitted with a new six-
speed transmission which handled the greater
torque of the new engines without increasing the
weight of the gearshift or the throw of the lever.
As an alternative to the manual transmission, both
911s could be specified with Porsche's Tiptronic
automatic transmission.

Porsche Active Suspension Management (PASM), optional on the Carrera, was standard on the Carrera S. At its 'normal' setting this active damper control system provided a good compromise between comfort and handling, while the 'sport' setting firmed up the suspension for more precise responses. The standard brakes were larger and more effective than before, and Porsche Ceramic Composite Brakes were optional on both cars. Another option was a 'Sports Chrono' package, which allowed the driver to vary the throttle pedal response, rev-limiter behaviour, suspension control and the Tiptronic gearbox's shift pattern.

Cabriolet arrives

Cabriolet versions of the Carrera and Carrera S followed at the end of 2004, with similar performance to the fixed-head models. Despite the reinforcements necessary because of the open roof, the cabriolet bodyshell weighed just 7kg more than the coupé's body. The fold-away roof could be opened and closed with the car moving at up to 31mph (50km/h).

In 2005 Porsche revealed four-wheel drive Carrera 4 versions of the latest 911. Now Porsche fans the world over wait for the next in the line, the 997 Turbo, which promises to be one of the fastest and most exciting supercars yet built by Porsche – or by anyone.

Left: The classic 911 shape and rear engine location have been retained for the new 911.

Bottom left: The flat-six engine now develops 325bhp in the Carrera, 355bhp in the Carrera S.

Below: At the front the 997 sees the return of classic oval headlamps and a stronger 'face'.

Specification	Porsche 911 Carrera S
Engine location	Rear, in-line
Configuration	Flat six
Bore and stroke	99 x 82.8mm
Capacity	3824cc
Valve operation	Twin overhead camshaft per cylinder bank
Horsepower	355bhp @ 6600rpm
Transmission	Six-speed manual or Tiptronic auto
Drive	Rear
Chassis	Steel monocoque
Suspension – front	MacPherson strut
Suspension – rear	Multi-link and coil spring
Brakes	Ventilated disc
Top speed	182mph (293km/h)
Acceleration	0-62mph (100km/h): 4.8 seconds

BMW M6

**Top speed
155mph***
250km/h

*electronically
limited

*Right: BMW's SMG
transmission handles the
awesome power of the M6's
V10 engine.*

*Below: A shorter wheelbase
and lower centre of gravity
make the M6 even quicker
on a twisty road than the
M5 saloon with which it
shares its engine.*

BMW's 6-series coupé range, announced
in 2003, was topped by a high-
performance M6 version in 2005. It
shared with its M5 cousin a 5.0-litre V10 engine
revving to over 8000rpm and developing more than
500bhp, which would have given it a top speed of
205mph (330km/h) had an electronic limiter not
intervened at 155mph (250km/h).

The 90-degree V10 featured BMW's dual-
VANOS system, which optimised the valve timing
over the engine's very wide usable speed range.
The engine management system, the most powerful
fitted to any production car, monitored combustion
by applying a small voltage to the spark plug
electrodes during the exhaust stroke – ionized gas
created during combustion allowed current to flow
– so the system could detect any misfires and
juggle engine settings to suit. So powerful was the
new engine that it started up in a comfort-orientated
mode offering 'only' 400bhp. By pressing a
'power' button the driver could select a sports
program which delivered the engine's full power
and sharpened up its response.

The new engine was mated to a seven-speed
Sequential M Gearbox or 'SMG' transmission. The

driver could select gears manually using paddles mounted on the steering wheel, or the system could be left in a fully automatic mode. In total the driver had a choice of 11 different transmission control modes, each offering a different choice of gearchange characteristics.

The M6 offered Electronic Damper Control with three different settings, and Dynamic Stability Control with an 'M Dynamic' mode tailored to the sporting driver. A speed-sensitive locking differential and huge cross-drilled disc brakes with aluminium calipers sitting inside new 19-inch forged alloy wheels further underlined the M6's potential. BMW claimed that the M6 could lap the demanding Nürburgring Nordschleife in around eight minutes, which amply demonstrated the capabilities of the car's chassis – greater even than those of the M5 saloon. The coupé's more responsive handling was the result of a shorter wheelbase and a lower centre of gravity, the latter aided by a carbon-fibre roof panel – the first in a series-production car.

Until BMW decides to apply its considerable engineering talents to an outright supercar, the M5 and M6 will be its most exciting machines – and they will continue to demonstrate that Munich's engineers are amongst the most capable designers of fast cars in the world.

Above: As on the M5, quadruple tailpipes hint at the M6's potential.

Left: BMW's new V10 engine delivers over 500bhp from its 5.0 litres – so much that it automatically starts up in a 'comfort' mode offering only 400bhp.

Specification	BMW M6
Engine location	Front, in-line
Configuration	V10
Bore and stroke	92 x 75.2mm
Capacity	4999cc
Valve operation	Twin overhead camshaft per cylinder bank
Horsepower	507bhp @ 7750rpm
Transmission	Seven-speed SMG sequential
Drive	Rear
Chassis	Steel monocoque
Suspension – front	MacPherson strut
Suspension – rear	Multi-link with coil spring
Brakes	Ventilated disc
Top speed	155mph (250km/h)
Acceleration	0-62mph (100km/h): 4.6 seconds

Maserati MC12

**Top speed
205mph**
330km/h

*Below: The MC12's styling
was developed by Maserati's
own design team, from an
original concept by
Giugiaro. The blue and
white colour scheme recalls
a Maserati sports car livery
from the 1960s.*

Maserati's return to international motor racing in 2005 was with a competition version of its own very exclusive supercar, the MC12 – or perhaps more accurately, the MC12 is a road-going version of the company's GT1 racer. It will be available in the traditional Maserati colours of white with blue stripes, which derive from the livery of the American Casner team which raced Maserati sports cars in the early 1960s. But under the long-tailed, trident-badged bodywork the MC12 hides a secret – it is largely derived from its stablemate, the Ferrari Enzo.

Both cars are based on a composite monocoque structure, though with slightly different materials: the Ferrari's tub was made from a carbon, fibre and aluminium honeycomb sandwich, while the Maserati's used a carbon/nomex honeycomb sandwich. The MC12's structure was stiffened up to allow the roof panel to be made removable. The MC12 body is much wider and much longer than that of the Enzo and it carries a full-width wing above its tail, all of which is designed to maximise aerodynamic downforce for the racing versions. Developed by Maserati's own Frank Stephenson-led team from an original Giugiaro design, the MC12's styling reflects that of other Maserati models. The nose, in particular, has a strong link with Maserati's road going GT and Spyder and carries Maserati's trident symbol in its air intake.

The Maserati is powered by essentially the same 5998cc, 65-degree V12 engine as the Enzo, though modifications to suit GT1 racing regulations reduce the power output to 'only' 623bhp. The multi-mode six-speed electro-hydraulically

operated transmission is also the same as that in the Ferrari, though it now carries the 'Maserati Cambiocorsa' name tag.

In August 2004 Maserati presented the 25 road-going MC12s necessary to qualify for GT racing, along with the racing versions which would be entered in the GT1 championship. The racing MC12s made their debut at Imola that year, though with homologation not yet completed they could not score championship points. Andrea Bertolini and Mika Salo brought their car home in second place ahead of the Johnny Herbert/Fabrizio De Simone car in third. Homologation was ratified in October, and the Maserati finished first and second in their championship debut at Zhuhai in China the following month.

The racing MC12s quickly pulled out a huge lead in the GT1 championship, which they put beyond doubt with a 1-2-3 victory in the eighth round in Instanbul in September 2005. The MC12 had done its job, and done it well.

Above: MC12 is based on the Ferrari Enzo, but with a strengthened structure to allow the roof to be removable.

Left: Long-tail bodywork with a full-width rear wing provide maximum downforce for the racing versions.

Specification	Maserati MC12
Engine location	Mid, in-line
Configuration	V12
Bore and stroke	92 x 75.2mm
Capacity	5998cc
Valve operation	Twin overhead camshaft per cylinder bank
Horsepower	623bhp @ 7500rpm
Transmission	Six-speed sequential semi-auto
Drive	Rear
Chassis	Carbon-fibre and aluminium honeycomb monocoque
Suspension – front	Double wishbone and coil spring
Suspension – rear	Double wishbone and coil spring
Brakes	Ventilated disc
Top speed	205mph (330km/h)
Acceleration	0-62mph (100km/h): 3.8 seconds

TVR Sagaris

**Top speed
195mph**
314km/h

During the 1990s TVR announced itself as a major force in the specialist sports car market, designing a succession of ever faster machines which received rave reviews for their raw driving appeal. At the same time the Blackpool company became more independent, putting into production its own engines rather than rely on tuned versions of the ageing Rover V8.

From the Griffith, Chimaera and Cerbera of the early 1990s TVR moved on to the wild Tuscan and the (slightly) more refined Tamora in 2000, both using the Speed Six engine which had been designed for TVR by engine specialist Al Melling. The T350 which followed was based on the Tamora chassis and running gear, and was available in coupé (T350C) and targa-top (T350T) guises. Originally designed with motor sport in mind, the

Sagaris was a wider, more powerful and more aerodynamically efficient version of the TVR T350 which was unveiled at the end of 2003.

The Sagaris was powered by the 4.0-litre version of the Speed Six engine which had already been seen in the Tuscan S. With four valves per cylinder operated by twin chain-driven overhead camshafts this engine delivers 400bhp, and includes such refinements as dry-sump lubrication to allow it to be mounted lower in the chassis avoiding any potential oil-surge problems in hard cornering. While the suspension systems front and rear were essentially the same layout as those of the T350, the Sagaris had wider tracks and the suspension systems had undergone considerable further tuning.

Under the skin, then, the Sagaris followed much the same pattern as previous TVRs, but in its

Below: The outlandish Sagaris shape was developed in-house by TVR, as a more aerodynamically efficient version of the T350 – originally with motor sport use in mind.

styling and its aerodynamic performance there were significant changes. Revised bodywork front and rear improved stability at speed by generating extra downforce, and certainly added to the dramatic appeal of the car's styling.

Prospective buyers queued up to try the Sagaris when TVR dealers got hold of their demonstrator cars in the summer of 2005, proving that TVR's latest cars are as exciting as anything that has yet emerged from Blackpool. Since TVR came under the new ownership of Russian billionaire Nikolai Smolenski the revised Tuscan 2 and the Sagaris have been brought to the market, and the even faster and more dramatic Typhon is on the way. TVR, it seems, is still accelerating…

Specification	TVR Sagaris
Engine location	Front, in-line
Configuration	In-line six
Bore and stroke	N/A
Capacity	3996cc
Valve operation	Twin overhead camshafts
Horsepower	400bhp @ 7000rpm
Transmission	Six-speed manual
Drive	Rear
Chassis	Tubular steel
Suspension – front	Double wishbone with coil springs
Suspension – rear	Double wishbone with coil springs
Brakes	Ventilated disc
Top speed	195mph (314km/h)
Acceleration	0-60mph (96km/h): 3.7 seconds

Left: Sagaris is covered with intakes, slots, and aerodynamic devices. It is only available as a fixed-roof coupé, and went on sale in the summer of 2005.

Far left: The Sagaris' interior is swathed in leather, as in most TVRs of the last two decades. The instrument layout is more conventional than that of the Cerbera.

Left: The 4.0-litre Speed Six engine in the Sagaris develops up to 400bhp, and powers the car to a top speed of 195mph (314km/h).

Jaguar XK

**Top speed
155mph***
250km/h

*limited

*Below: Jaguar's new XK,
unveiled in 2005. The car
was shaped by Ian Callum,
designer of the Aston
Martin DB7 and Vanquish.*

 The new Jaguar XK is the most technically
advanced Jaguar ever built, and the latest
in a long and illustrious line of fast and
luxurious sports cars from the Coventry firm.

The first sight of the XK was in the form of the
Advanced Lightweight Coupé concept, unveiled at
the Detroit Auto Show in January 2005. The
concept's powerful stance and clean-cut lines were
unmistakably the work of talented Scottish designer
Ian Callum, now heading Jaguar's design team
after a successful period with the British
engineering group TWR, where he was responsible
for several Aston Martin designs. The Advanced

Lightweight Coupé blended classic Jaguar styling
cues such as the oval grille opening – recalling the
1960s E-type – with modern coupé proportions and
a tighter, more assertive shape than the existing XK.

Later in the year, at the Frankfurt show, the
production version of the new XK made its world
debut. It was based around Jaguar's Lightweight
Vehicle Technology, the innovative aluminium
monocoque construction which had already been
seen in the XJ saloons. The bodyshell was riveted
and bonded together from pressed, cast and
extruded aluminium components, giving remarkable
strength but also lightness. The new car was 31 per

Left: The lightweight all-aluminium construction of the new XK gives it a 10 per cent improvement in power to weight ratio compared to the previous car.

cent stiffer than the old XK, and offered a 10 per cent improvement in power to weight ratio.

It was fitted with a developed version of the all-aluminium 4.2-litre AJ-V8 engine already seen in Jaguar saloons, mated to a six-speed 'Sequential Shift' automatic transmission which the driver could operate using steering wheel-mounted paddle switches. With 300bhp on tap and that lightweight body, the new car proved to be almost as fast over a standing quarter mile as the supercharged 400bhp XKR version of the previous generation.

The new XK offered improvements not just in performance but also in many other areas, from interior space and practicality to exhaust emissions and safety. Even pedestrian safety has been improved, with a new Pedestrian Deployable Bonnet System, which pops up a few inches if an impact is detected, to isolate the pedestrian from hard points in the engine bay.

Already a convertible version of the new XK has been announced to run alongside the hatchback coupé, featuring a roof which folds out of sight in just 18 seconds and two hidden aluminium roll hoops which pop up in the event of an accident. Now Jaguar fans wait for the next logical development – a supercharged XKR. With over 400bhp from the 'blown' AJ-V8 engine, it will be worth waiting for.

Left: The oval grille and curving bonnet shape are direct links with classic Jaguar sports cars of the 1950s and 1960s. The bonnet has a built-in pedestrian safety system.

Specification	Jaguar XK
Engine location	Front, in-line
Configuration	V8
Bore and stroke	86 x 90.3mm
Capacity	4196cc
Valve operation	Twin overhead camshafts per bank
Horsepower	300bhp @ 6000rpm
Transmission	Six-speed automatic
Drive	Rear
Chassis	Riveted and bonded aluminium monocoque
Suspension – front	Wishbones and coil spring
Suspension – rear	Wishbones and coil spring
Brakes	Ventilated disc
Top speed	limited to 155mph (250km/h)
Acceleration	0-60mph (96km/h): 5.9 seconds

Aston Martin V8 Vantage

**Top speed
175mph**
282km/h

Below: Aston Martin's new V8 Vantage shares the 'VH' structure which made its debut on the DB9 – and styling cues which go much further back into Aston history.

Aston Martin's miraculous rebirth was completed with the appearance of the V8 Vantage, first seen in concept form in 2003. By 2006 it was set to be rolling off the production line at Aston Martin's new Gaydon factory faster than any previous Aston, making the venerable British sports car maker a credible challenger to Ferrari not just in the speed and style of its products but also in its annual volume.

Like the DB9, which remains in production, the V8 Vantage uses Aston's VH platform of riveted and bonded aluminium, in this case supporting a two-seater body with aluminium, steel and composite outer panels. The styling combines classic Aston elements and a clear family resemblance to the DB9 and Vanquish with a new,

aggressive edge. Inside, the cabin again blends classic and modern with traditional leather trim, but up-to-the-minute instruments inspired by chronograph-watch design. At launch the V8 Vantage was only presented in hardtop, hatchback form but buyers who prefer the wind in their hair will not have to wait too long for a Volante convertible.

The V8 Vantage is front engined, with a 4.3-litre V8 which is related to Jaguar's V8 but has been so comprehensively modified that it is effectively a bespoke unit. The all-alloy engine's specification includes four valves per cylinder, variable-inlet valve timing and dry-sump lubrication. Like the V12 engines in the DB9 and Vanquish, the V8 is built at Aston Martin's dedicated engine plant at Cologne in Germany.

The power unit is mated to a cast-aluminium torque tube containing a carbon-fibre propshaft, which drives a six-speed transaxle. Automatic transmission is under development but for the moment V8 Vantage drivers will have to shift their own gears, and they will have only one engine spec to choose from – a 380bhp unit which propels the V8 Vantage to a claimed 175mph (282km/h), dispatching the standard 0-60mph (96km/h) sprint in 4.8 seconds along the way. But drivers who yearn for even greater performance need not worry, because Aston Martin are working on it: if the rumours are to be believed, a supercharged version of the V8 Vantage with 450bhp is already under development...

Specification	Aston Martin V8 Vantage
Engine location	Front, in-line
Configuration	V8
Bore and stroke	89 x 86mm
Capacity	4280cc
Valve operation	Twin overhead camshafts per bank
Horsepower	380bhp @ 7300rpm
Transmission	Six-speed transaxle
Drive	Rear
Chassis	Bonded aluminium monocoque
Suspension – front	Double wishbones and coil springs
Suspension – rear	Double wishbones and coil springs
Brakes	Ventilated disc
Top speed	175mph (282km/h)
Acceleration	0-60mph (96km/h): 4.8 seconds

Bugatti Veyron

**Top speed
252mph***
405km/h
*Claimed by
manufacturer

*Below: Bugatti concepts
with the EB218 four-door
saloon of 1999 top left and
the 1998 EB118 coupé
alongside it. In the left
foreground is the Chiron of
1999, stylistically the work
of Ital Design with input
from VW design chief
Hartmut Warkuss, who was
responsible for the Veyron's
stunning lines (right
foreground).*

This is the ultimate fast car! The fabulous Veyron supercar, which should finally reach production in 2006 after a long wait, is expected to obliterate existing speed records and assume the position of the world's fastest production car.

Bugatti's Volkswagen masters expect the Veyron to be capable of a top speed of no less than 252mph (405km/h), shading McLaren's F1, Koenigsegg's CCR and all the other pretenders to the crown. The Veyron is said to dispatch the usual 0-60mph (96km/h) sprint in less than three seconds, and hit 300km/h (which is 186mph) from rest in just 14 seconds…

This remarkable renaissance of the Bugatti marque is to the credit of Volkswagen and its charismatic chairman Ferdinand Piech. In September 1998 VW acquired the Bugatti name from Romano Artioli. It purchased Bentley and Lamborghini in the same year. Artioli, it will be

recalled, had produced the mid-engined four-wheel drive EB110 coupé in 1993 but his company had spectacularly collapsed in 1995.

Unveiled at Paris Motor Show

The new Volkswagen-initiated Bugatti has passed through a number of evolutionary phases. The first concept, coded EB118, appeared at the 1998 Paris Motor Show, only months after VW's purchase. It was based on an Ital Design-styled coupé version of a stillborn front-engined EB112 four-door saloon that Artioli displayed at the 1993 Geneva event. Under the bonnet was a complex 6.3-litre W18 cylinder engine, consisting of three rows of six cylinders, that developed no less than 550bhp.

Next, at the 1999 Geneva show, came the massive EB218 four-door saloon version which evoked some echoes of Artiolo's EB112 of six years before and was also styled by Giugiaro's

Left: Bugattis past and present: the Veyron, with its 8-litre 16-cylinder engine exposed, in company with a Type 51 Grand Prix Bugatti produced between 1931 and 1936. Note its classic horseshoe-shaped radiator which finds a modern interpretation on the Veyron. The famous Bugatti cast-aluminium wheels first appeared in 1924 and survived well into the following decade.

company. Recalling Ettore Bugatti's gargantuan 12.7-litre Royale of 1927, it was clearly targeted at Mercedes-Benz's revived Maybach and a new Rolls-Royce, the latter marque having been snatched from VW's grasp by rival BMW.

On reflection Piech decided that Ital Design's efforts were too derivative and lacked emotion. He wanted something more audacious and so looked in-house to his friend and VW design supremo Hartmut Warkuss. The resulting blue and black EB18.4 made its debut at the 1999 Tokyo Motor Show.

It represented nothing less than a root and branch rethink of the proposed Bugatti line. Out went the formal commodious saloon and in came a mid-engined sports coupé putting the new model four-square in the performance category.

Named Veyron in memory of French racing driver Pierre Veyron, who co-drove a 57C Bugatti to victory at the 1939 Le Mans race, this in turn lead to the evolutionary EB16.4 that was finished in striking red and black, a colour scheme reminiscent of Bugattis of the 1930s.

Below left: The Veyron's magnificent 90 degree W16 engine, effectively two V8s mounted side by side. Two of the four sequential KKK turbochargers can be seen centre left and the two intercoolers are mounted above the cylinder heads. The seven-speed gearbox was developed by British specialists Ricardo Engineering.

Specification	Bugatti Veyron
Engine location	Mid, in-line
Configuration	W16
Bore and stroke	86 x 86mm
Capacity	7993cc
Valve operation	Twin overhead camshafts per cylinder bank
Horsepower	987bhp @ 6000rpm
Transmission	Manual seven-speed
Drive	Four-wheel
Chassis	Unitary
Suspension – front	Wishbone and coil spring
Suspension – rear	Wishbone and coil spring
Brakes	Ventilated disc
Top speed	252mph (405km/h)*
Acceleration	0-60mph (96km/h): 3 seconds*

*Manufacturer's claim

Index